Footprint Handbook

Hava

SARAH CAMERON

This is
Havana

Of all the capital cities in the Caribbean, Havana has the reputation for being the most splendid and sumptuous. Before the Revolution, its casinos and nightlife attracted the megastars of the day. There may be no casinos now, but Havana's bars and clubs with their thriving music scene are still a major draw for foreigners and Cubans alike. Unlike most cities, Havana has not been subject to tacky 21st-century modernizations, partly because of a consistent lack of finance and materials. Low-level street lighting, relatively few cars (and many of those antiques), no (real) estate agents or Wendyburgers, no neon and very little advertising (except for political slogans), all give the city plenty of scope for nostalgia. Havana is probably the finest example of a Spanish colonial city in the Americas. Many of its palaces were converted into museums after the Revolution and more restoration work has been carried out since La Habana Vieja (the old city) was declared a UNESCO World Heritage Site in 1982, with hotels now occupying many of the grandest buildings. There is also some stunning architecture from the first half of the 20th century. That said, much of the city is fighting a losing battle against the corrosive effects of the sea air and housing for Habaneros is crumbling.

The recent rapprochement between the governments of Cuba and the USA has led to an influx of American tourists, keen to see what has been forbidden them for five and a half decades. However, there has been a boom in arrivals from the rest of the world too, with many wanting to see Cuba 'before the Americans arrive'. Be prepared for Havana to be 'full' and at least book accommodation in advance.

Although there are plenty of attractions to keep city-lovers occupied, short trips out into the countryside or to the beach are plentiful. West of Havana lie forested mountains, beautiful valleys and tobacco fields, where the red soil is turned by oxen and horses remain a common form of transport. Day trips and overnight stays provide an insight into rural life with visits to old coffee plantations, an orchidarium, waterfalls and opportunities for birdwatching and hiking. East of the city is the mega beach resort of Varadero, not the most beautiful of Cuba's beach destinations, but the 23-km peninsula offers relaxation and watersports for sun, sea and sand worshippers.

Sarah Cameron

Best of
Havana

❶ Museo Nacional Palacio de Bellas Artes

A fascinating collection of art divided between two buildings, one containing European and international art and artefacts, much of it left behind by wealthy families after the Revolution, and the other tracing the development of Cuban art from colonial times to the end of the 20th century. Page 39.

❷ Plaza Vieja

A beautifully restored 18th-century square with a central fountain, packed with museums, galleries, bars and restaurants.

A pleasant place to stop for a coffee or a beer during a tour of the old city to watch the world go by and admire the architecture. Page 45.

❸ Castillo del Morro

Standing on a headland at the mouth of the harbour, the huge, stout castle overlooks the city and along the Malecón, affording wonderful views. Together with other fortresses on both sides of the inlet, the Castillo del Morro protected the shipping of the Spanish Empire against pirates and invaders, with varying degrees of success. Page 46.

❹ Malecón

Day and night, the city's seafront drive
attracts fishermen, school children,
athletes, lovers and old cars. Hugely
photogenic, the light and atmosphere of
the 8-km esplanade changes from dawn to
dusk and on a windy day huge waves crash
over the sea wall to enliven the scene.
Page 49.

❺ Callejón de Hamel

An informal centre of *Santería* and Afro-
Cuban community art, the street's walls are
covered in murals and installation art, but
the area is known principally for its Sunday
afternoon *peñas*, when crowds come for
fun in the sun. Hot and steamy Afro-Cuban
music and dance and other activities
honour the different Orishas. Page 52.

❻ Plaza de la Revolución

The scene of Fidel Castro's marathon speeches and political parades, this enormous open space is surrounded by 1950s government buildings and overlooked by the iconic image of Che Guevara suspended on the side of the Ministry of the Interior. Page 53.

❼ Cementerio Colón

Intriguing tombs and extravagant statues characterize this enormous cemetery, one of the largest in the world. Built in 1871, the statues and other funerary architecture reflect changing tastes over nearly 150 years. Page 58.

❽ Jardín Botánico Nacional de Cuba

This 600-ha botanical garden showcases plants and trees from Cuba and around the world in a huge collection of tropical flora.

Spend a day away from the city touring the various zones of the garden and its glasshouses and have a leisurely lunch at the organic vegetarian restaurant. Page 61.

⑨ Sierra del Rosario

A biosphere reserve in the mountains, home to forests, waterfalls and a huge variety of birds and plants. Visit Las Terrazas, an ecological research station and ecotourism centre, or Soroa, where there is an orchid garden and excellent hiking to old plantations and other sites of historical and natural interest. Page 114.

⑩ Valle de Viñales

The steep-sided, limestone mogotes provide one of the most beautiful views in the world in the Viñales valley. Created over millions of years by erosion, the hills, caves and tunnels are fascinating to explore or just to sit and admire from a good vantage point with a mojito to hand. Page 125.

Route planner

Cuba is the largest island in the Caribbean, and Havana, with a population of over 2.1 million, is a sprawling city of many districts along the coast and inland. The three districts of most interest to the visitor are La Habana Vieja (Old Havana), a gem of Spanish colonial architecture; Centro Habana, which grew up in the 19th century when the old city walls were torn down; and Vedado, which expanded as a residential district in the 20th century. All three are linked by the Malecón, a wide highway and promenade along the seashore. Note that it can take some time to get out of the capital if you are planning excursions to the beach or into the countryside.

A weekend

have a capital time

The colonial city of Havana is unmissable. You need a day to see the old city with its palaces, mansions, museums and plazas. Everything is contained in a compact area and can be covered on foot. *Bicitaxis* (rickshaws) or horse-drawn carriages are available for tours, which are a useful way of getting an overview of the district before exploring on your own. A second day could be spent visiting the newer district of Vedado with its wide avenues and early 20th-century architecture as well as taking a stroll along the seafront Malecón. Don't overdo it, however, as you'll need plenty of energy to take in some of the nightlife in the music-mad city. Clubs are late-night affairs and Cubans rarely show up before midnight.

One week: Havana and around

sea and salsa

Spend the first couple of days getting your bearings and seeing the most important sights, then a couple more days exploring some of the suburbs as well as taking in a theatre or ballet performance, music concert or jazz club. Use the capital as a base for day trips out to the countryside or to the beaches along the coast east of the capital: Playas del Este, Jibacoa and the resort of Varadero.

Playas del Este can be reached by the hop-on, hop-off bus and are close enough for an afternoon's relaxation on the sand. Varadero is a 3½-hour bus journey, but can be done in a day and tours are offered.

Two weeks: Havana and the west of Cuba

diving, hiking and revolutionary history

With two weeks you could spend more time in the western province of Pinar del Río and not limit yourself to day trips. Places within striking distance of Havana include the lush green valley of Viñales, with its steep-sided limestone hills, and the fields of top-class tobacco around Pinar del Río. You could stay a night at Las Terrazas eco-lodge en route and visit the colourful orchid gardens at Soroa before heading up to the north coast beaches, untouched by mass tourism.

When to go

… and when not to

Climate

The high season is from mid-December to mid-April, when there are more dry days, more sunshine and less humidity. The season for hurricanes and tropical storms usually begins in August and can go on until the end of November. A serious hurricane does not come every year by any means, but in the last few years there have been several storms that have caused flooding and damage to houses and crops. There are also variations in climate on the island: it is hotter and drier in the east than in Havana, and wetter and cooler in the mountains than in the lowlands.

Northeast trade winds temper the heat, but summer shade temperatures can rise to above 30°C in Havana. Fortunately, most offices, hotels and leading restaurants are air-conditioned. In winter, average day temperatures drop to 20°C (68°F) and there may be a few cold days below 10°C (50°F), with a north wind. Average rainfall is noticeably greater in the west of the island; it falls mostly in the summer and autumn, but there can be torrential rains at any time. For Havana's weather chart, see page 31.

Festivals

In contrast with other Latin American countries, Cuba has no national religious festivals, although you will find some patron saints' days (often linked to *Santería*) celebrated in churches, such as **Día de la Caridad de Cobre** (8 September), Cuba's patron saint's day. Processions are usually limited to the church itself rather than around the streets of the town. Easter is an important time but **Christmas Day** was only reintroduced as a public holiday in 1997 prior to a visit from the Pope, having been banned after the Revolution. It has become a regular event in the Western tradition, with Christmas trees and tinsel, but a whole generation missed out on celebrating it and there is little awareness of what it signifies.

Public holidays are political and historical events and are marked by speeches, rallies and other gatherings, often in each town's Plaza de la Revolución.

New Year is celebrated everywhere as the anniversary of the 1959 Revolution, **Liberation Day**, when you can expect speeches, parades and parties, with lots of music and dancing, much of it outdoors.

Carnival is making a comeback in several towns, although it is not a pre-Lenten festival as in Trinidad or Rio de Janeiro. Despite limited budgets, carnival events are colourful, energetic and have a raw vibrancy. Parades are accompanied by music, drumming, dancing and competitions requiring lots of stamina. In Havana, carnival was suspended during the Special Period and then became a movable feast, but is now usually held in August.

Cuba has many cultural and sporting festivals, so there is nearly always something going on at any time of year. One of the most famous is the **Havana International Jazz Festival**, 'Jazz Plaza', in December, sponsored by Chucho Valdés with the Cuban Institute of Music and attracting the world's leading musicians. It is preceded by the **International Festival of the New Latin American Cinema**, when prize-winning films are shown at cinemas around Havana. This is the foremost film festival in Latin America showcasing the best of Cuban and Latin American films along with documentaries and independent world cinema.

The **International Ballet Festival of Havana** takes place every other year (28 October to 6 November 2016) and brings together dancers and choreographers from around the world in a non-competitive cultural exchange, with performances and workshops in theatres in Havana and other cities. The **International Festival Havana World Music** is a relatively new, but increasingly popular annual event held in March and attracting musicians from many far-flung countries as well as from Cuba.

Among the many sporting events, Havana's marathon, **Marabana**, in November, is popular with visiting runners. Its route, starting and finishing on the Prado and out along the Malecón, is particularly scenic. Competitive cycling has been huge since the 1960s, with the biggest race being **Vuelta a Cuba**, traditionally going through all the regions of Cuba. Economic hardship sometimes led to the cancellation of the race in years gone by, Guantánamo-La Habana in 2015 and Baracoa-La Habana in 2016.

What to do

Bus tour

There are myriad city tours offered around Havana, but for those on a tight budget or travelling alone, a good way to get a feel for the city is to get a day pass on the hop-on, hop-off **HabanaBusTour**. This is not a guided tour, although some sights are pointed out over a microphone in a rather garbled fashion, but with a map and your trusty guide book to hand, you can determine where you are. The bus is open-topped, providing excellent opportunities for photos from on high, but take sun screen, a hat, water and watch out for low trees along the way. The route takes you from the Parque Central in the old city west through the Plaza de la Revolución and past the Cementerio de Colón before heading out to Miramar. You can theoretically get off at any of the two dozen stops to explore (although drivers often don't bother to stop, or change the route on a whim), or simply stay on the bus for a couple of hours, take in the view and save your legs for another day. At CUC$10 per person, it is economical, but if there are three of you, you might prefer to hire a driver and visit places of your choice.

Classic cars

Do you dream of riding in an open-topped classic American car from the 40s or 50s with the wind in your hair and the sea spray cooling your skin, just like the Hollywood stars of old? In Havana this dream can come true. In the latest expansion of private enterprise in Cuba, there are now fleets of pristine, renovated Chevrolets, Cadillacs, Oldsmobiles and others, run by chauffeur-guides to provide you with that thrill. Whether you just want to arrive in style and have a pick-up from the airport and transfer to your accommodation, book a short trip along the Malecón, or spend a whole day touring as far as Viñales, anything can be arranged through an advance internet booking. Most of the guides speak English, are knowledgeable and are very friendly, offering an insight into Cuban life as well as giving background information on any sights you visit. The cars might not be 100% genuine antique under the bonnet, but they certainly deliver in atmosphere and style.

Cycling

Bicycles became the only reliable form of transport during the petrol shortages of the Special Period and they remain a common sight in both cities and rural areas. For active visitors, cycling is an increasingly popular way of exploring the country, because you can set off where

BACKGROUND

Music and dance

Tradition and roots

Cuban music, famously vibrant, is a marriage of African rhythms, expressed in percussion instruments, and the Spanish guitar. It is accompanied by an equally strong tradition of dance. There are four basic elements out of which all the other forms have grown. First of these is the *rumba*, one of the original black dances, which transferred from the plantations to the city slums around the end of the 19th century. Originating in eastern Cuba, *son* is the music out of which salsa was born. Buena Vista Social Club brought *son* to worldwide attention, while Los Van Van have long been the most popular exponents of salsa. *Danzón* was originally ballroom dance music and was the source for the cha-cha-cha, invented in 1948. The fourth tradition is *trova*, the itinerant troubadour singing ballads, which has been transformed post-Revolution into the *nueva trova* and made famous by singers such as Pablo Milanés and Silvio Rodríguez. The new tradition adds politics and everyday concerns to the romantic themes. There are many other styles, such as the *guajira* (the most famous example of which is the song, 'Guantanamera'), *tumba francesa* drumming and dancing, and Afro-Cuban jazz, performed by internationally renowned artists like Irakere and Arturo Sandoval.

Rhythm, ritual and reggaeton

From traditional *son* to Cuban rap via jazz and salsa, drums beat out the rhythm of the island's Afro-Caribbean heritage. The sacred *cueros batá* (the three drums used in

and when you please. Beyond the cities, quiet roads wind through flat or rolling countryside, where the majestic Royal palm towers over farmers' thatched cottages (*bohíos*) and oxen are still used to work the fields.

In Havana, you can cruise the cycle lane along the Malecón with the salt spray in your face and a bright yellow cocotaxi at your side. To get out to the beaches east of Havana, ride with your bike on the *ciclobus* through the tunnel under the harbour before picking up the Vía Blanca. For a multi-day trip to the Western Sierras, head out along Salvador Allende and Avenida Rancho Boyeros past the airport to San Antonio de los Baños and

the next day to Viñales. Side trips can be made in the Sierra del Rosario, with some demanding hill climbs.

If you don't want to go it alone there are many organized group tours, although you will need to bring your own bike. Most tours offer a fully supported programme and have a dedicated back-up team including tour leader, mechanic and support vehicle. Even better, luggage is carried for you while you cycle. The **Cuba Solidarity Campaign**, T020-72636452, www.cuba-solidarity.org.uk, runs an annual sponsored bike ride in western Cuba and delivers consignments of medical aid to a Havana Policlínico (local medical centre).

Santería rites) have been incorporated into mainstream bands, while performances of Yoruba and Congo devotional and profane song and dance are colourful spectacles, with Cubans fervidly chorusing the Santero chants and swaying to the infectious *guaguancó*. Carnival festivities are exuberant and colourful: the best is in Santiago in July, when rum-fuelled revellers take to the streets to dance the conga to ear-splitting drum music. More recently, reggaeton, a fusion of reggae, rap, Latin and electronic rhythms, has taken dance floors by storm, despite official reservations about its 'neoliberal' influence. It is street music with raunchy lyrics and a sensual beat, hugely popular with young Cubans. Cuban reggaeton can't be found in shops, nor on the radio; it is recorded independently at makeshift studios in people's homes and is distributed via home-made CDs and flash memory sticks. However, it is not a subversive political movement, and one artist, Yoandys 'Baby' Lores, has even composed a song, 'Creo' (I believe), dedicated to Fidel Castro.

Venues

In every town there is a Casa de la Trova, where you can find old-timers crooning the traditional songs, and a club or disco where the local youth party until the small hours. Bars are patrolled by trios, or other small groups, playing all the old favourites and tunes on request while trying to sell their CDs. The Casa de Cultura in any town is always a good place to find out about local concerts and other events, which are often held in the open air, even in the atmospheric shell of a ruined building awaiting funds for restoration.

Hiking

The mountains of the west of the island, the Sierra del Rosario and the Sierra de los Organos, have some of the most unusual geological features, as well as a wide variety of flora and very rewarding birdwatching.

The first months of the year are the best for walking, as they are drier and cooler. However, temperature varies with altitude: the higher you get, the cooler it will become, so take appropriate clothing. Also remember that in the rainforest there are few days when it does not rain, so expect to get wet. The months from August to November are the wettest, when the risk of hurricanes or tropical storms increases, but you can still encounter days when there is plenty of sunshine. At all times of year, it is best to start early, before it gets too hot. Always carry plenty of drinking water, some food, a hat and suntan lotion. Good footwear is essential and a walking stick is extremely useful on hilly forest trails. Good large-scale maps are non-existent so you are advised to take a guide when embarking on long walks. Not only will this prevent you getting lost, but you will learn a lot more about your surroundings, as many of the guides are professional botanists or ornithologists. If you are walking in national parks a guide is compulsory.

Where to stay

All hotels are state-owned. In the resort areas, the best are those with foreign investment or foreign management contracts. There are hotels to suit most budgets, even if they are basic at the lower end. Peso hotels are reserved for Cubans and are rarely available to foreigners, although Cubans are now permitted to stay in resort hotels if they have sufficient CUC$.

It is legal to stay with a Cuban family and rent a room as long as the family is registered and pays taxes. These places are known as *casas particulares*. There are also *casas particulares* reserved for the Cuban market, identifiable by the different coloured logo above the door. Cubans on holiday stay in campsites (*campismo*), which are cabins, not tents, a few of which accept foreigners.

Hotels

The **Gran Caribe** chain owns the four- and five-star grand old hotels, such as the **Nacional** and the **Riviera** in Havana. **Cubanacán** has upmarket, modern resort hotels, with an international standard of accommodation and facilities, as does **Gaviota**, owned by the military, which has most of the strategic beach areas. The Cubanacán group comprises all the **Brisas**, **Club Amigo**, **Cubanacán**, **Horizontes** and **Hoteles E (Encanto)** labels. Hoteles E are renovations of colonial mansions into boutique hotels in provincial towns and are some of the nicest places to stay at very reasonable prices. **Islazul** owns the two- and three-star, older hotels, often in the countryside. **Habaguanex** is in charge of the

Price codes

Where to stay	
$$$$	over CUC$150
$$$	CUC$66-150
$$	CUC$30-65
$	under CUC$30

Prices refer to the cost of one night in a double room in high season (15 December-15 March).

Restaurants	
$$$	over CUC$12
$$	CUC$6-12
$	under CUC$6

Prices refer to the cost of a two-course meal for one person.

renovation of colonial mansions in La Habana Vieja and their conversion into hotels, restaurants, bars, etc.

Most three-star hotels were built in the 1940s and 1950s and are showing their age, but some have been refurbished and are now considered four star. In remote beach resorts the hotels are usually all-inclusive and classify themselves as four or five star. At the cheaper end of the market you can expect old bed linen, ill-fitting sheets, intermittent water and electricity, peeling paintwork, crumbling tiles and indifferent service.

Accommodation for your first day in a hotel should be booked in advance of travelling. You have to fill in an address (any hotel will do) on your tourist card, and if you leave it blank you will be directed to the reservations desk at the airport, which is time consuming. A voucher from your travel agent to confirm arrangements is usual, and hotels expect it as confirmation of your reservation. This can be done abroad through travel agencies, accredited government agencies, or through **Turismo Buró** desks in main hotels. It's a good idea to book hotel rooms generally before noon. In the peak seasons, December to February and August, it is essential to book in advance. Lack of sufficient rooms has sometimes forced tourists to sleep in the plaza in Viñales in August. With the opening of the market to US tourists, this has become more critical as there are not enough good-quality rooms to meet demand.

At other times it is possible to book at the hotel reception. Prices given in the text are for a double room in high season (15 December-15 March); low-season prices are about 20% lower. Shop around for prices; travel agencies can get you a better deal than the hotel, which will usually offer you the rack rate. **Cubaism,** www.cubahotelbookings.com, offers real-time hotel availability and online reservations for a number of hotel groups.

Casas particulares/private accommodation

Cuba is geared more to package tourism than to independent visitors, but self-employment has opened up opportunities that can prove rewarding for the visitor. Lodging with a family is possible at CUC$20-40 per room depending on the season, the length of stay and the location, with the highest rates charged in Havana. Cubans are allowed to rent out rooms subject to health and hygiene regulations and incorporation into the tax system. Hustlers on the street will offer accommodation, but it is safer to arrange rooms through our recommendations or other contacts if you can. A guide or hustler (*jinetero*) taking you to a private home will expect CUC$5 commission per night, which goes on your room rate. Less obvious, but still an insidious form of touting is the networking of the *casa particular* owners. Most have an address book full of owners in other towns. If you ask whether they know someone in the next town you are going to, they will happily ring up a 'friend' and book a room for you. This may be a useful service, but you will be charged CUC$5 extra a night for the favour, a sum

Tip...
Take a torch. There may not be good street lighting in the area, let alone power in your house.

which will be sent to the first owner as his commission. Some owners take this so seriously that they travel around the country in low season, inspecting the properties they recommend and getting to know the families.

Private homes vary considerably. Houses in the town centre can be very noisy if your room is on the street and traffic starts at 0530. Colonial houses have no soundproofing and even a door shutting can be heard all over the house at 0600. Bear in mind that facilities often don't work, and there may be water and power cuts. The sheets don't always fit the bed; the pillows are often old and lumpy. Bathrooms should be exclusively for tourists' use, but towels are usually very small so take your own to complement theirs. Soap will probably be provided, but don't rely on it.

However, over the last few years *casa* owners have invested large amounts of money, time and effort into improving and expanding their visitor accommodation. The houses we list are in a good state of repair, newly painted and offer a private bathroom with new fixtures and fittings (although the water may still be tepid and the pressure poor), air conditioning and either a ceiling or free-standing fan and usually a fridge. Theft is not a problem, as the licence would be revoked if there was a serious complaint against the owner but you should always be careful with your belongings.

Food is nearly always better at a *casa particular* than in a state restaurant or private *paladar*. The family eats at a different time and the food is prepared in stages, but it will still be fresher and made from better ingredients than in a restaurant. Remember that what Cubans can buy with ration coupons is not enough to feed a visitor and any extra food has to be bought in CUC$. There are still no wholesale markets for private businesses to buy supplies and ingredients.

It is best to check that the *casa particular* you stay in is legally registered and pays taxes. All legal *casas particulares* should have a sticker on their front door showing two blue chevrons on a white background with *Arrendador Inscripto* written across it. Those with red triangles rent in pesos to Cubans only and it is illegal for them to rent to foreigners. If you stay at an illegal residence and it is discovered, the Cuban family will have to pay a huge fine. Illegal homestays are usually reported to the police by neighbours. All clients must sign and complete address and passport details in a Registration Book within 24 hours of arrival. This book must be made available to municipal inspectors.

If you have made a phone booking in advance and are arriving by Viazul, your host may come to the bus station with a taxi to collect you. This is not just for your benefit. A common scam is to steal guests, sometimes from the bus terminal and sometimes from outside the front door. If you are told by someone in the street that the owners no longer rent, or are full, or have asked this person to take you to another *casa*, do not go with them until you have rung the bell and checked the story with someone inside the house. *Jineteros* are very skilled at diverting you from your intended path. Some even change the numbers above the door to take you to another house where they will receive a commission.

Always reconfirm your booking with your *casa* owner the day before your arrival otherwise you may find the room has been let to someone else. If you have booked through an agency, the owner will get their money whether you turn up or not, but if you are arranging things independently and they don't hear from you, they will not want to lose that income. There are numerous booking agencies that reserve rooms in *casas particulares*. You will of course pay a premium on the room rate for the service, but with that you get convenience and peace of mind. Websites worth consulting include www.cubadirect. co.uk, www.airbnb.com, www.casaparticularcuba.org, www.cuba-junky.com, www.casaparticular.com and www.mycasaparticular.com. There are also local businesses, such as www.trinidadrent.com, and **Bed and Breakfast in Viñales** ⓘ *www.bbinnvinales.com*, now island-wide.

Camping

There are **Campismo Popular** ⓘ *www. campismopopular.cu*, sites all over the island, although not all are in operation. They are usually in nice surroundings and are good value. They

> **Tip...**
> Camping out on the beach or in a field is forbidden.

consist of basic cabins rather than tents and are designed for Cubans on holiday rather than foreigners. Many of them have been renovated and upgraded with games and sports equipment as well as improved food services. Campismo Popular has reservation offices all over the country and bookings should be made in the region where you want to stay.

Food
& drink

rice, beans and a bottle of rum

Food is not Cuba's strong point, although the supply of fresh food has improved in recent years. In Havana the Ministry of Agriculture has set up many *organopónicos* to provide the capital with fresh vegetables grown under organic conditions in order to avoid transport costs. However, although the peso food situation is improving, there are still shortages. It is not unusual to be told *"no hay"* ("there isn't any") at restaurants where you would expect the full menu to be available. (An Italian restaurant, for example, may not have any tomatoes, let alone the mozzarella and parma ham that are on the menu.)

Outside Havana shortages are not so bad, but the island is not self-sufficient. Shops sell mostly imported supplies in CUC$, such as tins of food from Spain, packets of biscuits, cookies and crackers. Farmers' markets are good places to buy fruit and vegetables. Tourists do not have access to local stores, or *bodegas*, as these are based on the national ration card system. Bread, rice, beans, sugar and coffee are rationed to Cuban families but they are not given enough to live on and have to purchase the balance at market prices. Milk is rationed only for children up to the age of seven. You can buy almost anything in CUC$.

Food

Beans (*frijoles*) are a staple of the Cuban creole (*criollo*) diet. The national dish is *congrís* (rice mixed with black beans), roast pork and yuca (*cassava*) or fried plantain. Rice with kidney (red) beans is known as *moros y cristianos*. Pork and chicken are the most common and cheapest meats available. Pork is traditionally eaten for the New Year celebrations, so in late December you'll see all the pigs that have been fattened up on people's balconies or smallholdings on the move in the backs of trucks, cars and bicycles to be sold privately or at the markets. Despite government investment in fisheries, seafood, such as lobster and shrimp, is reserved for the export and tourist markets. There is a story that the government tried to improve the diet of the Cuban people by reducing the price of fish, but all that happened was that the cats got fat; not even price manipulation could wean Cubans off their habitual diet of pork, rice and beans.

The most common side dishes are starchy root vegetables and plantain (*plátano*). The latter is ubiquitous, eaten ripe (*maduro*) or unripe (*verde*), boiled, mashed or fried. Most food is fried and can often be greasy and bland. Spices and herbs are not commonly used and Cubans limit their flavourings to onions and garlic. A marinade called *mojo* may be added to yuca to give it a bit of flavour. Salads in restaurants are mixed vegetables which are slightly pickled and not to everyone's taste. Shredded pickled cabbage and sliced cucumber are a common garnish to the main dish.

Cuba's range of tropical fruit is magnificent, so take advantage of whatever is in season. At the right time of year there will be a glut of avocado, banana (the smallest varieties are the sweetest), custard apple, guava, mango, orange, papaya, pineapple and soursop. The national fruit is the brown-skinned *mamey*, known elsewhere as *zapote*, whose bright pink-orange pulp is best made into juice. Fruit is generally served at breakfast and made into juices, but rarely used as a dessert except in ice cream. It is harvested in season and then disappears until next year, although some *casa particular* owners freeze things in times of plenty so that you can have mango or papaya juice at any time of the year.

Cubans are particularly hooked on ice cream, although it usually only comes in vanilla, strawberry or chocolate flavours. The ice cream parlour **Coppelia** can be found in every town of any size and is quite an experience, with long queues because of its popularity. There are other ice cream parlours for a change.

Drink

Rum is the national drink and all cocktails are rum based. There are several brand names and each has a variety of ages, so you have plenty of choice. Do not buy cheap firewater, or cane spirit, as it is unlikely to agree with you and you may be ill for a while. The good stuff is cheap enough.

Cuban beer is good, and there are regional varieties, which come in bottles or cans. The most widely available **beer** throughout the island is Cristal, made by **Cervecería Mayabe** in Holguín. Found in bottles or cans at 4.9% alcohol content, it costs CUC$1-1.15 in supermarkets and CUC$1.50-2.50 in bars. From the same brewery is Mayabe, with Ordinary at 3.5% and Extra at 5%, both costing the same as Cristal and also popular with more flavour. Sometimes you can find Mayabe beer in pesos cubanos, at 18 pesos. Hatuey, made in Havana, is reckoned by some to be the best of Cuba's many beers, named after an Amerindian chief ruling when the Spanish arrived, but it is very hard to find. Bucanero, from Holguín, is easily bought in the east of the island, 5.4% in bottles or cans. Tínimo (from Camagüey, good with more flavour than Cristal) is also difficult to find. In Havana and in Santiago de Cuba there are now state-owned micro-breweries which produce a range of beers priced for tourists rather than Cubans.

Cuban cocktails

Cubanito A cubanito is a Cuban version of a Bloody Mary, with ice, lime juice, salt, Worcester sauce, chilli sauce, light dry rum and tomato juice. Note that tomato juice is not always available everywhere.

Daiquirí A classic rum cocktail with a simple combination of lemon or lime juice and sugar syrup, served with crushed ice. Blended fruits, such as strawberries, can be added for variation.

Ernest Hemingway special An Ernest Hemingway special is light dry rum, grapefruit juice, maraschino liqueur, lime and shaved ice, blended and served like a daiquiri.

Havana Special A Havana Special is pineapple juice, light dry rum, maraschino liqueur and ice, shaken and strained.

Mojito To make a mojito, put half a tablespoon of sugar, the juice of half a lime and some lightly crushed mint leaves in a tall glass. Stir and mix well, then add some soda water, ice cubes, 1½ oz light dry rum and top up with soda water. Serve with a garnish of mint leaves and, of course, a straw.

Mulata A mulata is lime juice, extra aged rum, *crème de cacao* and shaved ice, blended together and served in a champagne glass.

Piña colada The old favourite, piña colada, can be found anywhere: coconut liqueur, pineapple juice, light dry rum and shaved ice, all blended and served with a straw in a glass, a pineapple or a coconut, depending on which tropical paradise you are in.

Saoco Another old recipe best served in a coconut is a saoco, which is just rum, coconut milk and ice.

Zombie One to finish the day off, and maybe even yourself, is a zombie, a mixture of ice, lime juice, grenadine, pineapple juice, light dry rum, old gold rum and extra aged rum, garnished with fruit.

Cuba produces **wines** under the Soroa label, grown and produced in Pinar del Río. Standards are improving thanks to Spanish technology and assistance. There is also a more expensive range sold for about CUC$9-10, including Cabernet Sauvignon, Chardonnay, Tempranillo and other grapes, produced with the help of a Spanish company in a joint venture. However, if you really want wine, an imported bottle is still your best option.

The locally grown coffee is good, although hotels often manage to make it undrinkable in the mornings. Some of the best coffee comes from back gardens and is home roasted.

Eating out

Cubans eat their main meal at lunch time, but they expect foreigners to eat at night. Generally, although restaurants have improved in the last few years, eating out in Cuba is not very exciting. Restaurants are more innovative in Havana than elsewhere and some of the *paladares* are eccentric in their tastes. While quality and style of cooking naturally varies, as a general rule you will get fresher food in *casas particulares* than you will in state restaurants, which have the reputation of recycling meals and reheating leftovers.

State restaurants/hotels

State-owned 'dollar' restaurants are recognizable by the credit card stickers on the door, where meals are about CUC$10-40, paid only in CUC$. Some can be quite good, and there are some international variations, including Italian, Spanish or French. You get what you pay for, and at the cheap end of the market you can expect poor quality, limited availability of ingredients and disinterested staff. Always check restaurant prices in advance and then scrutinize your bill: discrepancies occur in both the state and private sector.

Resort **hotels** tend to serve buffet meals, which can get tedious after a while, but breakfast here is usually good and plentiful and you can stock up for the day. If you're not eating at a buffet, service can be very slow; this applies regardless of the standard of the restaurant or hotel and even if you are the only customer.

Paladares/casas particulares

Paladares are privately owned restaurants that are licensed and taxed. Some very good family-run businesses have been set up, offering a three-course meal in Havana for CUC$10-20 per person, or less than that outside the capital. Portions are usually generous, but olives, coffee and other items are usually charged as extras, so be sure to check what the meal includes. You will always find pork and chicken cooked in a variety of ways and accompanied by several side dishes, including rice, salad, fried plantain, yuca or sweet potato. Some *paladares* also serve lobster (CUC$15-20), shrimp and fish, which are excellent value, fresh and tasty. There are also illegal *paladares*, which will serve meals with meat for CUC$3-5 per person. We do not list them.

The cheapest legal way of getting a decent meal is to eat in your *casa particular* (see Where to stay, above), although this is less common in Havana (where there are plenty of restaurants) than outside the capital. The food here

Tip...
Remember that if someone guides you to a *paladar* he will expect a commission, so you end up paying more for your food.

is generally of excellent quality and served in plentiful, even vast, portions. The hosts can usually cook whatever you want, with advance notice, so they are able to cater for vegetarians and special diets. There are still no wholesale markets in Cuba, so they spend a lot of time scouring the various food supply outlets every day to make sure they have a wide range of provisions for their guests. A meal is usually CUC$6-10; chicken and pork are cheaper than fish, shrimp and lobster. Many Cubans have no more than a cup of coffee for breakfast but will serve guests with coffee, fruit and/or fruit juice, bread, honey and eggs or a cheese and ham sandwich; at CUC$3-5, this is far better value than in a state hotel.

Fast food and peso stalls

For a cheap meal try one of the Cuban **fast-food** restaurants, such as **El Rápido** or **Burgui**, or a *cafetería*. As well as chicken and chips or burgers, they offer a range of sandwiches: cheese, ham, or cheese and ham, but they do come in different sizes. A sandwich in Havana costs about CUC$4, a coffee costs CUC$1. In a provincial town you can pay as little as CUC$2 for a sandwich and beer for lunch. There are **peso street stalls** for sandwiches, pizza and snacks; you'll need about CUC$10 converted to CUP$ for a two-week stay if you're planning to avoid restaurants entirely. In out-of-the-way places, you will be able to pay for food in pesos (CUP$), but generally you will be charged in CUC$.

Vegetarians

For vegetarians the choice of food is very limited, normally only cheese sandwiches, spaghetti, pizzas, salads, bananas and omelettes. Even beans (and *congris*) are often cooked with meat or in meat fat. If you are staying at a *casa particular* or eating in a *paladar*, they will usually prepare meatless meals for you with advance warning. Always ask for beans to be cooked in vegetable oil. Some vegetarians even recommend taking your own oil and lending it to the cook so that you can be absolutely sure that lard has not been used. Hotels usually have quite extravagant all-you-can-eat buffet spreads you can choose from.

Menu reader

boniato cream-coloured sweet potato

chicharritas thin slices of fried plantain

chirimoya custard apple

congri black beans with rice

frijoles beans

fruta bomba papaya

guineo banana

malanga starchy root vegetable, known as taro or dasheen in the English-speaking Caribbean.

mamey brown-skinned fruit, sometimes known as *zapote*.

mojo marinade or sauce made of onions, garlic and bitter orange or lime juice.

moros y cristianos kidney beans with rice

plátano plantain, eaten ripe (*maduro*) or unripe (*verde*), boiled, mashed or fried.

piña pineapple

potaje soupy black beans served with white rice

ropa vieja literally 'old clothes', but actually pulled or shredded beef flank, slow cooked with onions, peppers and tomatoes. Beef can often be tough in Cuba so this is a good way of tenderizing it.

tostones thick slices of plantain, fried, then squashed, then fried again.

yuca cassava

Improve your travel photography

Taking pictures is a highlight for many travellers, yet too often the results turn out to be disappointing. Steve Davey, author of Footprint's *Travel Photography*, sets out his top rules for coming home with pictures you can be proud of.

Before you go

Don't waste precious travelling time and do your research before you leave. Find out what festivals or events might be happening or which day the weekly market takes place, and search online image sites such as Flickr to see whether places are best shot at the beginning or end of the day, and what vantage points you should consider.

Get up early

The quality of the light will be better in the few hours after sunrise and again before sunset – especially in the tropics when the sun will be harsh and unforgiving in the middle of the day. Sometimes seeing the sunrise is a part of the whole travel experience: sleep in and you will miss more than just photographs.

Stop and think

Don't just click away without any thought. Pause for a few seconds before raising the camera and ask yourself what you are trying to show with your photograph. Think about what things you need to include in the frame to convey this meaning. Be prepared to move around your subject to get the best angle. Knowing the point of your picture is the first step to making sure that the person looking at the picture will know it too.

Compose your picture

Avoid simply dumping your subject in the centre of the frame every time you take a picture. If you compose with it to one side, then your picture can look more balanced. This will also allow you to show a significant background and make the picture more meaningful. A good rule of thumb is to place your subject or any significant detail a third of the way into the frame; facing into the frame not out of it.

This rule also works for landscapes. Compose with the horizon two-thirds of the way up the frame if the fore-ground is the most interesting part of the picture; one-third of the way up if the sky is more striking.

Don't get hung up with this so-called Rule of Thirds, though. Exaggerate it by pushing your subject out to the edge of the frame if it makes a more interesting picture; or if the sky is dull in a landscape, try cropping with the horizon near the very top of the frame.

Fill the frame

If you are going to focus on a detail or even a person's face in a close-up portrait, then be bold and make sure that you fill the frame. This is often a case of physically getting in close. You can use a telephoto setting on a zoom lens but this can lead to pictures looking quite flat; moving in close is a lot more fun!

Interact with people

If you want to shoot evocative portraits then it is vital to approach people and seek permission in some way, even if it is just by smiling at someone. Spend a little time with them and they are likely to relax and look less stiff and formal. Action portraits where people are doing something, or environmental portraits, where they are set against a significant background, are a good way to achieve relaxed portraits. Interacting is a good way to find out more about people and their lives, creating memories as well as photographs.

Focus carefully

Your camera can focus quicker than you, but it doesn't know which part of the picture you want to be in focus. If your camera is using the centre focus sensor then move the camera so it is over the subject and half press the button, then, holding it down, recompose the picture. This will lock the focus. Take the now correctly focused picture when you are ready.

Another technique for accurate focusing is to move the active sensor over your subject. Some cameras with touch-sensitive screens allow you to do this by simply clicking on the subject.

Leave light in the sky

Most good night photography is actually taken at dusk when there is some light and colour left in the sky; any lit portions of the picture will balance with the sky and any ambient lighting. There is only a very small window when this will happen, so get into position early, be prepared and keep shooting and reviewing the results. You can take pictures after this time, but avoid shots of tall towers in an inky black sky; crop in close on lit areas to fill the frame.

Bring it home safely

Digital images are inherently ephemeral: they can be deleted or corrupted in a heartbeat. The good news though is they can be copied just as easily. Wherever you travel, you should have a backup strategy. Cloud backups are popular, but make sure that you will have access to fast enough Wi-Fi. If you use RAW format, then you will need some sort of physical back-up. If you don't travel with a laptop or tablet, then you can buy a backup drive that will copy directly from memory cards.

Recently updated and available in both digital and print formats, Footprint's Travel Photography by Steve Davey covers everything you need to know about travelling with a camera, including simple post-processing. More information is available at www.footprinttravelguides.com

Havana
& around

Essential Havana and around

Finding your feet

Havana is situated in the western half of Cuba on the north coast, spreading largely west and south from the Bahía de Habana, which is linked to the Straits of Florida by a narrow inlet. **José Martí international airport**, the largest in the country, is 18 km southwest of central Havana and is the main hub for onward domestic flights to other parts of the island. All flights from abroad use Terminal 3, the newest terminal, with the exception of flights from Cancún which arrive at Terminal 2; domestic flights use Terminal 1. As many transatlantic flights arrive late at night, it can be sensible to arrange a transfer from the airport to your hotel in advance with your travel agent. The long-distance **Viazul bus station** for foreigners is based far away from the old city in Nuevo Vedado (southwest of Vedado) and a taxi will be needed to get to your destination. The central train station at the southern end of the old city was closed for renovation in late 2015, so trains were using **Estación La Coubre**, nearby. Both are within walking distance of hotels in La Habana Vieja or Centro Habana, but a taxi is advised at night. For further details see Transport, page 88.

Getting around

Havana is very spread out along the coast: it is more than 8 km from La Habana Vieja to Miramar along the Malecón (the seafront boulevard). Much of the city can be covered on foot, but most visitors restrict themselves to one district at a time. Local bus travel is not recommended for the uninitiated, involving complicated queuing procedures and a lot of pushing and shoving. Instead, the **HabanaBus** (see page 88) and taxis are the preferred method of transport for tourists, who pay in CUC$. Alternatives are to hire a classic car with driver, an overpriced, bright yellow *cocotaxi*, or even a *bicitaxi* (bicycle taxi) for short journeys. It is also possible to hire

scooters and cars to drive yourself, although you should exercise extreme caution on Havana's dangerous roads. For details of all these options, see Transport, page 88.

Guides

Many Cubans in Havana tout their services in their desperate quest for CUC$: they are a considerable nuisance and nearly all tourists complain of being hassled. If you feel you trust someone as a guide, make sure you state exactly what you want, eg private car, *paladar*, accommodation, and fix a price in advance to avoid shocks when it is too late. *Casas particulares* can often be a good source of information on reputable guides. You may find, however, that the police will assume your guide is a prostitute and prohibit him or her from accompanying you into a hotel.

Orientation

The city of Havana (population 2,204,300) has 200 districts in 15 municipalities, including 14,000 *manzanas* (blocks). These municipalities are: **Playa**, **Marianao** and **La Lisa** in the west; **Boyeros** in the southwest; **Plaza de la Revolución**, **Centro Habana**, **La Habana Vieja**, **Cerro** and **Diez de Octubre** in the centre; south-central **Arroyo Naranjo**; **Regla**, **San Miguel del Padrón** going eastwards; **Cotorro** in the southeast; and in the east, **Playas del Este** and **Guanabacoa**. The centre is divided into five sections, three of which are of most interest to visitors, **La Habana Vieja** (Old Havana), **Centro Habana** (Central Havana) and **Vedado**, linked by the Malecón, a picturesque thoroughfare along the coast.

Tip...
Don't forget to look up. Habaneros live in the open air and their balconies are as full of life as the streets below.

Tip...

Some museums charge for use of cameras and videos, others don't, but in order to film for professional purposes you must have permission from **Gestión Cultural de Patrimonio**, Oficios 8, T7-8644337.

Addresses

Streets have names in La Habana Vieja and Centro, but numbers or letters in Vedado and numbers in Miramar, although some of the main roads in Vedado are still referred to by names. An address is given as the street (*Calle* or *Avenida*), the building number, followed by the two streets between which it is located, eg **Hotel Inglaterra**, Prado 416 entre San Rafael y San Miguel. However, sometimes this is shortened to showing merely which corner it is on, eg **Hotel Florida**, Obispo 252 esquina Cuba. A large building will not bother with the number, eg **Hotel Nacional**, Calle O esquina 21. Cubans usually abbreviate *entre* (between) to e/ while *esquina* (corner) becomes esq.

When to go

The driest and least humid time of the year is between December and March, when you can have completely cloudless days. From July to August is the hottest time but most public buildings have air conditioning and there is usually a breeze along the Malecón. Rain falls mainly in May and June and then from September to October, but there are wet days all year round. In recent years, the worst storms have hit between September and November, destroying many of the decrepit houses in the city, but Havana is exceptionally well prepared for hurricanes and loss of life is rare. Many cultural festivals (jazz, ballet, film, etc) and sporting events (baseball, cycling, boxing, fishing, sailing, etc) take place throughout the year. There are also numerous festive days, for example José Martí's birthday (28 January 1853), which are not national holidays but are very important in Havana. New Year celebrations are a major event, coinciding with the anniversary of the triumph of the Revolution on 1 January 1959. Carnival is in August.

Time required

Two to three days is enough to get an overview of the different areas of the city and enjoy some of the nightlife, spending a day in Old Havana with time left over for visits to other districts. With a week you could do a couple of day trips, to the beaches to the east or even out to Las Terrazas or Viñales in the west.

Best cocktail spots

The pool at the Saratoga hotel, page 65
The garden at the Hotel Nacional, page 67
The rooftop bar at La Guarida, page 72
The bar at La Torre restaurant, page 73
El Delirio Habanero, page 81

Weather Havana

	High	Low	Rain
January	25°C	17°C	27mm
February	26°C	17°C	24mm
March	27°C	18°C	18mm
April	28°C	20°C	15mm
May	31°C	21°C	53mm
June	31°C	23°C	85mm
July	31°C	23°C	52mm
August	31°C	23°C	77mm
September	31°C	23°C	54mm
October	29°C	21°C	39mm
November	27°C	20°C	12mm
December	26°C	18°C	25mm

Havana

Most of Havana's sights of interest are in La Habana Vieja, the oldest part of the city. Around the Plaza de Armas are the former Palacio de los Capitanes Generales, El Templete and Castillo de La Real Fuerza, the oldest of all the forts. From Plaza de Armas two narrow and picturesque streets, Calles Obispo and O'Reilly, go west to the heart of the city around the Parque Central. To the southwest rises the white dome of the Capitolio (Capitol). From the northwest corner of Parque Central, a wide, tree-shaded avenue with a central walkway, the Paseo del Prado, runs to the fortress of La Punta. The Prado technically divides the old city from the largely residential district of Centro, although architecturally there is little distinction.

West of Centro is lively Vedado, with clubs, bars, theatres and hotels with murky pre-Revolution tales to tell. Vedado can be reached along Havana's beguiling oceanfront highway, the Malecón, which snakes westward from La Punta. Further inland is Plaza de la Revolución, with the impressive monument to José Martí at its centre and the much-photographed, huge outline of Che Guevara on one wall. West of the Río Almendares is Miramar, once an upper-class suburb, where embassies and hotels for businesspeople are located.

Reached by tunnel or ferry from La Habana Vieja, Casablanca is the area on the east bank of the harbour, dominated by the two massive fortresses of El Morro and La Cabaña.

La Habana Vieja (Old Havana)

colonial palaces and mansions now house boutique hotels, museums and galleries

The old city is the area with the greatest concentration of sights and where most work is being done to restore buildings to their former glory. New museums, art galleries, hotels, restaurants and shops are opening all the time in renovated mansions or merchants' houses. Several days can be spent strolling around the narrow streets or along the waterfront, stopping in bars and open air cafés to take in the atmosphere, although the nightlife is better in Vedado.

Plaza de Armas and around

This is Havana's oldest square and has been successfully restored to its original appearance. The statue in the centre is of the 'Father of the Nation', the revolutionary 19th-century landowner Carlos Manuel de Céspedes. On the north side of the Plaza are the **Palacio del Segundo Cabo, which was** the former private residence of the Captains General, and the former **Supreme Court**, a colonial building with a large patio. It is closed for renovation at present, with the support of the EU and UNESCO, and will become a centre for cultural relations between Cuba and Europe.

Castillo de la Real Fuerza ⓘ *O'Reilly entre Av del Puerto y Tacón, T7-8644490, Tue-Sun 0930-1700, CUC$3.* Just north of the plaza, this is Cuba's oldest building and the second oldest fort in the New World. It was first built in 1558 after the city had been sacked by buccaneers and was rebuilt in 1582. It is a low, long building with a picturesque tower from which there is a grand view.

El Templete ⓘ *Baratillo 1 entre O'Reilly y Narciso López.* In the northeast corner of the square is this small neoclassical church finished in 1828 (renovated 1997). A column in front of it marks the spot where the first Mass in Havana was said in 1519 under a ceiba tree. Allegedly, the bones of Columbus reposed in state under its branches before being taken to the Cathedral. A sapling of the same tree, blown down by a hurricane in 1753, was planted on the same spot. This tree was cut down in 1828 to be replaced by the present tree and the Doric temple. Habaneros celebrate the anniversary of the first Mass and the first town council of San Cristóbal de la Habana here every 16 November. It is also the starting point for all guided tours of La Habana Vieja.

Inside El Templete there are paintings by the Frenchman, Juan Bautiste Vermay, a pupil of the Master David and the first director of the Academia Nacional de Bellas Artes, founded in 1818. The paintings in El Templete are his greatest artistic work. They represent the first Mass celebrated on that spot, the first *Cabildo* (local council) and the consecration of the small temple.

South of El Templete on the east side of the Plaza is the small luxury hotel, the **Santa Isabel**.

Museo Nacional de Historia Natural ⓘ *Obispo 61, entre Baratillo y Oficios, Plaza de Armas, T7-863 2687, museo@mnhc.inf. cu, Tue-Sun 0930-1700, also Mon in Jul, Aug, CUC$3, guided visit CUC$4 including children over 5, CUC$1 if they visit the children's hall,*

Fact...
No Spanish king or queen ever visited Cuba in colonial times.

camera CUC$2. In a modern building on the south side of the square you will find lots of stuffed animals, with information (in Spanish) on Cuban bats, butterflies and endemic species. You can find out, for example, that a flock of 50,000 bats eats 200 kg a night, or that there are 87 species of cockroach, two-thirds of which are endemic. This is not the most exciting museum, especially if your Spanish isn't good enough to read the information provided. Outside the museum is a small, second-hand **book market** ① *daily 1000-1700.*

Museo de la Ciudad ① *Tacón 1 entre Obispo y O'Reilly, T7-869 7358, museologia@ patrimonio.ohc.cu, Tue-Sun 0930-1700, CUC$3, guided visit CUC$5.* On the west side of Plaza de Armas is the former **Palacio de los Capitanes Generales**, built in 1780, a charming example of colonial architecture. The Spanish Governors and the Presidents lived here until 1917, when it became the City Hall. It is now the historical museum of the city of Havana. The museum houses a large collection of 19th-century furnishings that illustrate the wealth of the Spanish colonial community, including large 'his and her' shell-shaped baths in marble. There are portraits of patriots, flags, military memorabilia and a grandly laid out dining room. The building was the site of the signing of the 1899 treaty between Spain and the USA. The nation's first flag is here, together with a beautiful sword encrusted

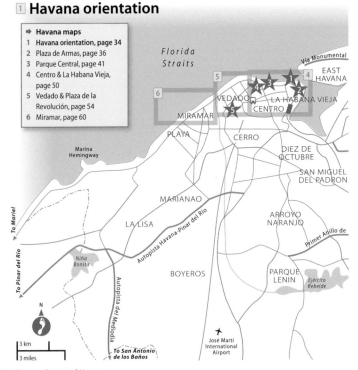

1 **Havana orientation**

Florida Straits

Vía Monumental

EAST HAVANA

VEDADO   LA HABANA VIEJA
CENTRO

MIRAMAR

PLAYA   CERRO

Marina Hemingway

DIEZ DE OCTUBRE

SAN MIGUEL DEL PADRON

MARIANAO

ARROYO NARANJO

LA LISA

Primer Anillo de

To Mariel

To Pinar del Río

Autopista Havana-Pinar del Río

Niña Bonita

Autopista del Mediodía

BOYEROS

PARQUE LENIN   *Ejército Rebelde*

N

3 km
3 miles

To San Antonio de los Baños

✈ José Martí International Airport

with diamonds belonging to Máximo Gómez. There is a curious portrait of Calixto García featuring his unusual wound: he was shot through the neck and the bullet emerged through his forehead. Also on display is the original slave freedom charter signed by Céspedes. The courtyard contains Royal palms, the Cuban national tree. Outside is a statue of the unpopular Ferdinand VII of Spain, with a singularly uncomplimentary plaque. In front of the museum is a collection of church bells.

Plaza de la Catedral and around

La Catedral de San Cristóbal de La Habana ① *Empedrado esq San Ignacio, T7-861 7771. Mon-Fri 0900-1700, Sat, Sun 0900-1200, Mass Mon-Fri 1800 in chapel (entrance on San Ignacio), Sat 1500 in chapel, Sun 1030 in main Cathedral. Cathedral tower CUC$1.* Northwest of the Plaza de Armas is one of Havana's most iconic and beautiful monuments, the Catedral de San Cristóbal de la Habana. Construction of a church on this site was begun by Jesuit missionaries at the beginning of the 18th century. After the Jesuits were expelled in 1767, the church was converted into a cathedral. On either side of the Spanish colonial baroque façade are bell towers: the left one (west) is half as wide as the right (east), which has a grand view.

The church is officially dedicated to the Virgin of the Immaculate Conception, but is better known as the church of Havana's patron saint, San Cristóbal de la Habana or the Columbus cathedral. The bones of Christopher Columbus were sent to this cathedral when Santo Domingo was ceded by Spain to France in 1795; they now lie in Santo Domingo (Dominican Republic). There is much speculation over whether the bones were indeed those of Columbus; they could have been those of his brother or son, but the Dominican Republic is convinced of their authenticity.

Centro de Arte Contemporáneo Wifredo Lam ① *San Ignacio 22, esquina Empedrado, just next to the cathedral, T7-8646282, divulgacion@wlam.cult.cu, free.* The work of Cuba's most famous painter can be seen here, along with changing exhibition programmes that feature mostly Cuban artists but also world masters. Lam directed most of his work to a non-Latin American audience. The building was renovated in 2009 and is a fine exhibition centre.

Opposite is the **Fundación Alejo Carpentier** ① *Empedrado 215 entre Cuba y San Ignacio, T7-8615506, www.fundacion carpentier.cult.cu, Mon-Fri 0800-1600,* which was the setting for Carpentier's novel *El Siglo de las Luces.* The foundation runs literary courses and there is a small museum

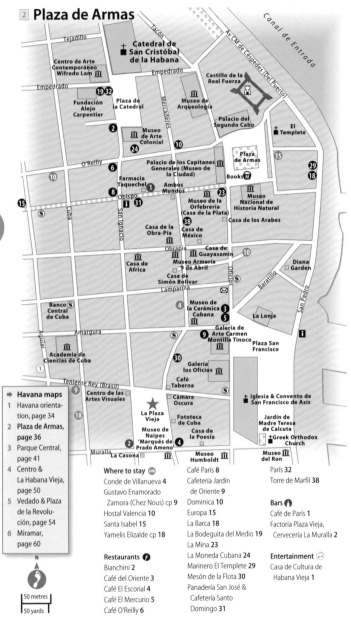

2 Plaza de Armas

Tejadillo

Tacón

Canal de Entrada

Av CM de Céspedes (Del Puerto)

Catedral de San Cristóbal de la Habana

Centro de Arte Contemporáneo Wifredo Lam 🏛

Empedrado

Castillo de la Real Fuerza

Empedrado

19 32

Fundación Alejo Carpentier

Plaza de la Catedral

Museo de Arqueología 🏛

Mercaderes

Palacio del Segundo Cabo

El Templete

2

Museo de Arte Colonial 🏛

24

O'Reilly

6

Palacio de los Capitanes Generales (Museo de la Ciudad) 🏛

10

Plaza de Armas

15

Bookstore 🏛

29

18

Farmacia Taquechel

8

1

Ambos Mundos

10

Museo de la Orfebrería (Casa de la Plata) 🏛

Museo Nacional de Historia Natural 🏛

15

Obispo

i

31

23

Cuba

Santa Ignacio

Casa de la Obra-Pía 🏛

38

Casa de México

Casa de los Arabes

Obrapía

Casa de Guayasamín 🏛

10

Casa de Africa 🏛

Museo Armería 9 de Abril 🏛

Diana Garden

Casa de Simón Bolívar

Lamparilla

Banco Central de Cuba 🏛

Museo de la Cerámica Cubana 🏛

4

3

5

La Lonja

Amargura

Galería de Arte Carmen Montilla Tinoco 🏛

9

Plaza San Francisco

i

Aguiar

Academia de Ciencias de Cuba 🏛

30

Galería los Oficios 🏛

Teniente Rey (Brasil)

9

Café Taberna

→ Havana maps

1 Havana orientation, page 34

2 Plaza de Armas, page 36

3 Parque Central, page 41

4 Centro & La Habana Vieja, page 50

5 Vedado & Plaza de la Revolución, page 54

6 Miramar, page 60

18

Centro de las Artes Visuales

★ La Plaza Vieja

Museo de Naipes 'Marqués de Prado Ameno'

2

La Casona

Muralla

Cámara Oscura

Fototeca de Cuba

Casa de la Poesía

Museo Humboldt 🏛

Iglesia & Convento de San Francisco de Asís

Jardín de Madre Teresa de Calcuta

Greek Orthodox Church

Museo del Ron 🏛

N

50 metres

50 yards

Where to stay 🛏
Conde de Villanueva **4**
Gustavo Enamorado Zamora (Chez Nous) cp **9**
Hostal Valencia **10**
Santa Isabel **15**
Yamelis Elizalde cp **18**

Restaurants 🍴
Bianchini **2**
Café del Oriente **3**
Café El Escorial **4**
Café El Mercurio **5**
Café O'Reilly **6**

Café París **8**
Cafetería Jardín de Oriente **9**
Dominica **10**
Europa **15**
La Barca **18**
La Bodeguita del Medio **19**
La Mina **23**
La Moneda Cubana **24**
Marinero El Templete **29**
Mesón de la Flota **30**
Panadería San José & Cafetería Santo Domingo **31**

París **32**
Torre de Marfil **38**

Bars 🍸
Café de París **1**
Factoría Plaza Vieja, Cervecería La Muralla **2**

Entertainment 🎵
Casa de Cultura de Habana Vieja **1**

of the writer's letters and books. Alejo Carpentier is revered throughout Latin America as the founder of Magical Realism.

Museo de Arte Colonial ⓘ *San Ignacio 61, Plaza de la Catedral, T7-862 6440, colonial@ patrimonio.ohc.cu, Tue-Sun 0930-1700, CUC$3, guide CUC$5 including use of camera and video.* In the former Palacio de los Condes de Casa Bayona is the exquisite colonial art museum, with exhibits of colonial furniture and other items, plus a section on stained glass.

Museo de Arqueología ⓘ *Tacón 12 entre O'Reilly y Empedrado, T7-861 4469, tony@ patrimonio.ohc.cu, Tue-Sat 0900-1700, Sun 0930-1300, CUC$1, CUC$2 with guide, CUC$15 to use video camera.* East of Plaza de la Catedral, the museum has displays on colonial archaeology uncovered during excavation works in La Habana Vieja and the bay. Exhibits feature Cuban and Peruvian aboriginal artefacts. The house was built in the 17th century but redesigned in 1725 by Juana Carvajal, a freed slave who inherited the building from her owner, Lorenza Carvajal. It was further expanded by the Calvo de la Puerta family, who acquired it in 1748. In 1988 it was restored and converted into a museum. Just outside, on the corner of Tacón and Oficios, is an archaeological excavation site, dug in 2006, with photos of the artefacts discovered there.

Castillo de la Punta and northern Habana Vieja
Castillo de la Punta ⓘ *Av del Puerto y Paseo del Prado.* Built at the end of the 16th century at the northernmost part of the old city to protect the entrance to the harbour, the Castillo del la Punta is a squat building with 2.5-m-thick walls. There are three permanent exhibition rooms covering the history of the castle, naval design and construction and marine archaeology, although the whole building was still closed for repairs in late 2015. On the seafront plaza in front of La Punta are metal floor plans of the local fortresses with numbers and a key. Opposite the fortress, across the Malecón, is the **monument to Máximo Gómez**, the independence leader.

The **Policía Nacional Revolucionario Comandancia General** is in another fortress in the block bounded by Cuba, Chacón, Cuarteles and San Ignacio. It is not open to the public but if you want to visit you can go to the offices of the **Centro Provincial de Selección PNR** ⓘ *Tulipán y Boyeros, Mon-Fri 0830-1700*, to get permission.

The Church of El Santo Angel Custodio ⓘ *Compostela 2 esq Cuarteles, T7-8610469, Mon-Fri 0900-1730, Sun 0830-1130, Mass Tue-Thu 1700, Mon, Fri, Sun 0900, currently being repaired.* The Church of El Santo Angel Custodio was built by the Jesuits in 1689 on the slight elevation of **Peña Pobre**, with the tower added in 1704. The original church was largely destroyed by a hurricane in 1846 but was restored and became the parish church in 1852. It was rebuilt and enlarged in its present neo-Gothic style in 1868-1870. It has white, laced Gothic towers and 10 tiny chapels, no more than kneeling places, the best of which is behind the high altar. There is some interesting stained glass depicting *conquistadores*. During the Christmas period an impressive Nativity scene is placed at the entrance. Famous

> **Tip...**
> There are two other old forts in Havana: **Atarés**, finished in 1763, on a hill overlooking the southwest end of the harbour; and **El Príncipe**, on a hill at the far end of Avenida Independencia (Avenida Rancho Boyeros), built 1774-1794, now the city jail. The finest view in Havana is from this hill.

BACKGROUND
The development of Havana

Havana was founded in 1519 on its present site at the mouth of a deep bay. In the colonial period, this natural harbour was the assembly point for ships of the annual silver convoy to Spain. Its strategic and commercial importance is reflected in the extensive fortifications, particularly on the east side of the entrance to the bay where there are two large fortresses, El Castillo de los Tres Reyes del Morro, built in 1589-1630, and San Carlos de la Cabaña, built in 1763-1774. On the west side of the canal are the smaller, 16th-century Castillo de la Punta and the Castillo de la Real Fuerza.

The city was prey to pirate attacks as well as being a pawn in European wars. In the 18th century, the British attacked Havana and held it from 1762 to 1763, but exchanged it for Florida. From that point, the city's importance as the gathering place for the silver convoy was superseded by trade. The local planters and merchants had briefly discovered the value of trading their crops with Britain and North America. From the second half of the 18th century to the end of the 19th century, ships came in to Havana carrying slaves, while exports of coffee, tobacco and, most importantly, sugar were the mainstay of the local economy.

From the beginning of the 19th century, the local sugar plantocracy began to move out of the walled city to build neocolonial villas or country estates in what are now the municipalities of Cerro, 10 de Octubre and the high part of Marianao. By the 1850s, the city walls had more or less collapsed and the Prado was absorbed into the old city instead of running outside its walls. The city expanded westwards from the 1870s onwards; the rise of Vedado reached its high point in the 1920s, when neoclassical, romantic and art nouveau villas with internal courtyards vied with each other for luxury and originality. The Colón cemetery reflects this bourgeois competitiveness.

By 1918, Miramar, on the western outskirts across the Río Almendares, now Playa municipality, began to take over as the salon of the city, with beach resorts, exclusive seaside clubs and, of course, casinos. Many wealthy Miramar residences are today occupied by embassies and government buildings, but there are also many abandoned villas. Major developments took place after the two World Wars, including the extension of Nuevo Vedado and the construction of high-rise buildings

people baptized here include José Martí in 1853, Amelia Goire (La Milagrosa), Alicia Alonso and Julián del Casal. It is also the setting for the last chapter of the novel *Cecilia Valdés*.

Museo de la Revolución
Refugio entre Monserrate y Zulueta, facing Av de las Misiones, T7-8624091/6, daily 0900-1600, CUC$8, guide CUC$2. Allow several hours, explanations are mostly in Spanish.

This huge, ornate building, topped by a dome, was once the Presidential Palace, but now contains the Museo de la Revolución. The history of Cuban political development is charted, from the slave uprisings to joint space missions with the ex-Soviet Union. The liveliest section displays the final battles against Batista's troops, with excellent photographs and some bizarre personal mementoes. The yacht *Granma*, from which Fidel Castro disembarked with his companions in 1956 to launch the Revolution, has been installed in the park facing the south entrance, surrounded by planes, tanks and other like the Focsa and the Hotel Nacional. The sea was regarded as a threat during most of Havana's history and only became an asset in the 20th century. The Malecón seafront drive was built in 1901, the tunnel to Miramar (replacing a bridge) in 1950, and the tunnel leading to Playas del Este, on the other side of the bay, in 1958.

After the Revolution, construction moved away from Havana to the rest of the country, which had been largely forgotten in preceding decades. However, new neighbourhoods were built in the east of the city in an attempt to improve living conditions. Both the Camilo Cienfuegos barrio, dating from 1961, and Alamar, from 1970, were built by microbrigades, with citizens helping to build their own apartments, schools and clinics. The decades since construction have taken their toll, however, and the tropical climate and sea winds have eaten into the concrete and metal structures, leaving these districts looking run down and depressed.

Contemporary Havana

Before the Revolution, Havana was the largest, the most beautiful and the most sumptuous city in the Caribbean. Today, it is rather run down and the weather has wreaked havoc on both pre- and post-Revolution buildings. Thanks to the government's policy of developing the countryside, it is not ringed with shanty towns like so many other Latin American capitals, although some reappeared in the 1990s. Nevertheless, the city is shabby and visitors are often taken by surprise by living conditions. Half the people live in housing officially regarded as sub-standard, and many buildings are shored up by wooden planks. In fact, thanks to renovation projects, the ancient palaces, colonnades, churches and monasteries are now in considerably better shape than the newer housing developments.

The old city is a United Nations World Heritage Site. Priorities include the restoration of the historic centre, under the auspices of UNESCO and the City Historian's Office, whose brief it is to rebuild communities in the widest sense of the word, with income from cultural tourism and aid from European NGOs. Restoration will encompass the Malecón, starting from the historic centre, where housing has been badly affected by salination and sea damage, and the Bosque de la Habana, crossed by the Río Almendares, now suffering from pollution and contamination, which is a potentially rich green belt, extending over several kilometres.

vehicles involved, as well as a Soviet-built tank used against the Bay of Pigs invasion and a fragment from a US spy plane shot down in the 1970s. Allow several hours to see it all.

★ Museo Nacional Palacio de Bellas Artes

T7-861 5777/863 9484, www.museonacional.cult.cu. Tue-Sat 0900-1700, Sun 1000-1400. Single museum ticket CUC$5 for foreigners, day pass to both museums CUC$8 (CUP$5 for Cubans), children under 13 free, accredited art students free, guide CUC$2 by prior reservation (T7-8639484 ext 105). No photography permitted in the galleries. Both museums have shops selling books, art and souvenirs.

This impressively extended museum has two separate buildings: the original 1954 Fine Arts Palace on Trocadero, which houses the Cuban art collection (Arte Cubano) from colonial times to the 1990s, including a section on the post-Revolution Art Schools; and the former Centro Asturiano, two blocks away on the east side of Parque Central, housing European and international art and ancient artefacts (Arte Universal). This is a truly spectacular museum and well worth a look.

Arte Cubano ① *Trocadero entre Zulueta y Monserrate*. Cuban paintings include the 20th-century painter Victor Manuel's *Gitana Tropical*, considered an important symbol of the Cuban vanguard. There are masterpieces by José Nicolás de la Escalera and Victor Patricio Landaluze from the colonial period and representations of modern-era Cuban paintings from Wifredo Lam and René Portocarrero. Exhibited works of more recent Cuban artists include those of Roberto Fabelo and Zaida del Río and some artists who have left the country. Start on the third floor with the colonial art and work your way down to the present day. On the ground floor there are also temporary exhibitions, a small shop and toilets.

Arte Universal ① *Centro Asturiano, San Rafael entre Zulueta y Monserrate*. On the east side of Parque Central, the older building was designed by the Spanish architect Manuel del Busto in the early 20th century and was fabulously renovated at the turn of the millennium (at an estimated cost of CUC$14.5 million) with huge marble staircases giving access to five floors. The large collection of European paintings, from the 16th century to the present, contains works by Gainsborough, Van Dyck, Velázquez, Tintoretto, Degas et al. One painting by Canaletto, *Chelsea from the Thames*, in the Italian room on the fifth floor, is in fact only half a painting; the other half of the 18th-century painting is owned by the National Trust in Britain and hangs in Blickling Hall, Norfolk. It is believed to have been commissioned in 1746-1748 by the Chelsea Hospital, which is featured in the Cuban half, but the artist was unable to sell it and cut it in two just before he died in 1768. The left half was sold to the 11th Marquis of Lothian, whose family owned Blickling Hall, where it has stayed ever since. The right half was bought and sold several times until it ended up with a Cuban collector, Oscar Cinetas, who donated it to the museum before the Revolution. A full-size photograph of the Blickling section of the panorama is now on display next to the Cuban section and a complete digital image of the two pieces has been shown at Blickling Hall.

The museum also has Greek, Roman, Egyptian and Etruscan sculpture and artefacts, many very impressive. The unharmed Greek amphora from the fifth century BC is considered remarkable. Additionally, there are rooms dedicated to Latin American art and 18th- and 19th-century paintings from the United States.

Among the museum's holdings are private collections left behind by rich Cuban families (including the Bacardí and Gómez Mena families and members of Batista's government) who fled Cuba soon after the 1959 Revolution. These include works by Spanish masters Sorolla and Zurbarán. However, it is rumoured that some of these collections were sold by the Cuban government during the economic crisis of the Special Period.

> **Tip...**
> Between the two galleries on Avenida de las Misiones, between Empedrado and San Juan Dios, is the wonderful art deco former Bacardí building, topped by its signature bat. A great view of it can be appreciated from the roof terrace of the Hotel Plaza.

Parque Central

This is a very pleasant park with a monument to **José Martí** in the centre. The north side is entirely occupied by the Iberostar Parque Central, while the Hotel Plaza is in the northeast corner. On its west side are the Hotel Telégrafo and the historic Hotel Inglaterra, which celebrated its 125th anniversary in 2000. Now a National Monument, it has had many famous former foreign guests over the decades, including Sarah Bernhardt in 1887, General Antonio Maceo (one of the heroes of the Cuban Wars of Independence) in 1890, and the authors Federico García Lorca and Rubén Darío in 1910. Next door, the **Gran Teatro**, a beautiful neo-baroque monument dating from 1838, reopened on New Year's Day 2016 after three years' closure with a performance of *Giselle* by Ballet Nacional de Cuba. It is now known as the **Gran Teatro de la Habana Alicia Alonso**. It is used by the National Opera and National Ballet and also houses the Teatro García Lorca, where Sarah Bernhardt once performed when it was called the Teatro Tacón. José Martí wrote of her performance, "Sarah is flexible, delicate, svelte. When she is not shaken by the demon of tragedy, her body is full of grace and abandon, when the demon takes her over, she is full of power and nobility… Where does she come from? From poverty! Where is she going? To glory!"

Capitolio and around

Paseo de Martí entre San Martín y Dragones. Closed for renovation.

South of the Parque Central, the Capitolio was built in the style of the US Capitol in Washington DC in 1929-1932 by the dictator Machado in an attempt to impress his US paymasters with his loyalty. The white dome over a rotunda is 62 m high, and inside is a 17-m statue of Jupiter, representing the state. This is the tallest interior statue in Latin America and the third largest in the world. A 24-carat diamond (or is it a fake?) is set into the centre of the floor in the entrance hall to pinpoint zero for all distance measurements in Cuba. The interior has large halls and stately staircases, all most sumptuously decorated.

The Capitol was initially used as the seat of parliament with the Senate and the House of Representatives meeting there, but these were dissolved after the

3 Parque Central

N

400 metres
400 yards

Where to stay
Iberostar Parque Central **11**
Saratoga **16**

Restaurants
A Prado y Neptuno **1**
El Castillo de Farnés **13**
El Floridita **14**
Hanoi **17**
La Piña de Plata **25**
Los Nardos **28**
Pastelería Francesa **33**

Bars
Bar Monserrate **4**
Casa del Escabeche **7**

➡ **Havana maps**
1 Havana orientation, page 34
2 Plaza de Armas, page 36
3 Parque Central, page 41
4 Centro & La Habana Vieja, page 50
5 Vedado & Plaza de la Revolución, page 54
6 Miramar, page 60

Revolution. More recently it housed the Cuban Academy of Sciences and the National Library of Science and Technology.

South of the Capitolio, and landscaped to show off the building to the best effect, is the **Parque Fraternidad**. It was originally called Parque de Colón, but was renamed to mark the VI Panamerican Conference in 1892. At its centre is a ceiba tree growing in soil provided by each of the American republics. Also in the park is a famous statue, sculpted in 1837, of La Noble Habana, the Amerindian woman who first welcomed the Spaniards.

There is still a cigar shop near the Capitolio at the former site of the **Partagas cigar factory** ① *Industria entre Dragones y Barcelona, T7-8668060, Mon-Sat 0900-1900*, where you can buy rum, cigars and coffee, but the factory itself has moved (see Centro, below).

Calle Obispo and Calle Obrapía

From the Parque Central you can walk back to the Plaza de Armas along Calle Obispo, now closed to traffic and one of the streets of La Habana Vieja which has seen most restoration, with many shops lovingly restored to their former splendour. There is a small **handicrafts market** on Obispo between Aguacate and Compostela, where they sell leather goods, clothes, ceramics and jewellery. Avoid buying coral, which is protected internationally. Sundays are particularly busy. Calle Obrapía, which runs parallel, has some magnificent colonial buildings, many of which are now museums and galleries.

The **Museo Numismático** ① *Obispo 305 entre Aguiar y Habana, T7-861 5811, numismatica@patrimonio.ohc.cu, Tue-Sat 0930-1730, Sun 0930-1300, CUC$1, cameras with permission*, is a coin museum which exhibits and sells coins, medals and documentation. The extensive collection of more than 1000 pieces, including rare notes and valuable cold coins, dates from the colonial period up to the Revolution.

Farmacia Taquechel ① *Obispo 155 entre Mercaderes y San Ignacio, T7-862 9286*, displays all manner of herbs, remedies and concoctions stored in porcelain jars, glazed and gilded with herbal motifs and meticulously arranged on floor-to-ceiling polished mahogany shelves. The original 1896 building was the workplace of Francisco Taquechel Mirabal.

Just west of the Plaza de Armas, the **Museo de la Orfebrería (Casa de la Plata)** ① *Obispo 113 entre Mercaderes y Oficios, T7-8639861, plata@patrimonio.ohc.cu, Tue-Sat 0930-1700, Sun 0900-1300, CUC$1, guide CUC$2*, has a silverware collection and old frescoes on the upper floor.

Head south on Oficios to reach the **Casa de los Arabes** ① *Oficios 16 entre Obispo and Obrapía, T7-861 5868, arabes@patrimonio.ohc.cu, Tue-Sat 0900-1700, Sun 0900-1300, free, donations welcome*, in a lovely building built in Mudéjar style with vines trained over the courtyard for shade. The collection includes a mosque, jewels, Saharan robes, gold- and silver-painted weapons and rugs.

West of here are a cluster of museums on Obrapía. **Casa de México** ① *Obrapía 116 entre Mercaderes y Oficios, T7-861 8166, mexico@patrimonio.ohc.cu, Tue-Sat 0930-1645, Sun 0930-1245*, also called **La Casa de Benemérito de las Américas Benito Juárez**, is more of a cultural centre than a museum, housed in a pink building draped with the Mexican flag. Exhibits include pre-Columbian artefacts and popular arts and crafts including ceramics from Jalisco.

Works donated to Cuba by the late Ecuadorean artist Oswaldo Guayasamín are displayed at the **Casa de Guayasamín** ① *Obrapía 111 entre Mercaderes y Oficios T7-861 3843, guayasamin@patrimonio.ohc.cu, Tue-Sat 0930-1700, Sun 0900-1300, donations welcome*. Exhibits are, generally, paintings, sculpture and silkscreens, but there are occasionally other exhibitions. Guayasamín painted a famous portrait of Fidel Castro.

On 9 April 1958 a group of revolutionaries of the Movimiento 26 de Julio attacked the business of Compañía Armera de Cuba on Mercaderes between Obrapía and Lamparilla. They were unsuccessful and four members of the group were killed. After the Revolution, the site was declared a National Monument in their honour and on 9 April 1971 it became a museum. The **Museo Armería 9 de Abril** ⓘ *Mercaderes entre Obrapía y Lamparilla, T7-861 8080, armeria@patrimonio.ohc.cu, Tue-Sat 0930-1700, Sun 0930-1300,* recreates the original business at the front, with some contemporary pieces, hunting and fishing accessories, including the collection of arms that Castro donated in the 1990s. At the back there is an exhibition on the events that took place there in 1958.

The **Casa de Simón Bolívar** ⓘ *Mercaderes 156 entre Obrapía y Lamparilla, T7-861 3998, bolivar@patrimonio.ohc.cu, Tue-Sat 0930-1700, Sun 0930-1230, free, donations welcome,* contains exhibits about the life of the South American liberator and some Venezuelan art.

Casa de la Obra-Pía ⓘ *Obrapía 158 entre Mercaderes y San Ignacio, T7-861 3097, obrapia@patrimonio.ohc.cu, Tue-Sat 0930-1630, Sun 0930-1230, no entry fee but donations welcome, photos free,* is a furniture museum, with examples from the 18th and 19th centuries, housed in a yellow building. It was built in 1665, then remodelled in 1793 by the Marqués de Cárdenas de Monte Hermoso, whose shield is over the door. The portico was made in Cádiz in 1793, but finished off in Havana. The building was restored in 1983.

The **Casa de Africa** ⓘ *Obrapía 157 entre San Ignacio y Mercaderes, T7-861 5798, africa@patrimonio.ohc.cu, Tue-Sat 0900-1700, Sun 0900-1300, free,* is a small gallery of carved wooden artefacts and handmade costumes. Sculpture, furniture, paintings and ceramics from sub-Saharan Africa are on display, including gifts given to Fidel by visiting African Presidents. There is also an exhibit of elements of African-Cuban religions.

Plaza San Francisco and around

Calle Oficios runs south of the Plaza de Armas to the Plaza San Francisco, dominated by the **Iglesia y Convento de San Francisco de Asís** ⓘ *Oficios entre Amargura y Churruca, T7-866 3638, sanfrancisco@patrimonio.ohc.cu, Tue-Sat 0930-1730, Sun 0930-1300, CUC$5 for museum and* campanario *(bell tower), guide CUC$3.* Built in 1608 and reconstructed in 1730, this is a massive, sombre edifice suggesting defence, rather than worship. The three-storey bell tower was both a landmark for returning voyagers and a lookout for pirates and has stunning views of the city and port. The **Basílica Menor de San Francisco de Asís** is now a concert hall (basilicamenor@patrimonio.ohc.cu, tickets for concerts are sold three days in advance) and the convent is a museum containing religious pieces. Restoration work continues. Most of the treasures were removed by the government and some are in museums.

The sculpture outside the church is of the eccentric *El Caballero de París* (Gentleman from Paris). The legendary vagrant with a deluded sense of grandeur was notorious throughout the city and affectionately embraced by Habaneros. He died in 1985 in Havana's psychiatric hospital. The sculpture was the work of José Villa who was also responsible for the John Lennon monument in Vedado, see page 58.

At the southern end of Plaza San Francisco, behind the church and convent, is the **Jardín de Madre Teresa de Calcuta** (Mother Teresa's Garden), and at the end of the garden is the Greek Orthodox Church.

Opposite San Francisco on the west side of the square, Nelson Domínguez, one of Cuba's most respected and prolific contemporary artists, has his own studio/gallery at the **Galería Los Oficios** ⓘ *Oficios 166 entre Amargura y Teniente Rey, T7-863 0497, daily 1000-1700.* Working in various mediums, he is primarily influenced by the natural environment and draws heavily on indigenous and spiritual symbolism. There are several other artists' galleries in this area, such as **Galería de Arte Carmen Montilla Tinoco** ⓘ *Oficios 162 entre Amagura y Teniente Rey, T7-866 8768, Tue-Sat 0930-1700, Sun 0930-1300*, housed in an early 18th-century building. It was originally used as a shop below and dwelling above, then briefly as the Consulate of Paraguay at the beginning of the 20th century, but it was ruined by fire in the 1980s. The **Oficina del Historiador**, with the help of the Venezuelan artist, restored it and opened it as an art gallery in her name in 1994. Nearby to the west is the **Museo de la Cerámica Cubana** ⓘ *Amargura y Mercaderes, T7-861 6130, ceramica@patrimonio.ohc.cu, Tue-Sat 0930-1700, Sun 0930-1300, free*, displaying Cuban ceramic art dating from the 1940s onwards.

On the northwest corner of the square, the Corinthian white marble building was once the **legislative building** where the House of Representatives met before the Capitolio was built. To the east, the newly restored Cuban Stock Exchange building, **La Lonja** (on the corner of Oficios and Plaza San Francisco de Asís), is worth a look, as is the new cruise ship terminal opposite.

Just north of the square, the British Embassy financed the construction of the **Diana Garden** ⓘ *Baratillo, near Plaza San Francisco, daily 0700-1900*, in memory of Diana, Princess of Wales. It is dominated by a concrete tube covered in ceramics in the shape of liquorice all-sorts which don't reach to the top, symbolizing a life cut short. There is also a sculpture of the sun, representing the happiness in her life, but one triangle is missing, her heart. Around the base of the pole are rings for sadness.

Museo del Ron ⓘ *Av del Puerto 262 entre Sol y Muralla, T7-861 8051, www.havanaclubfoundation.com, Mon-Thu 0900-1700, Fri-Sun 0900-1600, CUC$7, includes a drink, under 15s free, multilingual guides included.* Southeast of Plaza San Francisco, the **Fundación Destilería Havana Club** has a museum that explains the production of rum, from the sugar cane plantation to the processing and bottling, with machinery dating from the early 20th century. The museum is well laid out, dark and atmospheric. There is a wonderful model railway which runs round a model sugar mill and distillery, designed and made by prize-winning Lázaro Eduardo García Driggs in 1993-1994 and restored in 1999-2000. At the end of the tour you get a tasting of a six-year old **Havana Club** rum in a bar that is a mock-up of the once-famous **Sloppy Joe's**. There is also a restaurant and bar next door, a shop and an art gallery where present-day Cuban artists exhibit their work.

Museo Humboldt ⓘ *Oficios 254, esquina Muralla, closed for repairs in 2015.* The great explorer and botanist Federico Enrique Alejandro von Humboldt (1769-1857) lived here at the beginning of 1801 when he completed his calculations of the meridian of the city. His home is now a museum. Humboldt travelled extensively in Central and South America, paving the way for Darwin, who called him the greatest naturalist of his time. His scientific works were not confined merely to plants. His name has been given to the cold current that flows northwards off the coast of Chile and Peru, which he discovered and measured. He also made important contributions to world meteorology, to the study of vulcanism and the earth's crust and to the connection between climate and flora. In the process he discovered that mountain sickness is caused by a lack of oxygen at high altitudes. The last years of his life were spent writing *Kosmos*, an account of his scientific findings, which was soon translated into many languages.

Nearby, is the **Casa de la Poesía** ⓘ *Muralla 63 entre Oficios e Inquisidor, T7-862 1801, poeta@patrimonio.ohc.cu, Mon-Sat 0830-1730.*

★ La Plaza Vieja and around

This 18th-century plaza has been restored as part of a joint project by UNESCO and **Habaguanex**, a state company responsible for the restoration and revival of La Habana Vieja. The large square has a fountain in the middle and is overlooked by elegant balconies on many of the buildings.

The former house of the Spanish Captain General Conde de Ricla, who retook Havana from the English and restored power to Spain in 1763, can be seen on the corner of San Ignacio and Muralla. Known as **La Casona** ① *Centro de Arte La Casona, Muralla 107 esq San Ignacio, T7-861 8544, www.galeriascubanas.com, Tue-Sat 1000-1730,* it is a beautiful blue and white building with friezes up the staircase and along the walls and trailing plants in the courtyard. There is a great view of the plaza from the balcony, but in 2015 the upper floor was closed for repairs and restoration works. The Galería Diago displays naïf art and has a shop selling books, cards, catalogues, prints and art reproductions. On the south side there is also a museum of playing cards, **Museo de Naipes 'Marqués de Prado Ameno'** ① *Muralla 101 esq Inquisidor, T7-860 1534, naipes@patrimonio.ohc.cu, Tue-Sat 0930-1700, Sun 0930-1300.*

On the west side of the Plaza is the hugely popular microbrewery, **Cervecería La Muralla** (see page 78) and the **Centro de las Artes Visuales** ① *San Ignacio 352 entre Teniente Rey y Muralla, T7-862 5279, Tue-Sat 1000-1700,* which has a variety of art exhibitions. There are two galleries, Siglo XXI and Escuela de Plata.

On the north side of the square, on Teniente Rey, is a posh and expensive restaurant, **Santo Angel**, which has tables outside and is a pleasant place for an evening cocktail. In the northeast corner (Mercaderes y Teniente Rey) is the **Café Taberna** (T7-861 1637), the first coffeehouse to be established in Havana by the English, after they took the city in 1762. The café was named after its owner, Juan Bautista de Taberna. It remained in operation until the 1940s and was known as a place where merchant traders congregated. It was reopened in 1999 as a Benny Moré theme restaurant. Unfortunately the food is nothing special, rather greasy, and the service is poor.

On the top floor of the Gómez Vila building is the **Cámara Oscura** ① *Teniente Rey esq Mercaderes, Plaza Vieja, T7-866 4461, Tue-Sun 0930-1715, CUC$3, free for under 12s, presentations every 20 mins,* where lenses and mirrors provide you with a panoramic view of the city. Donated by Cádiz, this camera obscura is the first in the Americas and one of few in the world: there are two in England, two in Spain and one in Portugal.

In one of the converted mansions on the east side, the **Fototeca de Cuba** ① *Mercaderes 307 entre Teniente Rey y Muralla, T7-862 2530, Mon-Sat 1000-1700,* showcases international photography exhibitions. The old post office, also on the east side, dates from 1909.

Academia de Ciencias de Cuba ① *Cuba 460 entre Amargura y Brasil, T7-863 4824, closed for long-term renovations in 2015.* Housed in a strikingly ornate building northwest of the plaza, the museum contains displays about science in Cuba, the history of the Academy of Sciences and exhibits on the role of the medical profession during the Wars of Independence. It was previously known as the **Museo Histórico de las Ciencias Carlos J Finlay** after the eminent Cuban doctor who discovered that the mosquito was the vector of yellow fever in the late 19th century and helped to eradicate the disease in Cuba.

Convento de Santa Clara ① *Cuba 610 entre Luz y Sol, closed for repairs.* The convent of Santa Clara was founded in 1644 by nuns from Cartagena in Colombia. It was in use as a convent until 1919, when the nuns sold the building. In a shady business deal it was later acquired by the government and, after radical alterations, it became offices for the Ministry of Public Works until the decision was made to restore the building to its former glory. Work began in 1982, with the creation of the Centro Nacional de Conservación, Restauración y Museología (CENCREM), and is still continuing. The convent occupies four small blocks in La Habana Vieja, bounded by Calles Habana, Sol, Cuba and Luz, and originally had three cloisters and an orchard.

Southern Habana Vieja

The area is rather off the beaten track. Renovation works have not yet spread this far south, so it looks scruffy, and some people find it intimidating. It is much more a residential area than a tourist attraction, and, while there are plenty of churches, you won't find the museums and palaces typical of the northern part of the old city.

Opposite the central railway station, the **Museo Casa Natal de José Martí** ⓘ *Leonor Pérez 314 entre Picota y Egido, T7-861 5095, nataljmarti@patrimonio.ohc.cu, Tue-Sat 0930-1700, Sun 0930-1300, CUC$2, guided tour CUC$3*, is the birthplace of the country's great hero, with his full life story documented with photos, mementoes, furniture and papers. The tiny house has been devoted to his memory since a plaque was first put on the wall in 1899; it's been a museum since 1925 and was restored in 1951-1953.

Another attraction in the southern part of Old Havana is the vintage car museum, **Depósito de Automóviles** ⓘ *Desamparados (Av del Puerto) y Damas, T7-863 9942, automovil@patrimonio.ohc.cu, Tue-Sat 0930-1700, Sun 0930-1300, CUC$2, guided tour CUC$5*, which lovingly presents vehicles from the 19th and 20th centuries. There are a great many museum pieces including pre-Revolution US models, which are still on the road especially outside Havana, in among the Ladas, VWs and Nissans.

The church of **San Francisco de Paula** is on a traffic island on Avenida del Puerto (Desamparados). On the bay side of the road you will see some fine old steam engines, which have been put to rest outside the renovated warehouse, Almacenes San José. This is now the main handicrafts market in Havana (see Shopping, page 85), attracting coachloads of tourists to buy their souvenirs. There are hundreds of stalls where you can bargain for a good price and a waterfront café where you can get a drink overlooking the docks. Next door is another old warehouse, **Antiguo Almacén de la Madera y el Tabaco**, which has been converted into a microbrewery and restaurant/snack bar (see page 77).

Casablanca

two massive fortresses guard the entrance to the bay and afford lovely views of the city

From near the fortress of La Punta in the old city, a tunnel built in 1958 by the French runs east under the mouth of the harbour; it emerges in the rocky ground between the Castillo del Morro and the fort of La Cabaña, some 550 m away, where a 5-km highway connects with the Havana–Matanzas road.

★ Castillo del Morro

Ctra de la Cabaña, T7-8619727. Daily 0900-1900. CUC$6 plus CUC$1 for the guide, CUC$2 for the lighthouse (currently closed), children under 6 free, children 6-11 CUC$4. No charge for photos.

The Castillo del Morro (El Castillo de los Tres Reyes) was built between 1589 and 1630, with a 20-m moat, but has been much altered. It stands on a bold headland with the best view of Havana and is illuminated at night. It was one of the major fortifications built to protect the natural harbour and the assembly of Spain's silver fleets from pirate attack. The flash of its lighthouse, built in 1844, is visible 30 km out to sea. It now serves as a museum with a good exhibition of Cuban history since the arrival of Columbus.

On the harbourside, down by the water, is the **Battery of the 12 Apostles**, each gun being named after an Apostle. There is a bar here, open Monday to Saturday 1200-1900, which is worth a visit for the views of the harbour and the whole of Havana.

Fortaleza de San Carlos de Cabaña
T7-7911233. Daily 1000-2200, CUC$6, plus CUC$2 for cannon-firing ceremony 1800-2200. No charge for camera or video. Access as for Castillo del Morro, see above.

It is believed that around 1590, the military engineer Juan Bautista Antonelli, who built La Punta and El Morro, walked up La Cabaña hill and declared that "he who is master of this hill will be master of Havana." His prophecy was proved correct two centuries later when the English attacked Havana, conquering La Cabaña and thereby gaining control of the port. In 1763, after the English withdrew, another military engineer, Silvestre Abarca, arrived with a plan to build a fortress there. Construction lasted until 1774, when the fortress (the largest the Spanish had built until then in the Americas) was named San Carlos de la Cabaña, in honour of the king of Spain. It has a solid vertical wall of about 700 m with a deep moat connected to that of El Morro. The ditch is 12 m deep on the landward side and there is a drawbridge to the main entrance. From its position on the hill it dominates the city, the bay and the entrance to the harbour. In its heyday it had 120 cannon.

Inside are **Los Fosos de los Laureles**, where political prisoners were shot during the Cuban fight for independence. On 3 January 1959, Che Guevara took possession of the fortress on his triumphant arrival in Havana after the flight of the dictator, Batista. Every night the cannon are fired in an historical ceremony recalling the closure of the city walls to protect the city from attack by pirates. In the 17th century the shot was fired from a naval ship in the harbour, but now it is fired from La Cabaña at 2100 on the dot by soldiers in 18th-century uniforms, with the ceremony starting at 2045. There are two museums here, one about Che Guevara and another about fortresses with pictures and models, some old weapons and a replica of a large catapult and battering ram from the 16th to 18th centuries.

Essential Casablanca

Finding your feet

To cross the bay to Casablanca, join the left-hand ferry queue at Muelle Luz, opposite Calle Santa Clara. Security is very tight here since a ferry was hijacked in 2003 for an abortive attempt to get to Miami. Everybody is searched and there are metal detectors. The ferry crossing costs 10 centavos. Access to the Castillo del Morro is from any bus going through the tunnel (40 centavos or 1 peso): board at San Lázaro and Avenida del Puerto and get off at the stop after the tunnel, cross the road and follow the path up to the left. Alternatively, take the **HabanaBusTour** or a taxi, or it's a 20-minute walk from the Fortaleza de San Carlos de la Cabaña.

Tip...
You can walk from the Christ statue to the Fortaleza in 10 minutes and then, from there, on to the Castillo del Morro.

Other sights in Casablanca

Casablanca is also the site of a statue of a very human-looking Jesus Christ, erected in white marble during the Batista dictatorship as a pacifying exercise. To get there from the ferry dock, go up a steep, twisting flight of stone steps, starting on the other side of the plaza. You can get a good view of the harbour and Havana's skyline from **Parque El Cristo**, particularly at night, but be careful not to miss the last ferry back. Also in Casablanca you will find the **National Observatory** and the old railway station for the **Hershey line** trains to Matanzas.

Centro

ornate but crumbling 19th-century buildings

The state of the buildings in Centro Habana can be a shock to the first-time visitor; some streets resemble a war zone, with piles of rubble and holes like craters on the streets and pavements. Centro is not a tourist attraction, although many visitors end up staying here in one of the many *casas particulares*, conveniently placed between the architectural and historical attractions of La Habana Vieja and the nightlife of Vedado.

Centro is separated from La Habana Vieja by the Prado (although we have included those buildings on the west side of the avenue in the old city text, above). Centro's main artery is Calle San Rafael, which runs west from the Parque Central and is initially closed to traffic. This was Havana's 19th-century retail playground but today is spliced by ramshackle streets strewn with rubble and lined with decrepit houses. To the north, Centro is bounded by the seafront drive, the Malecón, which is in a dire state of repair because of buffeting sea winds, although renovation is underway in parts.

Barrio Chino

At the cross-section of Amistad and Dragones stands the gateway to Barrio Chino, a Cuban-Chinese hybrid. In its pre-Revolutionary heyday, this 10-block zone, pivoting around the Cuchillo de Zanja, was full of sordid porn theatres and steamy brothels. Now, a handful of restaurants strewn with lanterns, a colourful food market and a smattering of Chinese associations are all that remains of what was formerly the largest Chinatown in Latin America.

Quinta de los Molinos

Handsome Avenida Allende runs west from the corner of Parque de la Fraternidad to the high hill on which stands **El Príncipe Castle** (now the city jail). At the foot of the hill, on the border of Centro and Vedado, is the Quinta de los Molinos, which once housed the School of Agronomy of Havana University. The main house now contains the **Máximo Gómez Museum**, with displays on the life of the Dominican-born fighter for Cuban Independence. Also here is the headquarters of the association of young writers and artists (Asociación Hermanos Saiz). The gardens are a lovely place to stroll.

Partagás cigar factory

San Carlos 816 entre Sitios y Peñalver, 40-min tours Mon-Fri 0900-1300, CUC$10; tickets must be bought in advance in hotel lobbies. English, Spanish or French-speaking guides available, but you may have to wait until a guide is free in your preferred language.

ON THE ROAD
Cayo Hueso

Cayo Hueso is a run-down *barrio* lying in a triangle between Infanta, San Lázaro and the Malecón in Centro Habana. It was named by cigar factory workers returning from Key West and has nothing to do with bones (*huesos* in Spanish), although it was once the site of the Espada cemetery and the San Lázaro quarry. There are about 12,000 homes in the *barrio*, mostly tenements, which have been earmarked for restoration. As in La Habana Vieja, the renovation project also involves educating the community in its own particular culture and history.

In 1924, the cigar factory workers built a social club on San Lázaro, which became the site of the José Martí People's University. San Lázaro, with the University of Havana's wide stairway at its western end, was the site of fierce and determined student demonstrations from the late 1920s onwards. In the mid-1950s, Infanta was the Maginot line where the students faced Batista's troops. On 25 Jul 1956, Fidel Castro departed from Calle Jovellar 107 for the attack on the Moncada Garrison in Santiago de Cuba. There is a memorial plaque there now.

Cayo Hueso is now best known as a centre of *Santería* in the city, with Afro-Cuban art and music in abundance, especially on Calle Hamel (see page 52).

Relocated from its old position behind the Capitolio, the factory offers a behind-the-scenes look at cigar production. The tour can be interesting but is more often a shambles and not worth the entry free. You are taken up to the top floor where you stand in a corridor looking in through windows to where people are working. You briefly see the workers rolling cigars and get a cursory description of the components, but there is very little space and it is difficult to hear the guide over the loud music. Four different brand names are made here: *Partagás*, *Cubana*, *Ramón Allones* and *Bolívar*. These and other famous cigars can be bought at the Romeo y Julieta shop in a blue building a block away on the opposite corner (Monday-Saturday 0900-1700), as can rum (credit cards accepted). Do not buy black market cigars from your guide. Cigars are also made at many tourist locations (for example Palacio de la Artesanía, the airport, some hotels). Also see Cayo Hueso box, above.

> **Tip...**
> If your stay is not restricted to Havana, then you are far better off visiting the cigar factory in Pinar del Río (see page 122).

Museo Casa José Lezama Lima ① *Trocadero 162 entre Industria y Consulado, T7-863 4161, mlezama@cubarte.cult.cu, Tue-Sat 0900-1700, Sun 0900-1300, CUC$1, CUC$5 with guide*. This is the house where José Lezama Lima (1910-76) lived, one of the most important Cuban writers. There is a collection of his personal belongings and art by Cuban painters of the vanguard movement (La Vanguardia).

★ Malecón

The Malecón is Havana's oceanfront esplanade, which links Habana Vieja to the western residential district of Vedado. The sea crashing along the wall here is a spectacular sight when the wind blows from the north. On calmer days, fishermen lean over the parapet,

④ Centro & La Habana Vieja

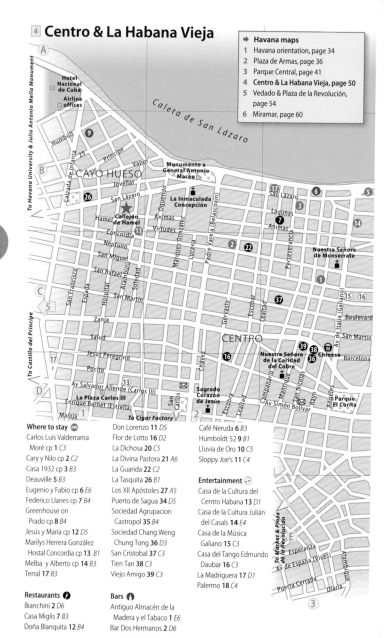

Where to stay 🛏

Carlos Luis Valderrama
  Moré cp **1** C3
Cary y Nilo cp **2** C2
Casa 1932 cp **3** B3
Deauville **5** B3
Eugenio y Fabio cp **6** E6
Federico Llanes cp **7** B4
Greenhouse on
  Prado cp **8** B4
Jesús y María cp **12** D5
Marilys Herrera González
  Hostal Concordia cp **13** B1
Melba y Alberto cp **14** B3
Terral **17** B3

Don Lorenzo **11** D5
Flor de Lotto **16** D2
La Dichosa **20** C5
La Divina Pastora **21** A6
La Guarida **22** C2
La Tasquita **26** B1
Los XII Apóstoles **27** A5
Puerto de Sagua **34** D5
Sociedad Agrupacion
  Castropol **35** B4
Sociedad Chang Weng
  Chung Tong **36** D3
San Cristóbal **37** C3
Tien Tan **38** C3
Viejo Amigo **39** C3

Café Neruda **6** B3
Humboldt 52 **9** B1
Lluvia de Oro **10** C5
Sloppy Joe's **11** C4

Entertainment 😊

Casa de la Cultura del
  Centro Habana **13** D1
Casa de la Cultura Julián
  del Casals **14** E4
Casa de la Música
  Galiano **15** C3
Casa del Tango Edmundo
  Daubar **16** C3
La Madriguera **17** D1
Palermo **18** C4

Restaurants 🍴
Bianchini **2** D6
Casa Miglis **7** B3
Doña Blanquita **12** B4

Bars 🍸
Antiguo Almacén de la
  Madera y el Tabaco **1** E6
Bar Dos Hermanos **2** D6

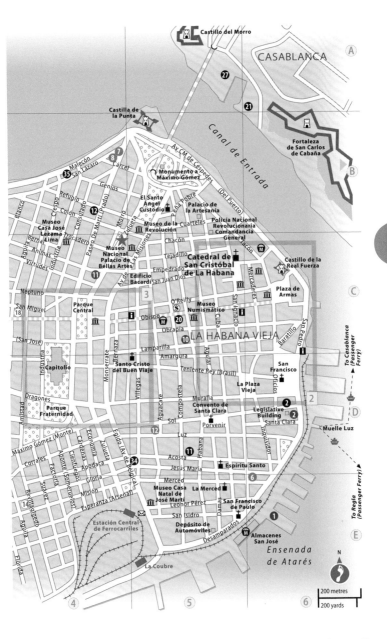

Castillo del Morro

CASABLANCA

Castilla de la Punta

Canal de Entrada

Fortaleza de San Carlos de Cabaña

Malecón

Cárcel

Monumento a Máximo Gómez

El Santo Angel Custodio

Palacio de la Artesanía

Museo Casa José Lezama Lima

Museo de la Revolución

Policía Nacional Revolucionaria Comandancia General

Catedral de San Cristóbal de La Habana

Castillo de la Real Fuerza

Museo Nacional Palacio de las Bellas Artes

Edificio Bacardí

Plaza de Armas

Parque Central

Museo Numismático

Capitolio

LA HABANA VIEJA

Santa Cristo del Buen Viaje

San Francisco

La Plaza Vieja

To Casablanca (Passenger Ferry)

Parque Fraternidad

Convento de Santa Clara

Legislative Building

Muelle Luz

Espíritu Santo

Museo Casa Natal de José Martí

La Merced

San Francisco de Paúla

To Regla (Passenger Ferry)

Estación Central de Ferrocarriles

Depósito de Automóviles

Almacenes San José

La Coubre

Ensenada de Atarés

N

200 metres
200 yards

lovers sit in the shade of the small pillars and joggers sweat along the pavement. On the other side of the six-lane highway, buildings which from a distance look stout and grand, with arcaded pavements, balconies, mouldings and large entrances, are salt-eroded, faded and sadly decrepit inside. Restoration is progressing slowly, but the sea is destroying old and new alike and creating a mammoth renovation task. Parts of the sea wall are also being rebuilt meaning that there is always construction work somewhere along the Malecón.

★ Callejón de Hamel

Among the alleyways of Cayo Hueso (see box, page 49) is Calle Hamel (an extension of Calle Animas, between Aramburu and Espada). It is the location of **Salvador González Escalona's art studio** ① *Hamel 1054 entre Aramburu y Hospital, T7-878 1661, www. afrocubaweb.com, www.havana-cultura.com, daily 0930-1800, free.* Salvador is a self-taught painter and sculptor, inspired by the history of the neighbourhood and its *Santería* traditions. He has painted large bright Afro-Cuban murals on the walls of Calle Hamel, combining a mixture of abstract and surrealist designs with phrases giving advice and warnings about danger, death and life. The project is affectionately called Callejón de Hamel and is recognized as the first open-air mural in Cuba dedicated to *Santería* and reflecting Afro-Cuban scenes. Salvador himself describes it as a community-based project, "from el barrio, to el barrio and with el barrio". As well as murals there are other surprises such as a typewriter pinned to the door of the gallery, painted drums and sculptures of corrugated iron and bike wheels.

Every Sunday 1200-1500 a free Peña Cultural Alto Cubana, known as **Peña de la Rumba del Cayo**, is held to honour the different Orishas. This is a very popular event, attracting large enthusiastic crowds. Other community activities at Callejón de Hamel include children's activities every other Saturday from 1000. There are a couple of *paladares* here, and a small bar in the street sells a unique rum cocktail called El Negrón. There's also a stall selling herbs with spiritual and curative roles within *Santería*.

Hamel 1108 is the home of singer-songwriter Angel Díaz and the birthplace of the musical genre known as *filín* ('feeling'). Nearby, Calle Horno was the site of the first cultural circle dedicated to Carlos Gardel (the Argentine maestro of tango) and is another centre for cultural activities.

Vedado

the best restaurants, bars and clubs can be found in this district of former wealth and decadence

The largely residential district of Vedado was built in the mid 19th century, funded by the massive wealth generated by the sugar industry. According to Cuban historian Hugh Thomas, between 1917 and 1925 money flooded into the capital as Cuba supplied the United States with its entire sugar needs following the First World War. Prosperity and decadence went hand in hand, as opportunistic officials grew rich on non-existent projects and gambling was allowed. The grand hotels and sumptuous houses of Vedado reflected the opulence of life under the dictatorship. However, imagination is now required to conjure up the glory days of these beautiful residences, with their magnificent but crumbling staircases, twisted wrought-iron work and patched or broken stained-glass windows.

BACKGROUND
Hotel Habana Libre

The hotels in Vedado harbour many secrets and tales from the past, Some, such as the Nacional, were built with Mafia money and were frequented by the mob during the decadent years before the Revolution. The **Havana Hilton** was inaugurated on 19 March 1958; its huge tower symbolized everything that was luxurious and profligate in the capital and attracted a high-flying and wealthy clientele. However, it had been open for barely one year before it was taken over by the victorious revolutionaries in 1959 and renamed the **Habana Libre**. The Continental Suite, room 2324, was used as the Revolution Headquarters for the first three months of 1959 and press conferences for foreign journalists were given here. Later, the first Soviet embassy in Havana occupied two floors. In the 1960s it was used for international meetings. Castro stayed in La Castellana Suite, room 2224, for the Tricontinental conference in December 1961.

Plaza de la Revolución is the place to be for any demonstration, political rally or festive occasion. It was the scene for most of Castro's marathon speeches in the days when they lasted for hours. Vedado is also the place to come for nightlife. This is where you'll find all the hottest clubs and discos, bars and floor shows. If you are a night owl, find yourself a hotel or *casa particular* here so that you can walk home in the early hours, after enjoying salsa, jazz, *son*, boleros, cabaret, a show, theatre, cinema, ballet or a classical concert – whatever takes your fancy.

★ Plaza de la Revolución

This vast open space looks more like a car park than the venue for some of the nation's most rousing speeches and memorable gatherings including the May Day parade. Surrounded by imposing 1950s buildings housing most of the more important ministries, it is a focal point for anyone wanting to understand the charisma of Fidel and his marathon speeches. Suspended on the outside of the **Ministry of the Interior** is the 30-m steel sculpture of Che Guevara seen in all photos of Havana, a replica of the iconic image originally shot in 1960 by the celebrated photographer Alberto Korda. The long grey building behind the Martí monument is the former **Justice Ministry** (1958), now the headquarters of the Central Committee of the Communist Party. The plaza was completely transformed for an open-air Mass held by Pope John Paul II in January 1998 with huge religious paintings suspended over the surrounding buildings.

Memorial y Museo a José Martí ① *Plaza de la Revolución, T7-859 2347, Mon-Sat 0930-1630, CUC$3, children under 12 free, lookout CUC$2 extra*. Overlooking the Plaza is the 17-m statue of the national hero, José Martí, carved from white marble extracted from La Isla de la Juventud. The enormous base of the monument is where Castro stood to address the people. Inside it is a beautifully restored and most impressive museum. Don't miss the lookout accessed by mirrored lift. This is the highest point in the city with good panoramic views of Havana. You should receive a certificate from the lift attendant on your descent.

➡ **Havana maps**
1 Havana orientation, page 34
2 Plaza de Armas, page 36
3 Parque Central, page 41
4 Centro & La Habana Vieja, page 50
5 **Vedado & Plaza de la Revolución, page 54**
6 Miramar, page 60

Where to stay 🛏

Alicia Horta cp 1 *B6*
Casa Betty et Armando
 Gutiérrez cp 2 *B6*
Casa Caprí (Eugenia y Rudel)
 cp 3 *A5*
Colina 4 *C6*
Daysie Recio cp 5 *B4*
Gisela Ibarra cp 6 *A4*
Jorge Coalla Potts cp 7 *B5*
Martha Vitorte cp 8 *B5*
Meliá Cohiba 9 *A3*
Mercedes González cp 10 *B5*
Nacional de Cuba 11 *B6*

Restaurants 🍴

Adela 1 *C4*
Café Laurent 2 *B6*
Coppelia 3 *B5*
Decameron 4 *B3*
Gringo Viejo 5 *B4*
Hurón Azul 6 *C6*
La Casona de 17 7 *B6*
La Roca 8 *B5*
La Torre 9 *B6*
Le Chansonnier 10 *B5*
Los Amigos 11 *B6*
Starbien 12 *B6*
Unión Francesa 13 *B3*

Entertainment 🎵

Bar Bohemio 1 *C2*
Cabaret Las Vegas 2 *C6*
Café El Gato Tuerto 3 *B6*
Café Teatro Bertolt
 Brecht 4 *B5*
El Cocinero 5 *B1*
El Gran Palenque Bar 6 *A3*
El Submarino Amarillo 7 *B3*
Hurón Azul 8 *A3*
Imágenes 9 *A4*
Jazz Café 10 *A3*
La Casona de Línea 11 *A4*
La Zorra y El Cuervo 12 *C5*
Salón Rojo 13 *B6*
Tikoa 14 *B3*

Museo Postal Cubano ① *Ministry of Communications, Plaza de la Revolución, T7-8828223, Mon-Fri 0800-1730, free.* The museum tells the history of the Cuban postal service. You will also find a collection of stamps and the story books of José Antonio de Armona (1765).

La Rampa and around

Calle 23, familiarly known as La Rampa, runs through Vedado from the Malecón at its eastern end, to the Cementerio Colón and the Río Almendares in the west. The eastern end is full of activity, overlooked as it is by the (in)famous **Hotel Nacional de Cuba** and **Hotel Habana Libre** (see box,

> **Tip...**
> The garden of the iconic Hotel Nacional is the place to drink cocktails while watching the sun set and the moon rise over the Malecón.

page 53). Airline offices and the International Press Centre cluster together alongside restaurants and nightclubs and the ice cream parlour **Coppelia** (see also page 75), which found movie fame in *Strawberry and Chocolate*. The parlour, which occupies a whole block, is a good example of the architectural creativity of the post-Revolution years. It was built by Mario Girona in 1966, based on an idea by Celia Sánchez Manduley, a heroine of the Sierra Maestra.

Tribuna Anti-Imperialista José Martí On the Malecón, close to the **Hotel Nacional**, the **Monumento al Maine** is a tribute to the 265 men who were killed when the *USS Maine* warship exploded in the bay in 1898. Close by, the Tribuna Anti-Imperialista José Martí was built during the Elián González affair and features a statue of Martí holding his son Ismaelillo and pointing towards the US Embassy, fronted by a veil of mirrored glass windows and patrolled by Cuban military personnel. The famous billboard of a fanatical Uncle Sam towering menacingly over a young Cuban patriot has been relocated behind the Embassy.

Pabellón Cuba ① *Calle 23 entre N y M, T7-832 4925, Tue-Fri 1400-2000, Sat, Sun 1000-2000.* The Cuban Pavilion is a combination of a tropical glade and a museum of social history, with live music and dancing held regularly. It tells the nation's story through a brilliant combination of objects, photos and the architectural manipulation of space. It also hosts the annual *Feria del Libro* in February (the main site is at La Cabaña), the *Cubadisco* music convention in May, a showcase for the latest Cuban music, and *Arte en la Rampa* in July, August and the first two weeks in September, with handicrafts and souvenirs for sale, music and dancing.

Universidad de Habana Just to the south of Calle 23, on the edge of Centro and Vedado, is Havana University. The neoclassical building was constructed in the early 20th century and is reached by an imposing stone stairway. A monument to **Julio Antonio Mella**, founder of the Cuban Communist Party, stands across from the university entrance. This area is full of students, helping to make it a lively and happening part of town. Near the university the **Museo Napoleónico** ① *San Miguel 1159 esquina Ronda, T7-879 1460, mnapoleonico@patrimonio.ohc.cu, Tue-Sat 0930-1700, Sun 0930-1230, CUC$3, guide CUC$5,* houses 7000 pieces from the private collection of sugar baron, Julio Lobo: paintings and other works of art, a specialized library and a collection of weaponry. Check out the tiled fencing gallery.

Avenida de los Presidentes

The Avenida de los Presidentes, or Avenida G, joins the Plaza de la Revolución in the south to the Malecón in the north, bisecting La Rampa on its way through to the sea. It is a magnificent wide boulevard with grand houses and blocks of apartments that are desirable places to live. Just north of the intersection with La Rampa is a statue of Salvador Allende, the murdered President of Chile. At the Malecón the avenue is blocked by a monument to Calixto García.

Museo de la Danza ① *Entrance on Línea esq G (Av de los Presidentes), T7-831 2198, musdanza@cubarte.cult.cu, Tue-Sat 1000-1700, CUC$2, guided tour CUC$1, CUC$5 to take photos.* The museum presents an engaging collection of items from the dancer Alicia Alonso's personal collection and from the Ballet Nacional de Cuba.

Casa de las Américas ① *Calle 3 52 esq G, T7-838 2706, www.casa.cult.cu, Mon-Fri 0830-1600 except the last Fri in the month.* This active and welcoming centre was founded in 1959 by Haydée Santamaría (1923-1980) for pan-American cultural promotion and interchange. It hosts a varied programme of seminars workshops and investigative studies in addition to running its own publishing house. Exhibitions of art from all corners of Latin America are held in the Galería Latinoamericana, while contemporary Cuban art is shown in the Sala Contemporánea. On the ground floor is the **Librería Rayuela** book and music shop and a small peso bookstall.

Next door is the **Galería Haydée Santamaría** ① *Calle G entre 3 y 5, alongside Casa de las Américas, T7-838 2706, closed for renovation 2015,* which displays the work of Latin American artists. There is a good representation of mostly 20th-century styles with over 6000 works of art including sculptures, engravings and photography.

Built in 1961 opposite the Casa de las Américas, the **Estadio José Martí** (Malecón entre Avenida de los Presidentes y J), is a good example of post-Revolutionary architecture; the sports ground shows a highly imaginative use of concrete, painted in primary colours.

Museo de Artes Decorativas ① *Calle 17 502 esq E, T7-832 0924, artdeco@cubarte.cult.cu, Tue-Sat 0930-1700, CUC$5 including Spanish- or English-speaking guide, or 1100-1630, CUC$3 without a guide, CUC$5 to take photos, CUC$10 for videos.* European and Oriental art from the 16th to the 20th centuries has been displayed at this French Renaissance-style mansion since 1964. It was originally designed by Alberto Camacho (1924-1927) for José Gómez Mena's daughter, who belonged to one of Cuba's wealthiest families. Most of the building materials were imported from France and the interior decoration was by House of Jansen. In the 1930s the mansion was occupied by Gómez' sister, María Luisa, Condesa de Revilla de Camargo, who was a fervent collector of fine art and held elegant society dinners and receptions for guests, including the Duke of Windsor and Wallace Simpson. Her furniture included a desk that had belonged to Marie Antoinette. Her valuable collections were found in the basement after the family fled Cuba following the Revolution in 1959.

There are 10 permanent exhibition halls with works from the 16th to 20th centuries including ceramics, porcelain (Sévres, Chantilly and Wedgewood), furniture (Boudin, Simoneau and Chippendale) and paintings. The Regency-inspired dining room is recommended viewing and includes a sumptuous dinner service that belonged to the dictator Batista. The attendants are very knowledgeable and informative about the exhibits, but only in Spanish.

Paseo

Further west, this is another of Vedado's grand thoroughfares, running south from the Mafia-built **Hotel Habana Riviera** on the Malecón to the Plaza de la Revolución. Many of the elegant mansions either side of the street have been converted into offices or embassies.

Casa de la Amistad ⓘ *Paseo 406 entre 17 y 19, T7-830 3114 ext 103. Bar and café Sun-Fri 0900-2200, Sat 0900-0100 for 'Noche Cubana' (CUC$3 including a cocktail).* This former mansion dating from 1926 was built by a wealthy plantation owner for his lover, later his wife, who left her first husband for him. (They were the first couple to divorce when it became legal in Cuba.) A beautiful dusky, coral pink building with gardens, it is now operated by **ICAP** (Cuban Institute for Friendship among the Peoples), which has a reasonably priced bar and cafeteria, with a live show on Saturday nights.

John Lennon Park ⓘ *Calle 17 entre 6 y 8.* The recently re-landscaped and renamed park just west of Paseo features a bronze statue of the Beatle sitting on a bench. It was sculpted by José Villa, who also sculpted the Che Guevara monument at the Palacio de los Pioneros in Tarará (see page 94). Words from Lennon's song 'Imagine' have been translated into Spanish and etched on the ground: *"dirás que soy un soñador, pero no soy el único"* ("You may say I'm a dreamer, but I'm not the only one."). It was inaugurated in December 2000 in a ceremony attended by Fidel Castro and Silvio Rodríguez (singer/songwriter and founder of the movement of *La Nueva Trova)*. Theft of the statue's glasses has meant there is now a 24-hour security guard, and the replacement glasses have been permanently fixed in place. Classical guitar concerts are sometimes held here.

★ Cementerio Colón

Entrance on Zapata y 12, T7-830 4517, daily 0800-1700. CUC$5 entrance including photos, CUC$1 for good map.

Constructed in 1871, the 56-ha city of the dead is the second largest cemetery in the world. It was designed by the Spanish architect, Calixto de Lloira y Cardosa, who was also the first person to be buried there. The Colón cemetery should be visited to see the wealth of funerary sculpture, much of it in Carrara marble, from the 19th and 20th centuries. Cubans visit the sculpture of Amelia La Milagrosa (Amelia Goire) at Calle 3 entre F y G and pray for miracles. The Chinese cemetery is at Avenida 26 y 31.

Miramar and further west *See map, page 60.*

this smart area is where diplomats and business people work and play

Miramar is some 16 km west of the old city on the west side of the Río Almendares and is easily reached via two road tunnels or bridges. Although there are many beautiful art nouveau and other houses from the early 20th century, the area is now being developed into a modern city with glossy new hotels for business people with state-of-the-art fitness and business centres. Most of the embassies are here, which always implies a certain status and level of comfort. It has the appearance of a wealthy suburb, with broad avenues and neatly aligned rectangular blocks.

Avenida Primera (first) runs closest to the sea, which is rocky and not recommended for bathing (use the hotel pool instead); Avenidas Tercera (third), Quinta (fifth) and Séptima (seventh) run parallel, with the tunnels to Vedado at the end of Avenidas 5 and 7. Some of the best restaurants are in Miramar and there are good nightlife venues too, including the internationally famous **Tropicana** cabaret show to the south.

Rigoberto Mena is one of Cuba's most respected contemporary artists, and his studio, **Estudio Galería Rigoberto Mena** ① *Calle 21 esq 54, T7-2025276, 5241 5737 (mob)*, just south of Miramar, houses a fantastic collection of abstract art. His style is deceptively simple: a meticulous composition of brilliant colours radiating from dark backgrounds.

Marina Hemingway
Off Av 5, Santa Fé, 20 mins by taxi (CUC$10-15) from central Havana.

The Marina Hemingway tourist complex in the fishing village of **Santa Fé** is the largest marina in the country and offers fishing and scuba-diving trips as well as other water- and land-based sports. It also hosts numerous fishing competitions and regattas. Also here is the Hemingway International Nautical Club, a social club for foreign executives based in Cuba. Another club in this area is the **Club Habana** (Sol Meliá) ① *Av 5 entre 188 y 192, Playa, T7-2750100, 7-2750300-9.* The main house dates back to 1928 and was the Havana Biltmore Yacht and Country Club. It is very posh but has lots of facilities on land and in the water.

Southern suburbs
modern architecture and green space

Instituto Superior de Arte (ISA)
Calle 120 1110 entre 9 y 13, Cubanacán, T7-208 8075, vrri@isa.cult.cu. Visits must be arranged by tour agencies (Paradiso), a specialist guide is provided. Independent visitors should phone or email at least 2 days in advance.

The Instituto Superior de Artes (ISA), which combines schools of visual art, modern dance, ballet, music and drama, is located in the grounds of the former Havana Country Club in Cubanacán, southwest of Miramar. Architects will be interested in this 'new spatial sensation', which was an ambitious project of the early 1960s. Three architects, Ricardo Porro, Roberto Gottardi and Vittorio Garati, were involved in the revolutionary design, which was to be constructed using domestic rather than imported materials.

Some parts of the scheme were not completed and others have since been abandoned (they were not entirely practical), but you can still visit the **Escuela Superior de Artes Plásticas**, which consists of a series of interlinked pavilions, courtyards and sinuous walkways designed by Porro. (Many people believe the layout takes the form of a woman's body, although some see it more as the womb itself, with a cervix-like fountain in the centre.)

There is also the **Escuela Superior de Artes Escénicas**, built by Gottardi, in the form of a miniature Italian hill-top town. It's rather claustrophobic and quite unlike Porro's sprawling, 'permeable' designs, which are full of fresh air and tropical vegetation. Porro's Dance School, although part of the same complex, is not accessible via the Country Club. The Clubhouse itself now serves as the Music School, since the 1960s Music School by Garati is now in ruins.

A lack of maintenance, water leaks, a faulty drainage system, structural defects, vegetation and vandalism have all contributed to the deterioration of both the finished and unfinished buildings and there is a lack of funds for planning a renovation programme and for carrying out repairs.

Parque Lenin

Northwest of Boyeros and the airport, T7-644 2721, Wed-Sun 1000-1700.

Parque Lenin is a huge green space on the edge of Havana, which is very popular as a weekend escape for Cuban families. There are lakes for boating, horses for riding, an amusement park (very popular) with a circus show, an aquarium and an upmarket

6 Miramar

➡ **Havana maps**
1 Havana orientation, page 34
2 Plaza de Armas, page 36
3 Parque Central, page 41
4 Centro & La Habana Vieja, page 50
5 Vedado & Plaza de la Revolución, page 54
6 Miramar, page 60

Gulf of Mexico

Maqueta de la Ciudad

MIRAMAR

Santa Rita

Av 5A

Estudio Galería Rigoberto Mena

N

300 metres
300 yards

Restaurants 🍴
1830 **1** *B6*
El Aljibe **2** *C3*
El Palio **3** *A3*
El Tocororo **4** *B4*

La Cocina de Lilliam **5** *D2*
La Esperanza **6** *A4*
La Fontana **7** *B1*

Entertainment ☺
Casa de la Música
  Egrem **1** *C4*
Club Almendares **2** *D5*
Don Congrejo **3** *A4*

restaurant. To the south is the botanical garden and Expocuba. Hiring bikes has been recommended as a good way to visit.

★ Jardín Botánico Nacional de Cuba

Km 3.5, Ctra Rocío, Calabazar, south of Havana beyond Parque Lenín, T7-697 9170, www. uh.cu/centros/jbn/index.html. Wed-Sun 0900-1600, but in practice you may not be allowed in after 1530. CUC$1, or CUC$3 if you take the 'train' with guide, children half price. Many hotel tour desks offer day trips with lunch for CUC$25. Taxi from Habana Vieja CUC$15-18 one way, good for groups.

The 600-ha botanical garden in Arroyo Naranjo is well maintained with excellent collections of Cuban and other tropical plants representing five geographical regions, including a Japanese area with tropical adaptations. It is part of the University of Havana and much scientific research takes place here. A multilingual guide will meet you at the gate, no charge, and you can take a 'train' tour along the 35 km of roads around the site in an open-sided, wheeled carriage towed by a tractor, which enables you to see the whole garden in about two hours. There are few signs, so it is not as informative as it might be, and a guide is helpful, describing unusual plants in the various zones. Several interconnected glasshouses are filled with desert, tropical and sub-tropical plants, and are well worth walking through. The garden's **organic vegetarian restaurant** uses solar energy for cooking (see Where to eat, page 77). There are also other restaurants and snack bars serving *criollo* food in CUP$ or CUC$.

El Río Club
(Johnnie's Club) **4** *B6*
Salón Boleros en
Dos Gardenias **5** *C3*

Salón Rosado Benny
Moré, La Tropical **6** *E3*
Tropicana **7** *E3*

BACKGROUND
Go before it changes

In August 2006 Fidel Castro had his 80th birthday. The occasion was to have been marked by national celebrations, parades and speeches, but shortly beforehand Castro made the surprise announcement that he was about to undergo major abdominal surgery and that he was handing over the reins of power temporarily to his brother, Raúl. The nature of his illness, operation and subsequent condition was shrouded in secrecy, with rumours of terminal illness and even his death circulating in Cuba and in Miami. By mid-2007, Fidel was well enough to receive foreign dignitaries and write articles on world issues. Nevertheless, he was still not seen in public and in 2008 the temporary handover of power became permanent. Raúl initially made attempts to liberalize the economy, allowing certain materialistic freedoms for Cubans with access to foreign exchange (permission to own laptops, stay in hotels, etc) and introduced bonuses for workers who exceed their targets, but was stymied by the arrival of three devastating hurricanes, which between them caused US$10 bn in damage. This, together with the world financial crisis and a dramatic fall in the price of nickel, completely stalled the economy and seriously hampered the government's room for manoeuvre. The celebration of the 50th anniversary of the Cuban Revolution on 1 January 2009 was a low-key, no-frills, low-budget affair. Hopes were raised when US President Obama took office and lifted travel restrictions on Cuban Americans visiting the island. However, he kept the US trade embargo in place to press Cuba to improve human rights and political freedoms. Castro agreed to talks on migration and other issues, but refused to make concessions.

In February 2013, Raúl Castro announced that at the end of his five-year term of office, in February 2018, he would retire. That prospect, together with President Obama leaving office in January 2017, appeared to galvanize bilateral negotiations. In 2014, secret talks were held at the Vatican and in Canada, facilitated by Pope Francis, and in December the two presidents announced the beginning of a process of restoring normal relations between the two nations. This was to include the lifting of some travel restrictions for US citizens, giving US banks access to the Cuban banking system, fewer restrictions on remittances and, importantly, restoring diplomatic relations. In January 2015, Cuba released 53 political dissidents. In April, Presidents

Obama and Castro met at the Summit of the Americas in Panama, and, following that, Cuba was taken off the US State Sponsors of Terrorism list. In July 2015 the Interests Section of both countries in Havana and Washington DC were upgraded to embassies. Charter flights from New York began, and four companies were approved to offer a chartered ferry service between Miami and Havana. However, the Cuban trade embargo remained in place, as it could only be lifted by a vote in the US Congress. Executive action could only lift some restrictions on travel and the import and export of goods between the two countries. In September, Pope Francis visited Cuba and the USA, saying Mass in Havana, Holguín and Santiago de Cuba.

Tourism to Cuba soared in 2015-2016, not only from US citizens on approved cultural or educational tours, but also from Europe and elsewhere as travellers rushed to see the island 'before it changes'. At the same time, however, there was another exodus of Cubans fleeing the country for the USA, fearing that if the Cuban Adjustment Act were to be eliminated, the 'wet foot, dry foot' route into the 'land of opportunity' would be closed to them and the annual quota of migrants would be abandoned.

The depth of the change in US-Cuba relations was underlined by the unprecedented visit to Havana in March 2016 of US President Barack Obama, accompanied by his family and an enormous delegation of business people. In addition to talks with President Raúl Castro and government officials, Obama held meetings with the private sector and gave a speech directly addressing the Cuban people. The mood was cordial and positive in terms of economic advancement between the two countries and several trade and investment deals were signed or discussed. Human rights issues were barely mentioned, to the disappointment of some, although nearly 500 people were arbitrarily detained during the visit, according to the Cuban Commission on Human Rights and Reconciliation. Criticism came also from another quarter, with a scathing article in *Granma* by Fidel Castro, expressing his disapproval.

In another sign of the changing times, Obama's visit was followed a few days later by the arrival of the Rolling Stones, who put on a free concert to some 1.2 million people both inside a sports stadium and outside watching giant screens. Rock music having been banned in the toughest period of the Revolution, the Stones' visit was symbolic of more than just another concert by a Western band. The ecstatic welcome was reminiscent of their 1960s heyday.

Tourist information

Oficina Nacional de Información Turística (Infotur)
Calle 28 303 entre 3 y 5, Miramar, T7-204 6635 and Guanabo, Av 5 entre 468 y 470, T7-796 6868, www.infotur.cu.
This is the headquarters of the national tourist board.

There is also a network of kiosks run by **Infotur**, which can provide you with information and maps. These are located at the **airport** (Terminal 3, T7-266 4094/642 6101, open 24 hrs); in **Habana Vieja** (Obispo entre Bernaza y Villegas, T7-866 3333, and Obispo y San Ignacio, T7-863 6884); in **Playa** (Av 5 y Calle 112, T7-204 7036, daily 0815-1615). At the **Santa María del Mar** office (Av Las Terrazas entre 11 y 12, Playas del Este, T7-797 1261/796 1111) you will find maps, excursions, internet, booking for hotels, souvenirs, but with no map of the area and with limited bus information, it remains to be seen how useful it's going to be.

The state tour agencies, such as **Cubatur** and **Havanatur**, are found in hotels and other locations. Their main task is to sell tours, but they can also make hotel reservations, sell tickets for buses, trains and planes and organize pick-ups and transfers. If you are staying in a *casa particular* you will probably find your host is a mine of useful information and can fill you in on all the gossip and background detail to enrich a stay in the capital.

Where to stay

Tourist hotels have a/c, 'tourist' TV (US films, tourism promotion) and restaurants with reasonable food, but standards are not comparable with Europe, and plumbing is often faulty or affected by water shortages. Payment for hotels used by tourists is in CUC$.

Several important hotel renovation projects have been completed by **Habaguanex** in La Habana Vieja and these are now elegant places to stay, becoming known as 'boutique' hotels. See www.habaguanexhotels.com for a full list of their hotels in Old Havana. Hotels in Vedado are some distance away from the colonial sights but are in a better district for nightlife. Miramar is further away still; hotels here are designed for business travellers and package tourists, but there are good restaurants, *paladares*, bars, clubs and Teatro Karl Marx.

La Habana Vieja
Hotels

$$$$-$$$ Conde de Villanueva – Hostal del Habano
Mercaderes 202 esq Lamparilla, T7-862 9293/4, www.habaguanexhotels.com.
Named after Claudio Martínez del Pinillo, Conde de Villanueva (1789-1853), a notable personality who promoted tobacco abroad and helped to bring the railway to Cuba. Just 9 rooms and suites around a peaceful courtyard, attractive red and green colour scheme, cigar theme with cigar shop, café, bar, good restaurant, highly regarded, friendly staff.

$$$$-$$$ Iberostar Parque Central
Neptuno entre Prado y Zulueta, on north side of Parque Central, T7-860 6627/9, www.iberostar.com.
Rooms and suites of international standard in 2 buildings connected by an enclosed walkway, excellent bathrooms, business centres, Wi-Fi, 3 restaurants, 4 bars, great view of Havana from pools on 9th floor of the Torre section and on 8th floor of the Colonial section, fitness centre, sauna, charming and helpful multilingual staff.

$$$$-$$$ Santa Isabel
Baratillo 9 entre Obispo y Narciso López, Plaza de Armas, T7-860 8201, www. hotelsantaisabel.com.

Beautiful 18th-century mansion, 27 luxury rooms, 10 of them suites, well-equipped bathrooms, rooms on 2nd floor have balcony overlooking plaza and those on the 3rd floor have a terrace, central patio with fountain and greenery and lobby bar. Wi-Fi. Good views from the **El Mirador** restaurant and the café.

$$$$-$$$ Saratoga
Paseo del Prado 603 esq Dragones, T7-8681000, www.hotel-saratoga.com.
The 1879 neoclassical façade of this corner plot masks a smart, modern hotel, favoured by celebrities such as Mick Jagger and Beyonce. Suites and rooms are comfortable and spacious but can suffer from traffic noise. The food is good with several dining options, from a tapas bar to an upmarket restaurant, and there's Wi-Fi in the Mezzanine Bar. Breakfast is comparatively expensive. The rooftop pool is particularly popular with views of the Capitolio, Parque Fraternidad and the Prado, great for sunset cocktails. Spa 0800-2000. Service nothing special.

$$$-$$ Hostal Valencia
Oficios 53 esq Obrapía, T7-867 1037, www.habaguanexhotels.com.
Joint Spanish/Cuban venture modelled on the Spanish *paradores*. 10 suites and rooms – some rather past their best – named after Valencian towns. Tastefully restored building, nicely furnished, pleasant courtyard with vines, music, good restaurant. Sister hotel, **El Comendador**, next door. The restaurant and bar on the corner is open from 1200 and serves pizza, *tortillas, empanadas*, etc, for lunch.

Casas particulares

$$ Eugenio y Fabio
San Ignacio 656 entre Jesús María y Merced, T7-862 9877, fabio.quintana@infomed.sld.cu.
6 rooms, all well-equipped and spacious but some are dark, overlooking interior courtyard, a/c, fan. House is stuffed with antiques and bric-a-brac and meals are served family style in an ornate baroque dining room. Roof terrace for sunset watching. Fabio and staff are very helpful and English is spoken. Breakfast CUC$8.

$$-$ Federico Llanes
Cárcel 156 Apto 3, entre San Lázaro y Prado, T7-861 7817, 5264 6917 (mob), fllanes@gmail.com.
Excellent location just off the Prado and a stone's throw from the Malecón. You have to climb 64 stairs up to the apartment on the 3rd floor but Federico, a former lawyer, is helpful with luggage as well as providing advice and information. 2 large, light rooms with tiled floors and heavy dark furniture, double beds, extra bed on request, a/c, fan, fridge, desk, safe box, English spoken, friendly household, good breakfast with lots of fruit and juice.

$$-$ Greenhouse on Prado
Cárcel 158 entre San Lázaro y Prado, T7-8617810, 5389 4652 (mob), jorgemc84@nauta.cu and on Facebook.
Jorge Muñoz Céspedes speaks English and is very helpful and friendly. Ground floor apartment in good condition. Large room with comfortable double and single bed, a/c, fan, good bedside lighting, safe box, desk, fridge stocked with water, beer and soft drinks, substantial breakfast, CUC$5.

$$-$ Gustavo Enamorado Zamora – Chez Nous
Teniente Rey (Brasil) 115 entre Cuba y San Ignacio, T7-862 6287, hostalcheznous@gmail.com.
3 spacious double rooms, 2 of which share a bathroom, the other is en suite, a/c, fan, TV, safe box, fridge, balcony overlooking street, roof terrace, parking, warm atmosphere. Gustavo and Kathy are kind and helpful, French, English and Russian spoken. In the building opposite they have another apartment with 3 rooms to rent with private bathroom and balcony – **Chez Nous Art Deco**, with the advantage of an elevator.

$$-$ Jesús y María
Aguacate 518 entre Sol y Muralla, T7-
861 1378, jesusmaria2003@yahoo.com.
Upstairs above the family and very private,
5 a/c bedrooms on 2 floors with double and
single bed, with fan, fridge, safe box. Top
floor rooms are the nicest. There is a terrace
where you have meals and a sunbathing
area. More of a hostal than a family home.

$$-$ Yamelis Elizalde
Cuba 518 entre Muralla y Teniente Rey,
T5331 9498 (mob), fllanes@gmail.com.
1 block from Plaza Vieja, this is a delightful
apartment renovated in 2015 with high
ceilings and tall windows. 2 rooms, each
with balcony overlooking the street, quiet
a/c, fan, safe box, fridge. Yamelis speaks
English and is a good cook, serving breakfast
and other meals on request. She lives here
with her little boy.

Centro
Hotels

$$$-$$ Terral
Malecón esq Lealtad, www.
habaguanexhotels.com.
Stunning position on Malecón, all rooms
have great view over the sea. Small new hotel
in a contemporary, chic style with spacious
rooms, good bathrooms and large windows.
Even the breakfasts are modern. Very good
service from cheerful staff. Only drawbacks
are traffic noise and a longish walk to the
sights (20 mins to Old Havana).

$$ Deauville
Galiano y Malecón, T7-866 8812,
reserva@hdeauville.gca.tur.cu.
144 basic rooms, temperamental lifts, noise
from Malecón but great view, balconies
overlooking sea and fortress, breakfast
included, helpful *buró de turismo*. Restaurant
Costa Norte offers dinner 1900-2200,
followed by a cabaret 2200-0230, Tue-Sun.
The pool is open to non-guests for CUC$5
including CUC$4 *consumo* (food/drinks) in

winter and CUC$10 including CUC$8 *consumo*
in summer, children under 3 free, snack bar.

Casas particulares

$$-$ Carlos Luis Valderrama Moré
Neptuno 404 entre San Nicolás y Manrique,
2nd floor, T7-867 9842.
Carlos and Vivian are former teachers,
friendly and helpful, he speaks English and
loves to talk about football. 1930s apartment
above a shop, 3 rooms, front room has
balcony overlooking street, good bathrooms,
a/c, fans, safe box, good food.

$$-$ Cary y Nilo
Gervasio 216 entre Concordia y Virtudes,
T7-862 7109, caridadgf45@yahoo.es.
Beautiful house with high ceilings, quiet,
spotlessly clean, Nilo has decades of
experience of hotel work and knows how
to treat his guests. 3 spacious rooms with
bathrooms, antique furnishings, colonial
style, quiet, good food, huge breakfasts.
No English spoken.

$$-$ Casa 1932
Campanario 63 bajos entre San Lázaro y
Lagunas, T7-8636203, 5264 3858 (mob),
www.casahabana.net.
A living museum stuffed with art deco
stained glass, antiques and a collection of
musical instruments in this beautiful house.
Luis Miguel speaks English and Italian and
is extremely informative. 3 a/c rooms of
different sizes and prices but all comfortable
and stylish with en suite bathrooms, safe box,
fan, fridge. Pleasant patio and terrace. Airport
pickup in vintage taxi can be arranged.

$$-$ Melba y Alberto
Galiano 115 Apto 81 entre Animas y
Trocadero, T7-863 5178, T05-264 8262 (mob),
barracuda1752@yahoo.es.
Unprepossessing entrance on street but
up on the 8th floor you're in another world
with views of the sea and city. 2 bedrooms,
1 with balcony and double bed, the
other with double and single bed, use
of kitchenette and living room, good

for families, charming hosts, excellent food, breakfast served on balcony, very comfortable and pleasant.

$ Marilys Herrera González – Hostal Concordia
Concordia 714 altos entre Soledad y Aramburu, T7-870 0608, http:// casaparticular.tripod.com.
3 a/c rooms with private bathrooms although not en suite, fridge, fan, safe box, use of kitchen, patio and roof terrace. All spotlessly clean and comfortable, laundry offered, Marylis (former Russian teacher) and Miguel (former aircraft engineer) are very kind and caring, they have travelled abroad and speak English, French and Russian.

Vedado
Hotels
The better hotels in Vedado are used by package tour operators and business travellers and are of a reasonable international standard. The cheaper hotels are basic, with intermittent electricity and poor water pressure, variable levels of cleanliness and security. For comfort and ambience you might prefer to forego the facilities of a hotel and opt for a *casa particular*, where you will get better food and service.

$$$$-$$$ Meliá Cohiba
Paseo entre 1 y 3, T7-833 3636, www.meliacuba.com.
International grand high rise that dominates the neighbourhood, 462 rooms and suites with every comfort, the higher rooms have the best views, very good service, shops, gym, healthclub, pool, gourmet restaurant, piano bar and Habana Café nightclub.

$$$$-$$$ Nacional de Cuba
O esq 21, T7-873 3564, www. hotelnacionaldecuba.com.
429 rooms, some renovated, generally friendly and efficient service, faded grandeur, dates from 1930, superb reception hall, note the vintage Otis high-speed lifts, steam room, 2 pools, restaurants, bars, shops,

business centre, exchange bureau, gardens with old cannons on hilltop overlooking the Malecón and harbour entrance, great spot for a sundowner, the hotel's tourist bureau is efficient and friendly.

$$ Colina
L y 27, T7-836 4071, commercial@colina. islazul.tur.cu.
Often used by students learning Spanish at the university opposite; there is no reason otherwise to stay here. 80 rooms, some of which have been renovated, others have poor water pressure and broken fittings, street noise, reasonable breakfast.

Casas particulares

$$ Alicia Horta
Línea 53 entre M y N, Apto 2, T7-832 8439, aorta@infomed.sld.cu.
Alicia is a doctor, she and her daughter María are friendly and speak English, French and German, 3 rooms, 1 has an en suite bathroom, the other 2 share a bathroom, good for families. Large terrace/balcony overlooks Paseo.

$$ Casa Betty et Armando Gutiérrez
21 62 entre M y N, Apto 7, 4th (top) floor, T7-832 1876.
A penthouse with elevator which opens directly into the apartment. Very convenient for *paladares* and nightlife, very close to Hotel Nacional. Large and comfortable a/c rooms with 2 beds, big bathrooms, balcony. A delightful place to stay. Armando and his wife, Betty, have been renting for 20 years, they speak French, German and English and are knowledgeable on history and culture.

$$ Daysie Recio
B 403 entre 17 y 19, T7-830 5609.
Spacious, light and clean. 2 airy rooms with interconnecting bathroom, 1 has a terrace overlooking the backyard, both have double and single bed, a/c, fridge, English spoken. Daysie is a vivacious hostess and this is a good option for families or groups of up to 6.

$$ Gisela Ibarra

F104 altos entre 5 y Calzada, T7-832 3238.
Straight out of the 1950s, marble staircase, balconies, very high quality, wonderful old rooms with original furnishings, a/c, fan, fridge and safety box. Gisela is an excellent hostess, running a very proper, quiet and traditional home in a residential neighbourhood. Huge, filling breakfast for CUC$5, laundry service offered. If she is full, her daughter Marta Díaz runs another *casa* just round the corner on Calzada 452 Apto 5, same price but rooms are smaller, darker and hotter.

$$ Jorge Coalla Potts

I 456 Apto 11 entre 21 y 23, T7-832 9032, 5283 1237 (mob), www.havanaroomsrental.com
2 a/c rooms on ground floor, 1 large with 2 beds, 1 smaller with double bed, comfortable, good mattresses, new bathrooms, lots of hot water, ceiling fan and fridge, ample breakfasts. Excellent location close to the bars and restaurants of Vedado. Generous and fascinating hosts, Jorge and Marisel, and their daughter, Jessica, are mines of information and speak English. If they are full, Jorge will find somewhere else for you to stay.

$$ Martha Vitorte

G 301 Apto 14, 14th floor, entre 13 y 15, T7-832 6475, martavitorte@hotmail.com.
High-rise building near corner with Línea, 1 apartment on each floor, referred to as 'horizontals', beautiful modern building, very spacious, 3 rooms, en suite bathroom, a/c, security safe in each room, balcony on 2 sides for panoramic views of Havana, sea and sunsets, Martha is a retired civil servant and speaks some English and French. She also rents an independent apartment on Línea 453 entre E y F, piso 10, with 2 bedrooms and a terrace.

$$ Mercedes González

21 360 Apto 2A, entre G y H, T7-832 5846, mecylupe@hotmail.com.
Mercedes runs 2 identical *casas* on the same floor of the apartment block, with terrace,

elevator, laundry service. 5 airy rooms, a/c, fan, good bathrooms, 3 rooms have a balcony, smart, helpful and friendly, good location, near park.

$$-$ Casa Caprí (Eugenia y Rudel)

Calle 11 161 entre L y K, T7-830 5160, crisjo@infomed.sld.cu.
Right next to the US Embassy. 2 good-sized rooms with a/c and private bathrooms as well as 2 sitting areas for guests. Very cheerful and helpful family, some English spoken.

Miramar
Hotels

There is a string of 4-star hotels west along the coast that are used by package tour operators; guests are often here for the first and last nights of their stay in Cuba before being whisked off round the island. They are not particularly convenient for visiting the old city, but you do get a sea view. Miramar is also popular with business people; hotels are of an international standard and the area is quiet at night.

$$$$-$$$ Meliá Habana

Av 3 entre 76 y 80, T7-204 8500, www.meliacuba.com.
Not quite as luxurious as the Meliá Cohiba, but still the best in this area, with the biggest swimming pool in Havana and a free shuttle service to Old Havana 0930-2130. Rooms and beds are huge and sea view rooms have a balcony with lovely view, but the pool and garden view rooms are quieter.

Casas particulares

$$ Villa Reina

Calle 80 916 entre 9 y 11, T7-209 4951, 5280 2303 (mob), www.villa-reina.com.
Detached 1960s house in its own garden where you can sit and relax. Bedrooms are upstairs in 2 sections and living areas downstairs. Rosi, Carlos and Marielena are welcoming and helpful and provide a good breakfast. In a quiet residential area but

within easy reach of *paladares*, hotels, Av 5 and transport to other parts of Havana.

$$-$ Nieves y Marlen
Calle 3 9401 entre 94 y 96, Apto 2, T7-203 5284.
Clean, spacious and modern apartment, a/c, fridge in room, balcony.

Where to eat

Snacks and fast food
In addition to the excellent and varied *paladares* and more predictable state restaurants listed below, there are many street stalls and places where you can pick up cheap snacks priced in CUP$. These are good for filling a hole at lunchtime, but don't expect a culinary masterpiece. One of the best options is pizza fresh from the oven, which usually costs over CUP$10 in a private cafeteria but is just CUP$3-5 in a state snack bar; they can be very greasy, so take plenty of napkins. Very sweet juice drinks cost CUP$2 per glass. There are also many fast-food outlets throughout the city: **El Rápido** (red logo) is clean with fast service and numerous locations; **Burgui** serves hamburgers and fried chicken. Branches of **DiTú** are all over the city, open 24 hrs, selling pieces of chicken by weight.

La Habana Vieja
Restaurants

$$$ A Prado y Neptuno
Prado y Neptuno, opposite Hotel Parque Central, T7-860 9636. Daily 1200-2400.
Italian and Cuban food, excellent tiramisu and good pizza and pasta. Sports on TV at the bar. Good views over Parque Central.

$$$ Dominica
O' Reilly esq Mercaderes, T7-860 2918. Daily 1200-2400.
Italian and international, very smart, set menus CUC$25-30, pasta from CUC$6, pizza CUC$5.50-9 depending on size, vegetarian options, outdoor seating nice for lunch, credit cards accepted.

$$$ El Castillo de Farnés
Monserrate 361 esq Obrapía, T7-867 1030. Restaurant daily 1200-2400, bar 0800-2400.
Tasty Spanish and international food, reasonable prices, good for tapas, *garbanzos* and shrimp, also Uruguayan beef and chateaubriand. Castro came here at 0445, 9 Jan 1959, with Che and Raúl. Very small restaurant, eat inside or on the street.

$$$ El Floridita
Obispo esq Monserrate, next to the Parque Central, T7-8671300. Daily 1130-2400.
A favourite haunt of Hemingway, this is now a very elegant bar and restaurant as reflected in the prices (CUC$6 for a daiquirí), but well worth a visit if only to see the sumptuous decor and 'Bogart atmosphere'. In the corner of the bar is a life-size bronze statue of Hemingway, and on the bar, also in bronze, are his glasses resting on a open book. Live music.

$$$ La Barca
Av del Puerto esq Obispo, T7-866 8807, comercial@temple.habaguanex.cu. Daily 1200-2400.
Just down from El Templete but cheaper, overlooking the road and the harbour opposite the old yacht club with outdoor seating. Good variety on the menu with some Spanish dishes, seafood and steaks.

$$$ La Bodeguita del Medio
Empedrado 207 entre Cuba y San Ignacio, near the cathedral, T7-867 1374.
Restaurant 1200-2330, bar 1030-2300. It is here that Hemingway allegedly inscribed the now famous line "*Mi mojito en La Bodeguita, mi daiquirí en El Floridita*". It has since been claimed that one of Hemingway's drinking buddies Fernando Campoamor, the owner of *La Bodeguita*, hired a calligrapher to write the line as a lucrative tourist con, but it's still worth sampling a mojito at the bar (rum, crushed ice, mint, sugar, lime juice and carbonated water – CUC$5). The food is poor and expensive, but very popular.

$$$ La Mina
On Obispo esquina Oficios, Plaza de Armas,
T7-862 0216. Daily 1000-2400.
Very much on the tourist trail but a lovely
spot to sit and soak up the atmosphere,
traditional Cuban food, sandwiches, lots of
liqueur coffees, outdoor seating with live
Cuban music.

$$$ Marinero El Templete
Av del Puerto 12-14 esq Narciso López, T7-866
8807, comercial@templete.habaguanex.cu.
Daily 1200-2400.
Eat inside or outside with view over the
road to the harbour, pleasant, understated
elegance. Good food, international with
Cuban flavours, meat, fish or lobster.

$$$ París
San Ignacio 54 esq Empedrado,
Plaza Catedral, T7-867 1034.
Restaurant and snack bar daily 1200-2400.
Expensive, small portions, slow service,
but has selection of national dishes, tables
outside take up most of the square, lovely
location, worth stopping here for a coffee
when visiting the cathedral.

$$$-$$ Europa
Obispo esquina Aguiar. Daily1200-2400.
International and Cuban food, the most
expensive dish is *grillada de mariscos* at
CUC$11.95. Lots of cheaper options CUC$3-6,
although sometimes things run out. Good
music and dancing.

$$$-$$ La Piña de Plata
Bernaza esq Obispo, T7-867 1300 ext 134.
Daily 1200-2400.
Small and smart a/c restaurant with Wi-Fi if
you have a *tarjeta*. Full range of Cuban dishes,
chicken, pork, fish, shrimp and lobster, also
pasta, pizza. Good food, well presented.
Piña colada is the bar's speciality.

$$$-$$ Mesón de la Flota
Mercaderes 257 entre Amargura y
Teniente Rey, T7-863 3838.
Restaurant-cum-tapas bar with wooden tables
and impassioned flamenco *tablaos* 1200-1500

and 2000-2200. Reasonably priced menu with
wide selection of Spanish dishes and plenty
of fish and seafood, including paella, but the
tapas choices are better value than the main
dishes. Try the feisty *patatas bravas*.

$$$-$$ Torre de Marfil
Mercaderes 115 entre Obispo y Obrapía,
T7-867 1038. Daily 1200-2200.
Generally good-value Oriental cuisine
with food surpassing anything that
Chinatown has to offer in terms of
authenticity, decked out with colourful
lanterns and Chinese paraphernalia.

$$ Café del Oriente
Oficios y Amargura, T7-860 6686.
Daily 1200-2400.
High-class food with a reasonably priced
set menu and elegant surroundings.

$$ Café El Mercurio
Next to to Café del Oriente. Daily 1200-2400.
Informal, pleasant terrace.

$$ Los Nardos (Sociedad Juventud Asturiana)
Paseo del Prado 563 entre Dragones y
Teniente Rey, opposite the Capitolio,
T7-863 2985. Daily 1200-2400.
Not obvious from the street but look out
for the waiters at the entrance. Dining room
upstairs lined with cabinets containing old
football trophies, cups from 1936, while
the heavy wooden furniture is reminiscent
of a rancho. At one end are chefs in white
hats busy in the kitchen while at the other
you are overlooked by the stained glass
windows of a pool room. Not a great option
for vegetarians: plenty of meat, pork, lamb
or Uruguayan steak, although there is also
fish and assorted vegetables. Popular with
Cubans and foreigners, large, filling portions,
background music is limited to golden
oldies played 2-3 times during the meal. In
the same building are **El Trofeo**, 2nd floor,
serving Cuban and international food, big
portions, a little cheaper than Los Nardos,
good mojito CUC$2.20, and **El Asturianito**
for Cuban and Italian food, good pizzas

CUC$3-7. If you find a queue outside for Los Nardos, explain that you are going to El Asturianito and they will let you through.

$$ Puerto de Sagua
Bélgica (Egido) 603 esq Acosta, T7-867 1026.
Nautical theme, a cafetería serving dishes such as *arroz Puerto de Sagua* for CUC$6, and a more upscale restaurant specializing in seafood.

$$-$ Hanoi
Brasil (Teniente Rey) 507 y Bernaza, T7-867 1029. Daily 1200-2400.
A simple restaurant with plain furnishings but a little gem, serving typical Cuban food, excellent value for money with main dishes at less than CUC$5, mojito for CUC$2. Plenty of food, the rice and beans are good and the garlic on the potatoes will keep away vampires. Vegetarian option of beans, rice, salad and root vegetables with a *criollo* sauce, CUC$3.50. Live music after 1900, nice atmosphere, welcoming service, popular with Cubans and foreigners.

Paladares

$$$-$$ Don Lorenzo
Acosta 260A, entre Habana y Compostela, T7-861 6733. Daily 1200-2400.
Not a cheap option with fish and meat dishes at CUC$5-15 and vegetarian options for CUC$5-6, but one of the most extensive menus, with over 50 dishes offered, all types of meat and fish with a huge variety of sauces, Basque-style, French-style, cider, fruity, almond, etc. An entertaining night when it's full, good for people-watching from the 2nd floor. Watch out for tourist pricing and high service charges added to the bill.

$$$-$$ Doña Blanquita
Prado 158 entre Colón y Refugio, T7-867 4958. Open from 1200.
Run by English-speaking lawyer, the dining room is upstairs, with a neon sign and a lovely view of the Prado. Eat inside with fan or on balcony if dry. Good location but food

nothing special, consisting of simple Cuban food done to a formula: pork, chicken or eggs CUC$7-9, beer CUC$2.

$$$-$$ La Moneda Cubana
San Ignacio 77 entre O'Reilly y Empedrado, T7-867 3852. Open 1200-2300.
Limited choice, good fish with salad, beans and rice with fried banana, and usually good salads prepared for vegetarians. Menus for around CUC$8-10. More notable for the rooftop terrace which gives spectacular views of Havana and particularly the firing of the cannon at 2100. There is also an elegant dining room in colonial style if it is raining.

Cafés and bakeries

Bianchini
Sol 12 entre Oficios y Av del Puerto (beside the Rum Museum) and Callejón del Chorro, San Ignacio 68, Plaza de la Catedral, http:// dulceria-bianchini.com. Daily 0900-2100.
For sweet and savoury baked goodies, delicious quiches, cakes, pastries, croissants, biscuits, all hand made. The chocolate is organic from Baracoa, every cup of coffee is made with freshly ground beans, and fresh juices are unsweetened. Happy hour 1400-1500 for cut-price coffees.

Café El Escorial
Mercaderes 317 esq Muralla, escorial@enet.cu. Daily 0900-2100.
Coffees CUC$0.75-3.50, also coffee beans at CUC$3.25 for 250 g, plus ice cream, juices, soft drinks and sweets. Sit inside or out overlooking Plaza Vieja, if you can get a seat. Popular location.

Café O' Reilly
O'Reilly 203 entre Cuba y San Ignacio. Daily 0900-2100.
Coffee in various forms, sandwiches, drinks and cocktails. Coffee beans and ground coffee also sold by weight. Upstairs bar being renovated in 2015 as an Irish pub, with a balcony and live music.

Café París
Obispo y San Ignacio. Daily 0900-0100, live music 1200-2400.
Serves reasonably priced food and snacks, prices vary, make sure you see a menu. Seating inside with band or outside on the street for watching the world go by, popular, lively, fun.

Cafetería Jardín del Oriente
Amargura entre Mercaderes y Oficios. Daily 1100-2300.
Comida criolla, sandwiches, wine, juices and soft drinks at reasonable prices.

La Dichosa
Obispo esq Compostela. Daily 0900-2400.
Good place for breakfast, CUC$3.50, or a snack, CUC$2-4. Full meals available for lunch and dinner. Live music 1200-2200.

Panadería San José y Cafetería Santo Domingo
Obispo 161 entre San Ignacio y Mercaderes, T7-860 9326. Daily 0700-2400.
Bakery and café.

Pastelería Francesa
Between the Hotels Telégrafo and Inglaterra on the Prado.
Smorgasbord of pastries and cakes in a peach-coloured dining room. Popular, some of the better cakes have gone by lunchtime. The hot *pan au chocolat* and *pan con pasas* (raisins) are particularly good.

Casablanca
Restaurants

$$$ La Divina Pastora
Fortaleza de la Cabaña, T7-860 8341. Daily 1200-2300.
Expensive, upmarket state restaurant, food praised for its presentation but it tastes good too. However, the view is what makes this restaurant special. Sit indoors or in the open air overlooking cannon pointing out over the water towards La Habana Vieja and along the coastline. Great at lunchtime or for sunset-watching.

$$$-$$ Los XII Apóstoles
Near El Morro, T7-863 8295. Daily 1200-2345.
Fish and good *criollo* food, good views of the Malecón. The 12 apostles are the 12 cannon on the ramparts.

Centro
Restaurants

$$$-$$ Sociedad Agrupación Castropol
Malecón 107 entre Genios y Crespo, T7-861 4864. Daily 1200-2400.
Beautiful central patio on ground floor where food is cooked over coals, the mixed grill for 2 people is CUC$19.90. Upstairs, lobster, fish or meat dishes and an extensive wine list are served on a balcony overlooking the Malecón or in a/c dining room with a show at night Thu-Sun 2200-0300, cover CUC$5.

Paladares

$$$ Casa Miglis
Lealtad 120 entre Animas y Lagunas, T7-864 1486, www.casamiglis.com. Daily 1200-0100.
Swedish fusion cuisine, including Swedish meatballs, although there are other international dishes such as Mexican chilli, Greek souvlaki, pizza or cous cous. There's a small but excellent bar if you don't want to eat. Eclectic Scandinavian design. Very popular. Look for the Swedish flag hanging outside.

$$$ La Guarida
Concordia 418 entre Gervasio y Escobar, T7-866 9047, www.laguarida.com. Lunch daily 1200-1600, dinner 1900-2400 with reservation.
Film location for *Fresa y Chocolate* and popular with tourists, many of whom would not normally enter such a dilapidated building. The grand old marble staircase leads past drying laundry to a smart but quirky historic dining room on the 3rd floor. Consistently good food, *filet mignon*, seafood and vegetarian paellas are delicious. Main courses are around CUC$15, lobster is CUC$22, and, as you are charged for everything, even bread, this is more expensive than an average

paladar. It is always busy but you can go up to the glamorous rooftop bar even if you don't have a reservation, wonderful at sunset. A Cuba libre is CUC$3.50. Don't miss a visit to the bathroom.

$$$ La Tasquita
Espada 208 entre Jovellar (27 de Noviembre) y San Lázaro, T7-873 4916. Daily 1200-2400.
Run by Santiagüera Aralicia. Wonderful food and great atmosphere. House special for CUC$8 is a pork steak stuffed with ham, cheese and chorizo, served with a sweet and sour sauce and all the trimmings, including a drink, dessert and coffee. Other dishes of chicken, fish, pasta, pork, etc. Good for vegetarians with delicious sweet potato and Cuban fried eggs, served on mountains of rice and beans, plus good salads. Potent mojitos. No smoking.

$$$ San Cristóbal
San Rafael 469 entre Lealtad y Campanario, T7-860 1705, sheyla9010@gmail.com. Mon-Sat 1200-2400.
President Obama and family dined here during their visit in Mar 2016. Eclectic decor, walls filled with photos, clocks, religious icons, paintings, even a zebra skin. The food is tasty, nicely presented and the service is excellent. Complimentary rum and cigars often finish the meal.

Barrio Chino
At Zanja y Rayo, 1 block west of Galiano, there are several restaurants in a small street with tables inside or outside and menus on view; you will be pestered for your custom. Food can be very good if there is sufficient water, cooking gas and ingredients – shortages affect all the restaurants around here – but do not expect authentic Chinese cuisine or you will be disappointed. Chop suey or chow mein is about the most Oriental you can get. 'Sweet and sour' dishes are not recommended as they are very sweet and fruity. Spring rolls bear no relation to anything you might find in China. Lots of flies during the daytime. All prices in CUP$ or CUC$. Meals around CUC$5-10.

$$$-$$ Flor de Lotto
Salud 313 entre Gervasio y Escobar, T7-860 8501. Daily 1200-2400.
Although it looks Chinese from the decor, in fact this is a good Cuban restaurant with some Asian flavours such as sweet and sour sauce or chicken with pineapple. There's a wide-ranging menu with everything from tasty staples such as *ropa vieja*, to lamb, rabbit and lobster, all served in large portions. Popular, with queues at weekends. Main courses around CUC$4.50-8.

$$$-$$ Tien Tan (Templo del Cielo)
Cuchillo 17, entre Zanja y San Nicolás, T7-861 5478, taoqi@enet.cu. Daily 1100-2400.
Always full. The chef is from Shanghai, but this is still Cuba so don't expect much in the way of authenticity. Cheapest dish CUC$1, most expensive around CUC$25.

$$$-$$ Viejo Amigo
Dragones 356 entre Manrique y San Nicolás. Daily 1200-2400.
Combination Chinese/Cuban/international restaurant and pizzeria. Good food, pleasant service, nice restaurant upstairs with a friendly atmosphere. Portions are huge so ask them to box up what you can't eat.

$$ Sociedad Chang Weng Chung Tong
San Nicolás 517 entre Zanja y Dragones, T7-862 1490. Bar, café and restaurant, daily 1200-2400.
Part of the **Sociedad China de Cuba**, Chinese and *criollo* food. They have an all-you-can-eat international buffet upstairs including soups, roast meats, vegetables, pizza, pasta, salads etc for CUC$8.80, or you can order à la carte.

Vedado
Restaurants

$$$ La Torre
17 y M, Edif Focsa, T7-838 3089. Daily 1200-2400.
The a/c, glass-enclosed bar and restaurant on the 33rd floor of the Focsa building serves the best French food in Havana,

about CUC$40 per person but worth it. Go for a drink at the bar even if you don't want to eat there: bar prices are no higher than elsewhere (mojito CUC$3); the view is free and, as this is the highest point in the city, you get the full panorama.

$$$ Polinesio
Hotel Habana Libre, with access from the street, T7-834 6100. Daily lunch 1200-1530, dinner 1900-2230.
Dark and cool, a mix of Chinese and Indonesian dishes, CUC$12-20, also a good happy hour 1700-2000.

$$ La Casona de 17
17 60 entre M y N, T7-838 3136. Daily 0830-2400.
Elegant peach mansion with colonial terrace, once home to Castro's grandparents. House dish is *arroz con pollo a la chorrera*. Also good is *paella Casona*, or there is always a half roast chicken (a bit greasy) with bacon, rice'n'beans, chips and salad. Large servings. Adjoining Argentine *parillada* serves up mixed grills. Nice for a relaxing lunch. Owned by a cooperative, all staff have a stake and service is good.

$$ Unión Francesa
17 esq 6, T7-830 6515.
Attractive colonial building on the corner of Parque John Lennon, eat inside with a/c or on the veranda overlooking the garden, relaxed, nice atmosphere, photos of Fidel and Chirac, economical with set menus for CUC$5 (main course with bread, rice, vegetables and a drink) or CUC$10 (plus salad, dessert), but some items are not always available.

$$-$ La Roca
21 102 esq M, T7-8363219. Daily 1200-0200. Fri, Sat CUC$10 cover includes CUC$7 consumo.
Restored 1950s building with stained-glass windows dating from when it was a guesthouse. Sleek but stark dining room serves an international menu for a range of budgets: onion soup CUC$1, spaghetti carbonara CUC$2.50, plus more expensive

dishes. Set menu is excellent value at CUC$3.75-4.50 for drink, main course and dessert, plus piano music while you eat. It's very popular so best to get there before 1900. Evening entertainment on some nights.

Paladares

$$$ Adela
Calle F 503 entre 21 y 23, T7-832 3776.
Call ahead for opening hours. Adela is an artist and this *paladar*, though legal, is primarily an art gallery. Clients come to buy art and stay to eat. Appetisers include cinnamon-baked bananas, fried *malanga*, corn and chorizo stew, although the choice of main course is limited. A meal costs around CUC$20-25 per person.

$$$ Café Laurent
Calle M 257 entre 19 y 21, T7-8312090, see Facebook. Daily 1200-2400.
Smart penthouse restaurant much in demand so reservations are essential and are checked before you get in the lift. Get a table on the covered terrace if you can, to enjoy the view and the billowing white curtains. Light, bright decor during the day becomes chic and romantic at night. The international food is very good and nicely presented, not overly expensive with fish and shrimp around CUC$12.50, but you are charged for bread and side dishes so expect to pay CUC$25 per person without wine.

$$$ Decameron
Línea 753 entre Paseo y 2, T7-832 2444.
Unprepossessing on the outside but the dining room is pleasant and full of antiques. Extensive menu and good wine list, Cuban and international dishes, large portions.

$$$ Hurón Azul
Humboldt 153 entre O y P, T7-836 3636. Lunch and dinner.
The small, cosy dining room is decorated with works by local artists. Food and service are good, with large portions of Cuban dishes, reasonably priced.

$$$ Le Chansonnier
J 257 entre 15 y Línea, T7-832 1576,
www.lechansonnierhabana.com.
Very smart and contemporary bar and
restaurant design in elegant 1890 building,
fabulous international food and reasonable
prices. Outdoor seating too. Dress up to
come here.

$$$-$$ Gringo Viejo
21 454 entre E y F, T7-831 1946,
gringoviejocuba@gmail.com. Daily 1200-2300.
Nice atmosphere with wall-to-wall cinema
memorabilia, red checked tablecloths and
hanging plastic grapes and strings of garlic,
good portions, main course of fish, chicken,
pork and other meats with fruity or spicy
sauces accompanied by rice, beans and salad.

$$$-$$ Los Amigos
M entre 19 y 21, opposite Victoria,
T7-830 0880. Daily 1200-2400.
Good Cuban food, *ropa vieja* is
recommended, but check your bill. Dine
among Christmas decorations, religious
artefacts and wind chimes. Convenient
location for après-dining entertainment,
popular with locals and ex-pats.

$$$-$$ Starbien
29 205 entre B y C, T7-8300711.
Mon-Sat 1200-1700, 1900-2400.
A 2-storey green and white 1930s house has
been converted into a moden contemporary
restaurant and bar, serving some of the best
food in Havana. Chef Osmani has trained
abroad but now offers elegantly presented
Cuban food. A lunch special of 5 courses and
a drink for CUC$12 can't be beaten. There's
a bar upstairs with a small terrace. Service is
excellent. Always full, reservations advised.

Bakeries and ice cream parlours

Coppelia
23 y L, T7-831 9908, 833 3160.
Tue-Sun 1000-2200, or daily Jul/Aug.
A visit to the most famous ice cream parlour
in Cuba is recommended, see also page 56.
It has capacity for 707 seated ice cream lovers,

with several separate outdoor areas to eat
in, each with its own entrance and queue in
the surrounding streets, or inside in La Torre.
It's extremely popular with Cuban families.
If you pay in CUP$, you will almost certainly
have to queue for an hour or so, particularly
at weekends, but this is not unpleasant as
the characteristic *copey* trees provide plenty
of shade. A dedicated attendant (brown
uniform) controls the queue and directs you
into the seating area as tables become free.
Alternatively, pay in CUC$ in the Fuente de
Soda kiosks outside (said to be open 24 hrs
but often closed after midnight), although
this can work out extremely expensive. Bring
your own plastic spoons for the tubs as they
invariably run out. The ice cream (CUC$2
for small portion) comes in many different
flavours depending on availability (chocolate
is still the top flavour) and styles (all come
with a glass of water): *ensalada* (mixture of
flavours), *jimaguas* (twins), *tres gracias*. After
devouring your 1st choice you can stay and
order a 2nd portion without queuing. There
is also an a/c area within Coppelia called
Las Cuatro Joyas, where you pay by weight
in CUC$. Alternatively, sample Coppelia ice
cream in the tourist hotels and restaurants
and in some dollar food stores.

Pain de París
Línea entre Paseo y A, also Plaza de la
Revolución. Daily 24 hrs.
Good coffee served *cortadito* or *con leche*,
croissants and *señoritas de chocolate*
(custard slices).

Miramar and further west
Restaurants

$$$ 1830
Malecón y 20 (officially 7 1252 entre 20 y 22),
T7-838 3090/1/2. Daily 1200-2400.
Bar, restaurant and nightclub in a
wonderful setting at the mouth of the Río
Almendares, one of the best places for
dancing. International and Cuban cuisine,
from CUC$12 for a local dish, to CUC$16.25
for tenderloin with blue cheese sauce, and

lobster at CUC$30. Cabaret shows Mon-Sat 2200-0300, Sun 1800-2400, and local bands.

$$$ El Aljibe
7 entre 24 y 26, T7-204 1583. Daily 1200-2400.
Originally opened in 1947 as Rancho Luna, it attracted '50s movie stars like Eva Gardner and Errol Flynn with its secret recipe for roast chicken with a bitter orange sauce. The restaurant closed in 1961, but reopened again as a state-owned restaurant in 1993 and the original owner Sergio García Macías began to bring his famed *pollo al Aljibe* to a new generation of movie stars, including Jack Nicholson, Steven Spielberg and Danny Glover. Open, breezy, framework design with thatched roof and friendly atmosphere. Generous portions of delicious black beans, rice, fried potatoes and salad, with more if you want, CUC$12 per person. Good wine cellar. There is a cigar store attached if you want a fine rum and a cigar after your meal.

$$$ El Rancho Palco
Av 19 y 140, Playa, T7-208 9346. Daily 1200-2200.
Set in a lovely jungle garden west of Miramar, near the Palacio de las Convenciones, this is very popular with ex-pats for its Argentine steaks, good barbecued chicken, meats, typical *criollo* cuisine and international food. Good live music is provided by a trio.

$$$ El Tocororo
18 302 esq Av 3, T7-204 2209. Daily 1200-2400, bar 2000-0300.
Named after the national bird of Cuba. Old colonial mansion with nice terrace and a great house band. Prices fluctuate between CUC$20 and CUC$30. It used to be one of the best restaurants in town but is now on the tour party circuit and quality can be haphazard.

$$$ La Cecilia
5 entre 110 y 112, T7-202 6700. Daily 1200-2400, dance shows Fri-Sun 2200-0300.
Good international and Cuban food, mostly in an open-air setting. There are dance shows by top-level companies in the **Sala de Fiestas de la Cecilia** at the weekend and live bands with dancing outside, cover charge depends on who is performing. Can get very busy with tour parties.

$$$ La Ferminia
5 18207 entre 182 y 184, T7-273 6555. Daily 1200-2400.
A beautiful neoclassical residence with an elegant atmosphere. Best for meat eaters as this is a *churrasquería*. Salads are brought to the table and then staff come round with skewers of pork, beef, chicken and chorizo. Vegetarians should call beforehand to coordinate a menu.

Paladares

$$$ La Cocina de Lilliam
48 1311, entre 13 y 15, T7-209 6514. Sun-Fri 1200-1500, 1900-2300, closed 2 weeks in Aug, 2 weeks in Dec.
Very good, imaginative Cuban and Spanish food with tables outside but under cover in a lovely garden. Great appetizers and fresh fish, lots of vegetables, all beautifully presented. Popular with locals, reservations recommended, main course plus beer CUC$20-30, usually excellent service.

$$$ La Fontana
3-A 305 esq 46, T7-202 8337. Daily 1200-2400.
Lovely leafy setting with fish pools between the tables outside, fountains, exposed brickwork and stone, modern and chic. Good Cuban food, extremely popular, ask for the *menú de la casa*, about CUC$25 per person. Good grilled and barbecued meat and fish, extensive wine list. Arrive early or make a reservation, essential at night. A contemporary basement lounge bar stays open late.

$$$-$$ El Palio
Av 1 entre 24 y 26.
Italian and Cuban cuisine, notably fresh fish and seafood with a choice of creative sauces and good vegetables. Portions can be rather small, however, and the atmosphere is lacklustre. Eat in the open air or indoors.

$$$-$$ La Esperanza
16 105 entre 1 y 3, T7-202 4361.
Mon-Sat 1900-2330.
Small sign, very popular, traditional food, excellent cocktails, meal and drinks CUC$10-15 per person, plus 10% service, reservations advisable, run by Hubert and Manolo in their inviting 1950s period living room surrounded by their paintings and antiques.

Southern suburbs
Restaurants

$$ El Bambú
Jardín Botánico Nacional de Cuba (see page 61). Lunch served daily 1400.
Cuba's only organic vegetarian restaurant. Eat as much as you like from a selection of hot and cold vegetarian dishes for CUC$12, including drinks. Water and waste food is recycled and the restaurant grows most of its own food.

$$-$ La Casa del Dragón
Cortina de la Presa y 100, Boyeros (off the main road to the right soon after entrance from Arroyo Naranjo, look for the sign), T7-6443713. Wed-Sun 1200-1700.
Chinese restaurant with bamboo furniture and good food priced in CUP$, making it cheap, beer priced in CUC$. There is also a *ranchón* where they serve *comida criolla*. Nice walks nearby.

Bars

Many restaurants listed above have bars attached. Ordinary bars not on the tourist circuit will charge you in CUC$, if they let foreigners in at all. Even so, the prices in most places are not high by Caribbean standards: national brands of beer usually cost CUC$1-1.50 (or CUP$10-18, Tínima being the most expensive); imported beers cost CUC$2-3.

You will find musicians in most bars. Many play only 3 or 4 songs, then come round with the collecting bowl trying to sell their CDs before moving on, to be replaced by another band who do the same thing. Have a ready supply of small change for tips.

La Habana Vieja

Antiguo Almacén de la Madera y el Tabaco
Desamparados (Av del Puerto) esq Paula.
An old timber and tobacco warehouse converted into a microbrewery and restaurant/snack bar. You can get a cold pint of beer for CUC$2 and sit inside with the machinery and vats or outside by the water. The service is slow and the food nothing special, but it is still a good place to stop for a break in a city tour or after shopping at the handicraft market next door. It is vast, so there will always be room for you.

Bar Dos Hermanos
Av del Puerto esq Sol, opposite the ferry terminals, T7-8613514 ext 104. Daily 1100-2300.
Beside the rum museum. A trio and a quartet alternate each night and play traditional Cuban music.

Bar El Louvre
Hotel Inglaterra, Prado 416, Parque Central, T7-860 8595. Daily 1200-2400.
A pleasant place for an outdoor evening drink, where you can watch the sun going down catching the cream stone of the Museo de Bellas Artes through the Royal palms. Roving live musicians don't stay long and expect a generous tip, making your excellent CUC$3 daiquirí rather pricey. Slow service.

Bar Monserrate
Monserrate y Obrapía, T7-860 9751. Daily 1200-2400.
Draft beer CUC$2, imported beer about CUC$2.50, mojito CUC$3, plenty of flavour but not very generous shots of rum, food available, interesting to sit and watch comings and goings.

Café de París
Obispo 202 esq San Ignacio. Daily 0900-0100.
Predominantly tourist clientele but good location for people-watching.

Casa del Escabeche
Obispo esq Villegas, T7-863 2660.
Daily 1000-2300.
Tiny bar but popular and welcoming, house quartet from 1200, cocktails CUC$3, Cristal and Bucanero CUC$1.50.

Cervecería La Muralla
Factoría Plaza Vieja, San Ignacio esq Muralla,
T7-866 4433. Daily 1200-2400.
This popular microbrewery is a great place for a midday breather or a sundowner during or after your walk round the city. You can sit inside or out on the plaza listening to live music. Their own beer is CUC$2 in a pint mug, or you can buy a larger tube to share. Slow service.

El Floridita
Obispo esq Monserrate, next to the Parque Central, T7-8671300. Daily 1130-2400.
See Restaurants, above.

La Bodeguita del Medio
Empedrado 207 entre Cuba y San Ignacio,
near the cathedral, T7-867 1374.
Bar daily 1030-2300.
See Restaurants, above.

Lluvia de Oro
Obispo esq Habana. Daily 0900-2400.
Good place to drink rum and listen to loud recorded rock music or salsa, live music 1230-1600, 1830-2300, food is also served.

Museo del Ron
Av del Puerto 262 entre Sol y Muralla,
T7-861 8051.
2 bars with nightly music, 0900-2100, serve good Cuba Libre and sometimes showcase quality live bands.

Sloppy Joe's
Zulueta 252 entre Animas y Virtudes,
T7-866 7157.
A popular bar in the 1930s has been recreated by the state in a smarter guise aimed at the tourist market. The name comes from the sandwich served there, which is filled with *ropa vieja*, other food includes tapas and hamburgers. You'll pay CUC$5 or so for cocktails and CUC$2.50 for a beer. Drinks are cold and good, but service is extraordinarily slow.

Centro

Café Neruda
Malecón entre San Nicols y Manrique,
T7-864 4159. Daily 1000-2400.
Habaguanex has used the shell of an old building for this modern open-air bar with artistic flair. It's very popular with young Habaneros, who queue at weekends when they're taking a break from a stroll along the waterfront. Reasonable prices: mojitos and daiquirís CUC$2, meals CUC$6-8, snacks available.

Humboldt 52
Humboldt 52 entre Infanta y Hospital,
T5295 4893 (mob) and see Facebook.
Daily 1700-0300.
Havana's first official gay bar is welcoming to all. There's entertainment on most nights, with drag shows, karaoke, salsa and DJ nights. Screens show music videos, there's a dance floor and plenty of seating, with a back room for smoking.

Vedado

Bar Bohemio
21 entre 12 y 14, T7-833 6918.
Former ballerinas from the Ballet Nacional de Cuba have created this beautiful tapas bar in a lovely Vedado mansion with huge windows, high celings and tiled floors, spacious and comfortable, also a terrace outside. Extensive list of some 60 cocktails and a cigar menu. Happy hour 2000-2200. Gay friendly.

Casa de la Amistad
Paseo 406 (see page 58).
Bar with a beautiful garden extension, tasty cheap light meals optional, very peaceful surroundings.

El Cocinero
26 entre 11 y 13, T7-832 2355. Daily 1200-0200.

Contemporary industrial chic at this rooftop bar under the chimney of a disused vegetable oil factory. A place for the young and fit, as you have to climb 3 flights of a spiral staircase to get there. Popular with affluent young Cubans. Food is available on a lower terrace, indoors or open air, but it's best for drinks and tapas. English spoken, good, friendly service.

Hotel Nacional de Cuba
O esq 21, T7-873 3564.
If it's a nice evening, opt for a sunset cocktail at a table in the garden overlooking the Malecón, an ideal spot for looking out for old cars and watching the moon rise over the sea.

La Torre
17 y M, at top of Edif Focsa, T7-838 3089. Daily 1200-2400.
Have a drink at the bar on the 33rd floor even if you don't want to eat at the restaurant (see above). Day or night, this is a terrific place for a cocktail.

Entertainment

Cabaret
Cabaret Las Vegas, *Calzada de Infanta 104, Vedado, T7-836 7939.* Daily gay show 2300-0400, CUC$3, matinée Fri 1600-2000, CUP$20.
Copa Room, *Habana Riviera, Paseo y Malecón, Vedado, T7-834 4225 for reservation. Thu-Sun 2030-0300.* Part of the nightclub scene since before the Revolution. Traditional music including the boleros of Benny Moré. Glitzy Cuban cabaret *A lo Riviera*, skimpy outfits and sequins.
Parisien, *Hotel Nacional, Vedado, T7-873 3564. Daily 2200-0200.* Excellent show for CUC$35, lasts longer than **Tropicana** and of equivalent standard, make a reservation.
Salón Rojo, *Hotel Caprí, 21 entre N y O, Vedado, T7-833 3747.* The country's best musical groups play here, 2200-0400, CUC$10-35 depending on who is playing, drinks extra. The Caprí was Meyer Lansky and Lucky Luciano's turf in the days of the Mafia

wheeling and dealing in the 1950s. Scenes from the *Godfather II* were filmed here.
Tropicana, *72 y Línea del Ferrocarril, Marianao, T7-267 0110, reserves@tropicana.tur.cu. Daily 2030 until some time after midnight. Reservations 1400-2000. Tickets CUC$75, CUC$85 and CUC$95 (depending on location of seat), including ¼ bottle of rum, 1 bottle of cola and a small salad.* Internationally famous and open-air cabaret (entry refunded if it rains). Hotels sell entrance only, so it's best to take a tour, which will include transport, as a taxi from La Habana Vieja costs CUC$12. A snack or dinner can be added. Alternatively, if you fancy a cheap drink or snack go to **Rodneys** (daily 1200-0100), a 1950s bar and restaurant designed by Cuban painter, Nelson Domínguez, located just beyond the entrance.
Turquino, *Hotel Habana Libre, 25th floor, Vedado, T7-834 6100. Daily cabaret 2230-0300, CUC$10, last entry 0200, couples only.* Great setting with amazing views. The roof opens and you can dance under the stars. Expensive drinks at CUC$6.

Cinemas
Comprehensive weekly listings of all films posted in cinema windows Thu-Wed. There are several cinemas on La Rampa, Vedado; most have a/c.

Classical music and dance
Amadeo Roldán, *Calzada y D, Vedado, T7-832 1168.* The home of the **Orquesta Sinfónica Nacional** was closed for renovation in 2015.
Gran Teatro de la Habana Alicia Alonso, *Prado y San José, Parque Central, T7-861 3078, dir.gth@cubarte.cult.cu, CUC$10.* First opened in 1838 and reopened in Jan 2016 after renovation, this wonderful baroque building, which seats 1500 with 2 galleries, has seen countless famous performers on its stage. It is home to the **Cuban National Ballet** and **Opera** companies, who perform in the Sala García Lorca. The **Conjunto Folklórico Nacional** and **Danza Contemporánea** dance companies also perform here, and it hosts the **International Ballet Festival**.

Sala Hubert de Blanck, *Calzada 654 entre A y B, Vedado, T7-833 5962 (Casa de Ensayos), T7-8301011*. Specializes in classical and contemporary music concerts but has also staged contemporary dance companies, **Danzabierta** and **Danza Contemporánea**.
Teatro Nacional de Cuba, *Paseo y 39, T7-878 4275*. Concerts are held in the main theatre, but there's also a piano bar, **El Delirio Habanero**, upstairs, and the **Café Cantante** in the basement (for both, see Music and dance clubs).

Drama

All productions are performed in Spanish. Tourists pay in CUC$.
Sala Hubert de Blanck, *Calzada 654 entre A y B, Vedado, T7-833 5962 (Casa de Ensayos), T7-8301011*. Has staged major works by García Lorca and Cuban playwright Abelardo Estorino.
Teatro El Sótano, *K 514 entre 25 y 27, Vedado, T7-832 0630*. Contemporary drama, fringe theatre and home of the **Rita Montaner Company**.
Teatro Guiñol, M entre 17 y 19, Vedado, T7-832 6262. A children's theatre that specializes in marionette shows.
Teatro Mella, *Línea 657 entre A y B, Vedado, T7-833 5651*. Specializes in modern dance but stages lots of drama performances as well.
Teatro Trianón, *Línea entre Paseo y A, Vedado, T7-830 9648*. Small theatre in good condition, headquarters of **Teatro El Público**. The seats have quirky pull-out extensions for you to rest your thighs on.

Music and dance clubs

Havana is buzzing with musical activity. Rumba, conga, *son*, danzón, charanga, salsa – you'll hear it all. Cuba's greatest musicians converge on the capital's theatres and clubs, but there are also plenty of less star-studded venues to discover.

Havana clubs are late night/early morning affairs with most Cubans arriving around midnight and staying late. Expect queues at the weekends. Cubans dress up for club

nights and most clubs have a smart dress code, strictly enforced by the door staff. This includes no shorts or sleeveless T-shirts for men. No one under 18 is admitted. The emphasis is on dancing, be it salsa and Latin dance styles, R&B, hip hop, reggaeton, electronic or rock. Many places are frequented by *jineteros/as* and lone travellers have reported feeling uncomfortable with the unwelcome attention. Several venues now feature earlier shows, aimed at young Cubans, with entrance in CUP$. There are also some good jazz venues in Vedado.

Radio Taíno FM 93.3, an English- and Spanish-language tourist station, gives regular details of a wide range of venues and Cuban bands playing, particularly in the programme *El Exitazo Musical del Caribe*, daily 1500-1800 presented by Alexis Nargona. Information is also given on **Radio Ciudad de la Habana**, 94.9 FM, 820 AM, in Spanish, including up-to-the-minute salsa programmes and live music events on *Disco Fiesta 98*, Mon-Sat 1100-1300, and *Rapsodia Latina*, Mon-Fri 1630-1730. The newspaper *Opciones* has a listing of what's on and is sold in **Paradiso** (Calle 23 469 esq O, T7-8333921) and in the hotels where Paradiso has a office.

Centro

Callejón de Hamel, *Hamel entre Aramburu y Hospital, Centro Habana, T7-8781661*. A fast, kicking *rumba* show with invited guests and community artists every Sun 1200-1500. A responsive audience and electric jam sessions make this a hot venue, recommended (see page 52). Take lots of sun screen and water.
Casa de la Cultura del Centro Habana, *Av Salvador Allende 720 entre Soledad y Castillejo, T7-878 4727*. Phone for details as events vary considerably. Extensive programme from blasting rock to sedate *peñas campesinas*, frenetic rap to hip hop.
Casa de la Cultura Julián del Casals, *Revillagigedo entre Gloria y Misión, T7-8634860*. On the 4th Fri of every month 1600-1830 there is a Peña de Danzón with the Orquesta Siglo XX and others. On the

2nd Sat 1700-1900 there is a Peña de Boleros with different musicians of the genre.

Casa de la Música Galiano, *Galiano 255 esq Neptuno, T7-8608296/7, cmh-eco@egrem.cult.cu*. Music shop, restaurant and dance floor with popular salsa bands; the best place to come for salsa. Tue-Sun matinée 1700-2100, price depends on who is performing, evening performances daily 2300-0300, CUC$10-30.

Casa del Tango Edmundo Daubar, *Neptuno 309 entre Aguila y Italia, T7-863 0097*. Musical venue/museum with fascinating collection of tango memorabilia dating back to the 1940s, from record sleeves to all manner of Carlos Gardel idolatry. Also tango dance classes, ask for Ruben.

La Madriguera, *Quinta de los Molinos, Av Infanta esq Jesús Peregrino, entrance on Jesús Peregrino (Final), after crossing over Infanta. T7-879 8175*. This is the **Casa del Joven Creador de Ciudad Habana** and the headquarters of the **Asociación Hermanos Saíz in Centro**, with arts, crafts and musical workshops for all ages and talents. Hip hop, rap and traditional Cuban rhythms are all here; fascinating glimpse into Cuban youth culture. Sun 2000-2400 electronic music, free; alternate Fri and Sat 2000-2400, hip hop, free; once a month there is a Café-Teatro with different theatre groups.

Vedado

Café Cantante, *Basement, Teatro Nacional, Plaza de la Revolución, Paseo y 39, T7-878 4275. Matinées Tue-Thu 1700-2400, Mon 2100-0200, Fri, Sat 1600-2000, Sun 2000-0100, CUC$5-10 (depending on who is performing)*. Highly regarded venue, top bands play here and it's popular with local musicians and others in the business. Live bands perform at the daily matinées except Sun when there is recorded music. Matinées are particularly popular with

Cuban youth. At night there are live bands on Fri 2200-0300 and Sat 2200-0600. Start your night in **El Delirio**, see below, then head down to the basement for the last hour of **Café Cantante** (the doorman may let you in with no charge at this late hour).

Café El Gato Tuerto, *O entre 17 y 19, T7-838 2696. Daily 2200-0400, CUC$5. Son, trova, filín* and bolero are performed live at the 'One-eyed Cat' to a bohemian crowd. The funky, post-modern decor is bordering on pretentious. Local legends often perform on the intimate stage with audience participation encouraged. There is a restaurant upstairs open daily 1200-2400.

Café Teatro Bertolt Brecht, *Centro Cultural Bertolt Brecht, 13 entre I y J, T7-830 1354. CUC$2/CUP$50*. A large basement bar open every night, but for the latest music visit late on Tue, Thu, Fri nights for '*No se lo digas a nadie*' (Don't tell anyone), when contemporary fusion bands play live.

El Delirio Habanero, *5th floor, Teatro Nacional, Plaza de la Revolución, Paseo y 39, T7-878 4275. Matinée on Sat 1600-2000, CUC$5. Thu-Sun 2200-0300, CUC$5*. Piano bar upstairs (lift sometimes not working) where you can hear quality music by small traditional groups. Great views of floodlit José Martí monument and Plaza de la Revolución. Take the big red sofa seats under the windows. Busy at weekends with a mostly Cuban crowd; phone to reserve the best tables. Delicious cocktails, good-value snacks, attentive service. Recommended. Energetic clubbers leave here and head for the sweaty **Café Cantante** (see above) in the basement for the last hour.

El Gran Palenque Bar, *4 entre Calzada y 5, T7-830 3939/830 3060. Closed for repairs 2015*. On Sat at 1500-1700 the courtyard of this open-air café/bar is taken over by the acclaimed **Conjunto Folklórico Nacional de Cuba** for an upbeat rumba show: *Patio de la Rumba* (CUC$5).

El Submarino Amarillo, *17 esq 6, corner of Parque John Lennon. Mon 2100-0200, Tue-Sat 1400-1930, 2100-0200, Sun 1400-2200, CUC$5*. Beatle-themed decor, Pop Art on the walls, reasonable drinks prices, snacks available. No smoking. Some die-hard Beatles fans might find the cover bands a cringe, but it's all good nostalgic fun with music by the Beatles, Led Zeppelin, Queen, etc, plus plenty of heavy metal and lots of Cuban rock.

Habana Café, *Hotel Meliá Cohiba, Paseo entre 1 y 3, T7-833 3636. Daily show 2100-2400, CUC\$20 minimum, CUC\$30 with drinks, CUC\$50 with dinner and drinks (buy tickets in advance in the hotel lobby).* Very touristy and largely frequented by Meliá guests. A 1950s American pastiche has replaced the bombed-out disco. Old cars, small Cubana plane hanging from the ceiling, memorabilia on the walls, Benny Moré and Buena Vista Social Club music and large screen showing brilliant film of old Cuban musicians and artistes. Show is followed by a DJ who plays until 0200. Food expensive and not recommended, overpriced cocktails from CUC\$6.

Hurón Azul, *17 351 entre Av de los Presidentes y H, T7-832 4571.* The headquarters of UNEAC (artists' and writers' union) in a majestic, colonial mansion is an inviting hangout for the intelligentsia. The lovely, welcoming bar hosts regular upbeat afternoon *peñas*. Wed alternate between *Trova sin Traba* and *Peña del Ambia* 1700-2000. Sat bolero from 2100 onwards.

Imágenes, *Calzada 602 esq C, T7-833 3606. Daily 2130-0300. Matinée Fri-Sun 1500-2000, CUC\$1. Comedy Mon, Tue CUC\$3, Wed-Sun CUC\$5.* Intimate, classy piano bar, great for low-key evening, also stand-up comedy, karaoke, recorded music and games. Very popular, few tourists, reservations recommended for tables.

Jazz Café, *Galerías del Paseo esq 1, T7-838 3556. Daily 1200-0200. CUC\$10 consumo mínimo after 2030. 2 live performances at 2130 and 2300.* Sleek and savvy jazz venue with class acts, a laid-back welcoming ambience and a highly appreciative audience. Star-studded line-up includes legendary pianist Chucho Valdés. Excellent for jazz lovers.

La Casona de Línea, *Línea 505 entre D y E, T7-8305373, llaurado@cubarte.cult.cu.* A cultural institute in a grand old Vedado mansion, once the home of the family that owned the Cristal brewery, now the headquarters for the Teatro Estudio theatre group. On Sun at 2030 in the small patio, you can see up-and-coming singer/songwriters and bands performing. Cover CUP\$10. Call to see who is playing.

La Zorra y el Cuervo, *23 y O, T7-8332402, zorra.cha@tur.cu. Daily 2200-0200, CUC\$10 (including 2 cocktails).* 'The Fox and the Crow' is one of the best nights in Havana for jazz enthusiasts. The small, dark cellar space on La Rampa is entered through a fine reproduction of a red British telephone box. High-calibre jazz musicians play to an appreciative crowd. Get there before 2300 if you want a table with an unobscured view of the stage as there are pillars in the way. Cuban bands often feature visiting US musicians.

Tikoa, *23 entre N y O, T7-830 9973. Daily 2200-0300. Disco Fri-Sun CUC\$3, Mon-Thu CUC\$2.* All types of music. Wed matinee CUC\$1 1600-2000. Popular with travellers and locals, this small and sweaty basement club swings with a strong Afro-Cuban vibe.

Miramar

Casa de la Música Egrem, *Sala Té Quedarás, 20 3308 esq 35, T7-204 0447. CD shop daily 1100-2300. Music and dancing daily 1700-2100 (CUC\$5-15) and 2300-late (CUC\$10-25).* One of the top venues to listen to the cream of Havana's musical talent. The programme changes a lot so it's best to phone in advance to see who is on. Upstairs at the **Diablo Tun Tun** traditional and alternative music is played by small groups daily 2300-0600, CUC\$5-15. Food service from the *parrilla* daily 1200-2400.

Club Almendares, *Márgenes del Río Almendares, 49 y Av 28, Kohly, Miramar, T7-204 4990/7502.* Salón Chévere (*Disco Temba*), daily 2200-0300, CUC\$2 except Wed when

Tip...
Many of the *comparsa congas* parade regularly throughout the year down Paseo Martí and through La Habana Vieja.

it is CUC$5, all types of music. Swimming pool 0900-1800, CUC$10 including drinks of CUC$5. Mosquitoes can be troublesome as you are in the Bosque de la Habana.

Don Cangrejo, *Av 1 entre 16 y 18, T7-504 5002/204 3837. Daily 2300-0300.* A large open-air venue beside the sea with a rather inconvenient covered swimming pool in the centre. Cover CUC$5-20, depending on who is playing. Fri night is very busy and popular with young Cubans keen to see contemporary bands.

El Río Club, *A entre 3 y 5, T7-209 3389. Daily 2200-0400, CUC$5.* Locals still refer to it as *Johnnie's Club*, which it was called before the Revolution. The salsa disco is hot and sweaty, a favourite with Havana's dance crowd.

La Maison *Calle 16, 701 esq 7, T7-204 0124. Daily 2030-0050.* Live music in the lovely open-air patio of this luxurious mansion and fashion shows displaying imported clothes sold in their own boutique (see Shopping). The Piano Bar is open daily 2200-0400 for karaoke and comedy show as well as live music, CUC$5. There's also a swimming pool, bar and café open during the day.

Salón Boleros en Dos Gardenias, *7 esq 26, Miramar, T7-204 2353. Daily 2200-0500, CUC$5.* Upmarket *bolero* venue, 4-5 live shows every night, elegant, well-dressed crowd with popular Chinese and criollo restaurant and bars. Live singers with small bands.

Salón Rosado Benny Moré, *La Tropical, 41 y 46, T7-206 4799. Closed Mon-Thu.* Fri electronic music 1900-0400, CUC$2, Sat 2030-0300, CUC$2-5 depending who is on, Sun Discotemba 1700-2300, CUC$1 with live bands. Raunchy, popular dance venue with some of the best salsa in town.

Teatro Karl Marx, *Av 1 1010 entre 8 y 10, T7-203 0801, T7-209 1991.* Huge venue, famous for hosting the 1st rock concert by a Western band, Manic Street Preachers, who played here in 2001 in the presence of Fidel Castro.

Festivals

The most popular cultural events are the cinema and jazz festivals, but there are also several dance festivals as well as folk and classical music events. At the Marina Hemingway there always seem to be regattas and fishing tournaments in progress.

Jan Cubadanza is a twice-yearly dance festival with workshops and performances.
Feb Havana International Book Fair is held at La Cabaña castle. It's a commercial fair but is immensely popular with book-hungry families. Look out for new book launches. Also held in many cities around the island, www.cubaliteraria.com.
Cigar Festival, www.festivaldelhabano.com, is for true aficionados of *Habanos*. Held at the Palacio de las Convenciones. You can learn about the history of cigars and there are opportunities for visits to tobacco plantations and cigar factories.
Mar Bienal de la Habana is held over a month and takes place every 2 years (next in 2017), gathering over 200 artists from 40 countries in the Centro de Arte Contemporáneo Wifredo Lam, Centro de Arte La Casona, Parque Morro-Cabaña, Pabellón Cuba and other venues, www.bienalhabana.cult.cu.
Spring in Havana The **International Festival of Electroacoustic Music** features workshops and performances.
Apr Offshore Class 1 World Championship and the **Great Island Speedboat Grand Prix** are usually held during the last week at the Marina Hemingway, attracting powerboat enthusiasts from all over the world.
May Ernest Hemingway International Billfishing Tournament is one of the major events at the Marina Hemingway, www.internationalhemingwaytournament.com.
Festival Internacional de Poesía de La Habana is held at CubaPoesía, Hospital esq 25, www.cubapoesia.cult.cu.

Jun Festival Danzón Habana Latin American musicians and dancers celebrate *danzón* at the Teatro América, Centro Hispanoamericano de Cultura y Unión Fraternal, at the end of the month. Each year it is dedicated to a different Latin American country, ireartes@hotmail.com.

Jul Cuballet de Verano is a summer dance festival with workshops and courses for dancers and dance teachers, www.prodanza.cult.cu.

Aug Cubadanza, the 2nd of the year, with workshops and courses, see Jan for details.
Carnival Conga parades through the city.

Sep International Blue Marlin Fishing Tournament at Marina Hemingway. The marina fills up with mostly US fishermen eager to pit their strength against marlin and their fellow competitors, with lots of après-fishing social events.

Oct Havana International Ballet Festival is held every other year (2016) in the 2nd half of the month at the Gran Teatro, Teatro Nacional and Teatro Mella. Run by Alicia Alonso, head of the Cuban National Ballet, www.festivalballethabana.cult.cu.

Havana Theatre Festival takes place at theatres and plazas all over the city at the end of Oct and into Nov, featuring contemporary international and Cuban drama, workshops and seminars, organized by Cuba Escena, www.cubaescena.cult.cu.

Nov Havana Contemporary Music Festival is held at UNEAC and theatres mid-month, www.musicacontemporanea.cult.cu.
Marabana, Havana's marathon, takes place on the 3rd Sun of the month, www.inder.cu/marabana.

Dec International Festival of New Latin American Cinema shows prize-winning films (no subtitles) at cinemas around Havana. This is the foremost film festival in Latin America with the best of Cuban and Latin American films along with documentaries and independent cinema from Europe and the USA. The festival attracts big-name actors and directors, www.habanafilmfestival.com.
International Jazz Plaza Festival is held

at theatres and at the Casa de la Cultura de Plaza. It is one of the world's major jazz festivals with the best of Cuban and international jazz for CUC$5-10 per show. There are also events at the **Nacional** and the **Habana Libre**. There are masterclasses and workshops available and the event is organized by Grammy winner Jesús 'Chucho' Valdés, http://jazzcuba.com.

San Lázaro Pilgrims flock to the church in the small town of El Rincón (just south of the airport) on 17 Dec to ask Lazarus to cure them.
Christmas Day The conga parade is another chance to go wild with the *farolas* and *tambores*.

Shopping

Art

You need documentation to take works of art out of the country or you may have them confiscated at the airport; galleries will provide the necessary paperwork and even vendors in the market can give you the required stamp. The following are all in La Habana Vieja.

Casa de los Artistas, *Oficios 6 entre Obispo y Obrapía. Mon-Sat 1030-1630.* Several leading Cuban artists have their studios here which can be visited. There is also a gallery of contemporary art showcasing their work and that of others.

Centro de Desarrollo de las Artes Visuales, *San Ignacio 352 esq Teniente Rey, just off Plaza Vieja, T7-862 3533. Tue-Sat 1000-1700.* Exhibitions on 3 floors of established and up-and-coming artists. Experimental art has a home here.

Galería del Grabado, *at the back of the Taller Experimental de Gráfica de la Habana, Callejón del Chorro 62, Plaza de la Catedral, T7-864 6013, tgrafica@cubarte.cult.cu. Mon-Fri 1000-1630.* Original lithographs and other works of art can be purchased or commissioned directly from the artists. You can watch the prints and engravings being made and specialist courses are available for those who want to learn the skill for themselves, for 1 week, CUC$150, 2 weeks CUC$250,

1 month, CUC$500, contact Yamilys Brito Jorge, Especialista Principal.

Galería Forma, *Obispo 255 entre Aguiar y Cuba, T7-862 0123. Daily 0900-2100*. Formerly the bookshop, **Exlibris Swan** 1927-1960, now an art gallery belonging to the **Fondo Cubano de Bienes Culturales**, selling paintings, *artesanías*, ceramics, jewellery and sculpture.

Galería Víctor Manuel, *San Ignacio 56 esq Callejón del Chorro, Plaza de la Catedral, T7-861 2955. Daily 0900-2100*. A bit of a tourist trap selling mainstream representative art, rather than anything experimental, at high prices. However, you may still find something you would like to live with. The gallery is in the former Casa de Baños (public bath house).

Taller de Papel Artesanal, *Mercaderes entre Obispo y Obrapía, T7-861 3356. Mon-Sat 0830-1700, Sun 0830-1300*. Sells handmade paper as well as postcards and other items made from recycled paper. Workshops and courses in paper-making available.

Taller Serigrafía René Portocarrero, *Cuba 513 entre Teniente Rey y Muralla, T7-8623276, serigrafia@cubarte.cult.cu*. Another big workshop, making screen prints; again, you can watch them being made and buy things.

Terracota 4, *Mercaderes entre Obrapía y Lamparilla. Daily 1000-1800*. Studio and gallery of 2 ceramicists, Amelia Carballo and Angel Norniella.

Food

For food shopping, there is the **Focsa Supermarket** (on 17 entre M y N in Vedado, at the base of the big tower block) or the **Amistad** (on San Lázaro, just below Infanta in Cayo Hueso). The **Isla de Cuba** (on Máximo Gómez entre Factoría y Suárez), supermarket has the best selection of food in La Habana Vieja, with prices stamped on the goods to prevent overcharging. Farmers are allowed to sell their produce (root and green vegetables, fruit, grains and meat) in free-priced city *agromercados*. You should pay for food in CUP$. There are markets in Vedado at 19 y B and a smaller one at 21 esq J; in Nuevo Vedado, Tulipán opposite Hidalgo. There are busy food markets on the last Sun of every month in other Havana neighbourhoods and a new state market on the Plaza del Cerro, Vía Blanca y Boyeros opposite the Ciudad Deportiva entrance, Tue-Fri 0800-1800, Sat 0700-1700 and Sun 0700-1200, with a **Cadeca** exchange bureau, car and bike park.

Museo del Chocolate, *Mercaderes entre Teniente Rey y Amargura, La Habana Vieja, T7-866 4431. Daily 0900-2200*. Sells chocolate candy made on the premises, also offers hot and cold chocolate.

Handicrafts

Asociación Cubana Artesanos y Artistas (**ACAA**), *Obispo 411 entre Compostela y Aguacate, La Habana Vieja. Office T7-862 0655, Mon-Fri 1000-1500. Gallery, T7-8678577, and market daily 1000-1900*. Handicrafts, clothing, humidors, glassware and musical instruments.

Casa del Abanico, *Obrapía 107 entre Oficios y Mercaderes, La Habana Vieja, T7-863 4452. Mon-Sat 0900-1800*. Beautifully decorated fans for sale from luxury silk to everyday cotton. Lots of historical details. You can have one customized to your own design, just as the *criollo* ladies used to.

Palacio de la Artesanía, *Palacio Pedroso (built 1780) at Cuba 64 entre Peña Pobre y Cuarteles (opposite Parque Anfiteatro)*. A mansion converted into boutiques on 3 floors with musicians in the courtyard. A large selection of Cuban handicrafts is available. It also has things not available elsewhere, such as American trainers, as well as clothing, jewellery, perfume, souvenirs, music, cigars, restaurant, bar and ice cream. Visa and MasterCard accepted, passport required.

Handicraft markets

Many open-air markets, handicraft and tourist souvenir stalls and *ferias de artesanías* have sprung up.

Feria Almacenes San José, *Desamparados (Av del Puerto) entre Damas y San Isidro, La Habana Vieja. Daily 1000-1800*. Havana's largest craft market has a multitude of products: tourist souvenirs, clothing, paintings, carvings, crochet, ceramics, boxes, jewellery, T-shirts and baseball bats – the list is endless; if you can't find what you want, someone will know someone who has it. A platform for many talented young artists to show off their skills. You may pick up a bargain, or you may be asked to pay Miami-type prices. Also on the market site is a CADECA, a small music shop, a rum, tobacco and coffee outlet, a shop selling coins and antiques, and an office of ETECSA for phone cards; a second hand book stall is planned.

Feria del 23, *23 entre M y N, Vedado. Daily 0900-1700.* A varied selection, but carvings and beads predominate.

Feria del Malecón, *Malecón, entre B y C, Vedado. Tue-Sat 0930-1730, Sun 1000-1400.* Items include shoes and costume jewellery.

Music, cigars and souvenirs

Artex, *L esq 23, T7-838 3162. Mon-Sat 1000-2100, Sun 1000-1900.* Excellent music section with instruments and tasteful T-shirts and postcards.

Casa Cubana del Perfume, *Teniente Rey 13 entre Oficios y Mercaderes, La Habana Vieja, T7-866 3759. Mon-Sat 1100-1800, Sun 1100-1400.* Perfumes mixed on the premises. On the mezzanine is a little cafetería.

Casa de la Música Galiano, *Galiano 255 esq Neptuno, Centro, T7-860 8296, cmh-eco@egrem.cult.cu. Daily 1100-2300.* Shop specializing in music, extensive list of titles, past and contemporary.

Casa del Habano, *7 y 26, Miramar, T7-204 2353. Mon-Sat 1030-1830.* Full range of cigars, one of many state cigar shops. See box, page 120.

Casa del Tabaco y Ron, *Obispo esq Monserrate, La Habana Vieja, T7-866 8911. Daily 0900-1900.* Wide range of rums of all ages, plus tobacco and coffee.

EGREM, *Casa de la Música, see Music and dance clubs, above.* A good selection of CDs and music.

La Maison *Calle 16, 701 esq 7, Miramar, T7-204 0124.* Luxurious mansion with shops selling cigars, alcohol, handicrafts, jewellery and perfume. There is live music (see Entertainment) and fashion shows in the evening, displaying imported clothes sold in the boutique. However, as with all shops depending on imports, the quantity and quality of stock is variable and can be disappointing.

Longina Música, *Obispo 360 entre Habana y Compostela, La Habana Vieja, T7-862 8371. Mon-Sat 1000-1800, Sun 1000-1300.* You can buy drums and other instruments here as well as CDs and stereos.

Perfumería Habana, *Mercaderes 156 entre Obrapía y Lamparilla, La Habana Vieja, T7-861 3525. Mon-Sat 1000-1900, Sun 1100-1400.* Manufacture and sale of perfumes and colognes from natural essential oils. Aromatherapy massages also offered.

What to do

Baseball

Estadio Latinoamericano, *Pedro Pérez 302, Cerro, T7-870 6576.* South of the centre in Cerro district, this is the best place to see baseball (the major league level). Opened in the 1950s, it has a capacity for 55,000 spectators and is home to the 2 Havana teams, **Industriales** (Los Azules) and **Metropolitanos**. Days and times of games vary considerably, CUC$3 for the best seats and CUC$1 for the regular stand.

The *Serie Nacional* baseball season runs Aug-Nov, culminating in the national play-offs, followed a couple of weeks later by the *Liga Superior*, which lasts a month. Baseball games have a fanatical following and can last up to 3 hrs. Follow the evening's game by visiting the Parque Central in La Habana Vieja the next day, the traditional venue for groups of passionate fans to congregate and discuss match details using frantic hand gestures to illustrate their opinions.

Basketball

Estadio Ramón Fonst, *Av Independencia y Bruzón, Plaza de la Revolución, T7-881 4196.* Local team is **Capitalinos**. No fixed match dates.

Boxing

Sala Kid Chocolate, *Paseo de Martí y Brasil, La Habana Vieja, T7-861 1547.* The sports centre hosts regular matches during boxing season. Also here are judo, weightlifting, chess and handball; for international events it hosts tennis, boxing and badminton, when tickets are CUC$1. A monthly programme of events is on the noticeboard.

Golf

Club de Golf, *Calzada de Varona, Km 8, Capdevila, Boyeros, towards the airport, cgolf@continental.cubalse.cu.* The 9-hole course is par 35. CUC$30 for 18 holes (caddy charges CUC$6), CUC$20 for 9 (caddy CUC$3), CUC$10 for a 30-min lesson, club rental CUC$10. Non-members are welcome. For foreign residents or frequent visitors, club membership is CUC$45 a month after an initial fee of CUC$70, which gives you unlimited golf. There is also a 2-lane bowling alley, billiards (3 tables), tennis (5 courts, bring your own rackets, instruction available), squash and swimming pool, CUC$5 (CUC$8 in summer) including a drink, a bar (**Hoyo 19**, reserved for golfers and members) and a poor restaurant/snack bar, **La Estancia**.

Running

Entry to Havana's Marathon, **Marabana**, in Nov, is CUC$10, including a marathon jersey, see Festivals and events for details. Another race is **Terry Fox** on 2 Feb each year to raise money for cancer treatments.

Sports centres

Ciudad Deportiva, *at the roundabout on Av Boyeros y Vía Blanca, T7-881 6979. P2 bus passes outside.* The 'Sports City' is a large circular sports stadium seating 18,000 spectators for volleyball (very popular), basketball, martial arts and table tennis. The stadium is enclosed by a dome with a roof diameter of 88 m and was designed by architects Nicolás Arroyo and Gabriela Menéndez. The complex was inaugurated on 26 Feb 1958 and at the time was considered one of the world's best indoor sports facilities. Entrance usually CUP$2 for a seat and CUP$1 for the concrete benches in upper tiers, but it depends on the event. Buy tickets in advance at venue. International matches are usually a sellout. Great atmosphere, crowded, limited food and drink facilities. Large neon sign outside *'listos para vencer'* (ready to win).

Tour operators

There are lots of state-owned travel agencies, which cooperate fully with each other and have bureaux in all the major hotels. As well as local trips to factories, schools, hospitals, etc, tours can be arranged to destinations all over Cuba by bus or air, with participants picked up from any hotel in Havana at no extra charge.

Examples include a tour of the city's colonial sites (CUC$15, 4 hrs); a trip to the Tropicana cabaret; Cayo Largo for the day by air with boat trip, snorkelling, optional diving, lunch; Cayo Coco for the day with flight, all-inclusive package and changing room; Cayo Levisa day trip by bus and boat with snorkelling and lunch; Guamá and the Península de Zapata with a stop en route at the Finca Fiesta Campesina, tour of crocodile farm, lunch; Viñales and Pinar del Río, visiting mogotes, caves and tobacco factory, lunch; a day on the beach at Varadero with lunch, 10 hrs, and you get a changing room with shower and towel; Trinidad and Cienfuegos overnight, visiting the colonial city and the Valle de los Ingenios; ecological tour of Las Terrazas with walking and river bathing, lunch. Prices vary slightly between agencies and you can negotiate a reduction without meals.

Watersports

Marina Hemingway has 140 slips with electricity and water and space for docking 400 recreational boats.

Centro de Buceo La Aguja, *Marina Hemingway, T7-204 5280*. The dive centre takes up to 8 divers on the boat.

Club Habana (Sol Meliá), *Av 5 entre 188 y 192, Reparto Flores, Playa, T7-275 0100*. A club for permanent residents with annual membership of CUC$1500. Tennis, squash, pool, diving (with certification), windsurfing, training golf course, child care, shops, meetings facilities, sauna and massage, bar and restaurant, expensive. All motorized watersports were withdrawn in 2003 following a security clampdown.

Club Náutico Internacional 'Hemingway' (**Hemingway International Yacht Club**), *Residencial Turístico 'Marina Hemingway', Av 5 y 248, Playa, T7-204 6653, yachtclub@cnih. mh.cyt.cu*. Offers help and advice to visiting yachties. The club organizes regattas, sailing schools and excursions, as well as the Hemingway Tournament.

Transport

Air

José Martí International Airport is 18 km southwest of the city and has 3 terminals: Terminal 1 for domestic flights; Terminal 2 for flights from Cancún and Terminal 3 for all other international flights (for details, see Practicalities, page 135). There are no buses from Terminal 3 to the other 2 terminals (although it's just 5 mins in a taxi) and no public buses from Terminal 3 into Havana, but there are lots of taxis and taxi organizers waiting for you. As many transatlantic flights arrive late at night it can be sensible to arrange the transfer from the airport to your hotel in advance with your travel agent. However, it is cheaper to get a taxi when you arrive: CUC$25 is commonly asked to the old city; sharing a taxi with someone else will reduce the fare a bit. On the way back to the airport it is possible to arrange a regular taxi, which may work out cheaper, if you negotiate with the driver. Travelling by bus is not practical.

Bus

HabanaBusTour is a hop-on, hop-off tour bus service for foreigners, which travels 0900-2100 on 2 routes: T1 (CUC$10 per day) leaves from Almacenes San José (Feria de Artesanía on Av del Puerto) to the Plaza de la Revolución and out to Miramar (Av 5 y 112), while T3 (CUC$5 per day) leaves from the Parque Central and travels past the Fortaleza Cabaña, the Villa Panamericana and Alamar out to the Playas del Este.

Local Metrobuses (CUP$0.40) serve the suburbs, but the service has long been in crisis due to a lack of vehicles and fuel, and foreigners are not expected to use them. They are hot and sweaty and uncomfortably crowded at all times. *Habaneros* insist they carry more people than a Boeing 747 and refer to them as *La Película del sábado* (Saturday Night Movie) since they contain bad language, violence and sex scenes. This may be a slight exaggeration, but you should certainly be aware of pickpockets. If you insist on using the bus, then be sure to follow queuing etiquette at the bus stop. Discover who is last in line (*el último*, you have to shout loudly) for the bus you want, then ask him/her who they are behind (*¿detrás de quién?*). The queue may look disorganized, but it is actually highly functional: people mark their places and then wander off until the bus comes when everyone re-forms into an orderly queue. That's the theory. However, things may deteriorate at night, particularly if there has been a long wait, when the elbow becomes the preferred mode of queuing.

Long distance A/c tourist buses to most cities are run by Viazul, and leave from Av 26 entre Av Zoológico y Ulloa, Nuevo Vedado, T7-881 1413/881 1108/881 5652/881 5657, www.viazul.cu, with lots of intermediate stops. See also Practicalities, page 138. Viazul's terminal is small, with toilets and a poor snack bar upstairs; outside there's an **Etecsa** cabin for local and long-distance calls. **Taxis** wait outside the terminal and will cost around CUC$5-6 to La Habana Vieja or Centro.

Astro buses leave from the Terminal de Omnibus Interprovinciales, Av Rancho Boyeros (Independencia) 101 entre 19 de Mayo y Bruzón, by the Plaza de la Revolución, T7-870 9401/870 3397. However, foreigners are not allowed to use this service any more. **Viazul** buses often call in here after leaving their own terminal, but you can't rely on seats being available.

Car

Most of the hotels have car hire agencies in the reception area and many streets around tourist locations have unofficial 'supervisors' who monitor car parking spaces and expect a CUC$1 payment on your return. However, hiring a car is not recommended for getting around Havana, as roads are badly signed and there have been many accidents involving tourists driving rental cars, see Practicalities, page 139.

Instead, if you want the real experience, **Gran Car**, T7-8788784, rents classic cars (including Oldsmobiles, Mercury '54, Buicks and Chevvy '55) with driver for a maximum of 4 passengers. Under new regulations, you must negotiate the price with driver, usually CUC$25-30 per hr or more for cars without roofs (go for the Oldsmobile '52).

Motos (scooters) can be hired from **Transtur**, Av 7 esq 26, Restaurante Dos Gardenias, Miramar, T7-204 0646, 1 day CUC$25, 2-4 days CUC$23 daily, 5-12 days CUC$21 daily, 13-20 days CUC$18 daily, 21-29 days CUC$16 daily, 30 days CUC$14 daily. Returnable deposit of CUC$50.

There are **Cupet-Cimex** petrol stations (green logo) at Av Independencia y 271, Boyeros (near Terminal 2); Av Independencia esq Calzada de Cerro, Plaza (near Plaza de la Revolución); Paseo y Malecón (near Hotel Riviera), Vedado; L y 17, Vedado; Línea y Malecón, Vedado; 86 y 13, Miramar; 7, entre 2 y 4, Miramar; 112 y 5, Miramar, and Vento y Santa Catalina, Cerro. All are open 24 hrs and sell drinks, snacks and food.

Cycling

Cycling is a good way to see Havana, especially the suburbs; you can reach the Playas del Este beaches and surrounding countryside quickly and easily, although some roads in the Embassy area are closed to cyclists. The tunnel underneath the harbour has a bus designed specifically to carry bicycles and their riders, from Parque El Curita, Aguila y Dragones, to Reparto Camilo Cienfuegos after the tunnel. Take care at night as there are few streetlights and bikes are not fitted with lamps. *Poncheros*, small private businesses that crudely fix punctures, are everywhere.

Ferry

There are ferries from La Habana Vieja to **Casablanca** and **Regla**, CUP$0.10, which depart from Muelle de Luz, San Pedro opposite Bar Dos Hermanos. If you are facing the water, the Casablanca ferry docks on the left side of the pier and goes out in a left curve towards that headland, and the Regla ferry docks on the right side and goes out in a right curve. There are lots of security checks with X-ray machines and body searches following the 2003 hijacking of a ferry.

Taxi
Bicitaxi/cocotaxi In La Habana Vieja and Vedado, bicycle or tricycle taxis are cheap and a pleasant way to travel. A short journey will cost at least CUC$2. There is also the *coctaxi/*

cocomóvil. If you can handle being driven around in a bright yellow vehicle shaped like a coconut shell on a 125cc motor bike, then these are quick and readily available. They take 2 passengers, no safety belts, plenty of pollution in your face. The fare is fixed in CUC\$, but agree the fare before the journey. A typical fare from the Hotel Nacional to La Habana Vieja is CUC\$3. Less conspicuous are the **Rentar una fantasía** vehicles, using the same 125cc engine but the vehicle is designed as a pre-1920s motor car.

Cubataxi Taxis are plentiful and are a safe and easy way to travel around Havana, although they are relatively expensive. **Cubataxi**, T7-855 5555, is now the only state company. They wait outside most hotels and at the airport, or you can ask your hotel to call one. Cubataxi also have minibuses, or big taxis, T7-8831587, which take 7 people, useful if you are a group with lots of luggage. From Centro to the airport costs CUC\$25. There are also private taxis (*particulares*) you can hail on the street, see page 141.

Peso taxis Taxi *colectivos* ply their trade up and down main thoroughfares, usually stopping at bus stops to pick up passengers. They are large old American gas guzzlers in variable condition, usually poor, and everyone is squeezed in. Fixed CUP\$10 fare. These taxis can also be hired by foreigners if they have a licence.

Train

Rail services in Cuba are notoriously unreliable so the following departure and fare information is liable to change without warning. For further information, see Practicalities, page 137.

The **Estación Central on Egido** (Av de Bélgica) y Arsenal, on the edge of La Habana Vieja, is currently closed for renovation and trains for the east of the country are instead leaving from **Estación La Coubre** (Av del Puerto y Egido, get tickets in advance, T7-8603165, Mon-Fri 0830-1600, Sat 0830-1130, and take your passport), nearby.

Trains to **Pinar del Río** depart from Terminal 19 de Noviembre, Tulipán y Factor, Nuevo Vedado, T7-883 2769, every other day, 7-8 hrs, CUC\$6.50. However, a long-distance bus or dollar taxi will do the same journey in a fraction of the time.

The **Hershey** electric train (see page 95) with services to **Matanzas** starts from Casablanca departing daily 0445, 1221, 1635. Buy tickets at Casablanca booking office an hour before departure, CUC\$2.80 single to Matanzas, CUC\$1.40 to Hershey, but call first, T7-793 8888, because the service is 'informal'.

Tip...
The Estación Central has what is claimed to be the oldest engine in Latin America, *La Junta*, built in Baltimore in 1842.

East of
Havana

Several places of interest east of Havana can easily be reached as a day trip from the capital, with the option of staying a night or two if you wish. Readers of Ernest Hemingway novels will be fascinated to see his former home – now a museum dedicated to his memory – just as he left it, or Cojímar, the setting for his novel *The Old Man and the Sea*. The best beaches east of Havana are at Playas del Este, an easy cycle ride, bus or taxi from the city, or further afield at Jibacoa where you can explore the countryside as well as the sea. The once-prosperous and artistic city of Matanzas is well worth a visit and can be reached by the old Hershey electric railway line, making the journey as much of an adventure as the destination. The province of Matanzas is mainly associated with the mega-resort of Varadero beach. This tourist enclave is squeezed onto a finger of land stretching out into the Caribbean. All-inclusive deals make this a popular holiday spot, but for all that it represents of Cuba it might as well be another country.

Essential East of Havana

Finding your feet

There is an **international airport** at Varadero, which receives scheduled and charter flights from Europe and Canada. Matanzas is on the main railway line between Havana and Santiago. The Hershey electric railway line, which used to service the Hershey chocolate factory before the Revolution, also runs between Havana and Matanzas, but it breaks down frequently and timings are very approximate. More reliable than the train is the excellent bus service provided by **Viazul**, which uses the good road out from Havana along the north coast to Matanzas and Varadero.

Tip...

Public transport is notoriously scarce outside the main towns and tourist areas. Tourists from Varadero are herded on to tour buses for excursions, but to do your own thing, hire a car or pay a driver to take you around in his old Chevrolet taxi.

Tip...

Some places in Varadero accept euros (€).

Getting around

There are local trains from Matanzas to other towns in the province, but service is poor. Local buses run from Matanzas and Varadero, and there are plenty of tour buses to take you to the peninsula on an excursion, but car hire is recommended if you want flexibility. See also Essential Matanzas city, page 97, and Essential Varadero, page 106.

When to go

The winter season between December and April has the best weather, although, if there is a cold front off the eastern seaboard of the USA you can expect rough seas and a smaller expanse of sand as a result. This is also the most expensive season in the resorts. The wettest time of year is between September and November.

Havana to Matanzas

Afro-Cuban and Hemingway attractions plus miles of beaches for city escapees

Cojímar

The former seaside village, now a concrete jungle, featured in Hemingway's *The Old Man and the Sea*, is an easy excursion (15 minutes by taxi from central Havana). Hemingway celebrated his Nobel prize here in 1954, and there is a bust of the author opposite a small fort built in 1645. Unfortunately the wharf where he kept the *Pilar* was smashed by the hurricanes in 2008 and has not been repaired. The coastline (no beach) is covered in sharp rocks and is dirty because of effluent from tankers. **La Terraza**, founded in 1926, is a restaurant with a pleasant view, where Hemingway used to sit and pass time with the local fishermen upon whom he modelled his 'Old Man'.

Regla

Ferry from Muelle Luz (at the end of C Santa Clara), La Habana Vieja, or Ruta 6 bus from Zulueta entre Genios y Refugio, CUP$0.40.

Regla is to the east of La Habana Vieja, across the harbour. It has a largely black population and a long-standing and still active cultural history of Yoruba and *Santería* traditions. The main street, Martí, runs north from the landing stage up to the church on your left. In the church is the Santísima Virgen de Regla, the spirit (Orisha) who looks after sailors. Next to the church, the **Museo Municipal de Regla** ① *Martí 158 entre Facciolo y La Piedra, T7-797*

6989, *museoderegla@cubarte.cult.cu, Tue-Sat 0900-1800, Sun 0900-1300, CUC$2, with guide CUC$3, camera CUC$5, amateur video CUC$50,* has a room with information and objects of Yoruba culture. Three blocks further on is the **Casa de la Cultura** ⓘ *Martí 208, T7-797 9905,* which has very occasional cultural activities.

Guanabacoa

5 km east of Havana and reached by a road turning off the Central Highway. Take a CUP$0.40 bus: Ruta 195 (1 hr) from Calle 23 esq J, Vedado; Ruta 5 (1 hr) from 19 de Mayo; Ruta 3 from Parque de la Fraternidad, or a direct bus from Regla.

Guanabacoa is a small colonial town. Sights include the old parish church, which has a splendid altar, the monastery of San Francisco, the Carral theatre, the Jewish cemetery and some attractive mansions. Housed in a former estate mansion, with slave quarters at the back of the building, is the **Museo Histórico de Guanabacoa** ⓘ *Martí 108 entre Versalles y San Antonio, T7-797 9117, musgbcoa@cubarte.cult.cu, Mon-Sat 0930-1730, Sun 0900-1300, CUC$2, CUC$3 with guide, amateur video CUC$25.* The **Festival de Raíces Africanas Wemilere** is held here in the last week of November, each year dedicated to a different African country. Museum staff offer a 45-minute guided tour of the town (in Spanish) and there's sometimes folk dancing for groups.

The **Cementerio de Judíos** (Jewish Cemetery) was founded in 1906-10 and is set back behind an impressive gated entrance on the left on the road to Santa Fé. There is a monument to the victims of the Holocaust and bars of soap are buried as a symbolic gesture. Saúl Yelín (1935-1977), one of the founding members of Cuban cinema, is buried under a large flamboyant tree and you can also see the graves of the *Mártires del Partido Communista*, victims of the Machado dictatorship.

Museo Ernest Hemingway

Finca La Vigía, San Francisco de Paula, San Miguel del Padrón, 12.5 km from central Havana, T7-691 0809. Mon-Sat 1000-1700, closed rainy days. CUC$5 plus CUC$5 for a guide, children under 12 free, amateur video CUC$50. Getting there: Bus P7 from Parque Fraternidad and P2 from Línea y G, Vedado. The signpost is opposite the post office, leading up a short driveway. No toilets at the site.

Hemingway fans may wish to visit **Finca La Vigía**, where the author lived from 1939 to 1961, now the Ernest Hemingway Museum. Visitors are not allowed inside the plain whitewashed house, which has been lovingly preserved with all Hemingway's furniture, books and hunting collections, just as he left it. But you can walk around the outside and look in through the windows and open doors. A small annex building is used for temporary exhibitions and from the upper floors there are fine views over Havana. The garden is beautiful and tropical, with many shady palms. Next to the swimming pool (empty) are the gravestones of Hemingway's pets, shaded by a shrub. For details of the extraordinary joint US-Cuban project to restore the house and preserve Hemingway's papers, see the website of the Finca Vigía Foundation, http://fincafoundation.org/. Hemingway tours that include Finca Vigía are offered by tour agencies in the city for CUC$35. See also box, page 95.

Playas del Este

Day trips (minimum 6 people) from Havana cost about CUC$15 per person, but for small groups it's worth hiring a private car or a taxi. The HabanaBusTour, CUC$5, stops at Villa Bacuranao, Villa Tarará, Villa Mégano, Hotel Tropicoco, Hotel Atlántico and Hotel Arenal (see Transport, page 88).

This is the all-encompassing name for a string of truly tropical beaches within easy reach of Havana, which arguably surpass Varadero's brand of beach heaven. The only blot on the picture-postcard landscape is the ugly concrete mass of hotels, which erupt sporadically along the coastline.

Travelling east, the first stretch is the pleasant little horseshoe beach of **Bacuranao**, 15 km from Havana, which is popular with locals. At the far end of the beach is a villa complex with restaurant and bar. Then comes **Tarará**, famous for its hospital where Chernobyl victims have been treated, and which also has a marina and vast hotel complex, and **El Mégano**.

Santa María del Mar is the most tourist-oriented stretch of beach. A swathe of golden sand shelves gently to vivid crystal-blue waters, lined with palm trees, and dotted with tiki bars, sun loungers and an array of watersports facilities; the hip spot to chill out, flirt and play. For more undistracted sun worship, continue further eastwards to the pretty, dune-backed **Boca Ciega**, a pleasant, non-touristy beach 27 km from Havana. At the weekend, cars roll in, line up and deposit their cargo of sun worshippers at the sea's edge transforming the beach into a seething mass of baking flesh.

For a more authentic seaside ambience, head to the pleasant, if rather more rough-hewn (avoid the sewage canals), beach of **Guanabo**. Most facilities here are geared towards Cubans and it can get very busy during the national holiday season of July and August. The small town of Guanabo is very laid-back, there is no hassle and it also has a lush, green park between Avenida 474 y 476 and a children's playground. Generally, it is cheaper than Santa María del Mar and it's where a cluster of *casas particulares* are located, although there is little to do in the evening. The quietest spot of all is **Brisas del Mar**, at the east end of the stretch.

Cheap packages and all-inclusive holidays can be booked to Playas del Este from Canada and Europe, which can be good if you want to combine a beach holiday with excursions to Havana. However, most people report getting fed up after a few days of sitting on the beach here and the food is monotonous, so if you are the sort of person who likes to get out and about, avoid the all-inclusive deals.

Santa Cruz del Norte and around

The main road along the coast towards Matanzas and Varadero is called the Vía

BACKGROUND
Hemingway's Havana

Marlin fishing, gambling, beautiful prostitutes: these were the things that attracted Ernest Hemingway to Cuba in 1932. At first he stayed at the Hotel Ambos Mundos in Havana, but his visits became so frequent that he decided to buy a property. In 1940 he bought Finca Vigía, a 14-acre farm outside Havana. The staff included three gardeners, a Chinese cook and a man who tended to the fighting cocks Hemingway bred.

During the Second World War, Hemingway set up his own counter-intelligence unit at the Finca, calling it 'the Crook Factory'; his plan was to root out Nazi spies in Havana. He also armed his fishing boat, the *Pilar*, with bazookas and hand grenades. With a crew made up of Cuban friends and Spanish exiles from the Civil War, the *Pilar* cruised the waters around Havana in search of German U-Boats. The project surprisingly had the blessing of the US Embassy, who even assigned a radio operator to the *Pilar*. With no U-Boats in sight for several months, the mission turned into drunken fishing trips for Hemingway, his two sons and his friends.

When Hemingway returned to Cuba after more heroic contributions to the war effort in France, he wrote the book that was to have the biggest impact on the reading public, *The Old Man and the Sea*, which won him the Pulitzer Prize in 1953. This was a period of particularly heavy drinking for Hemingway: early-morning scotches were followed by numerous papa dobles (2½ jiggers of white rum, the juice of half a grapefruit, six drops of maraschino, mixed until foaming) at the Floridita, absinthe in the evening, two bottles of wine with dinner, and scotch and soda till the early hours in the casinos of Havana.

When the political situation under Batista began to grow tense in 1958, a government patrol shot one of Hemingway's dogs at the Finca. By then he was older and wearier than he had been during the Spanish Civil War and he quietly went back to his home in Idaho, from where he heard the news of Fidel Castro's victory. Hemingway made a public show of his support for the Revolution on his return to Cuba. He met Castro during the marlin fishing tournament, which the new president won.

Hemingway's last days at the Finca were taken up with work on *The Dangerous Summer*, a long essay about bullfighting, but his thoughts frequently turned to suicide, and he left for Florida in 1960. After the Bay of Pigs US-backed attempted invasion in 1961, the government appropriated the Finca. Hemingway committed suicide in the USA in 1961.

Bibliography: *Hemingway*, Kenneth S Lynn (Simon & Schuster, 1987).

Blanca. There are some scenic parts, but you also drive through quite a lot of industry, such as the rum and cardboard factories at Santa Cruz del Norte, a thermal electricity station and many smelly oil wells. The Hershey Railway runs inland from Havana, more or less parallel to the Vía Blanca, and is an interesting way to get to Matanzas. This electric line was built by the Hershey chocolate family in 1917 to service their sugar mill, which became known as the Central Camilo Cienfuegos after the Revolution; it was dismantled following the decline in the sugar industry.

From Santa Cruz del Norte, you can drive inland, via the former Central Camilo Cienfuegos, to Jaruco and the Parque Escaleras de Jaruco. The *escaleras* (stairs) are geological formations in the limestone, set in a very picturesque landscape with caves, forests and other rocks to see. There is a hotel in the park, but it is for Cubans only. The restaurant at the entrance is only open at weekends for lunch, but there is a nice coastal view from the terrace.

Jibacoa

Continuing east from Santa Cruz del Norte, some 60 km east of Havana is Jibacoa beach, which is good for snorkelling as the reefs are close to the shore. It is also a pretty area for walking, with hills coming down to the sea, making it a pleasant place to go for a weekend away from Havana. There is a pleasant, adults-only, all-inclusive hotel, **Memories Jibacoa**, www.memoriesjibacoa.com, and one of the best campsites, **Campismo Los Cocos**, which is very popular with Cubans in the summer months.

Some 14 km east of Jibacoa is the **Marina Puerto Escondido**, at Vía Blanca Km 80, which has boat trips, fishing, snorkelling, scuba-diving and a cafetería.

Matanzas city and around

palaces and theatres, castles and caves

Matanzas (population 115,000) is a sleepy city with old colonial buildings, a remarkable pharmacy museum and a legendary musical history. It sits on the Bahía de Matanzas and is freshened by the sea breeze.

On the opposite side of the bay is the busy, ugly industrial zone, consisting of oil storage facilities, chemical and fertilizer plants, sugar, textile and paper mills and thermal power stations. Both the rivers Yumurí and San Juan flow through the city; walk along the riverside at dusk to watch the fishermen or to take in the tranquillity of your surroundings and listen to the murmur of fellow observers. Most of the old buildings are between the two rivers, with another colonial district, Versalles, to the north of the Río Yumurí. This area was colonized in the 19th century by French refugees from Haiti after the revolution there. The newer district, Pueblo Nuevo, also has many colonial houses.

Parque de la Libertad

Parque de la Libertad is the main square, with a statue of José Martí in the middle and dominated by the former **Palacio del Gobierno** on its eastern side. The **Sala de Conciertos José White** is on the northern side, and next to it is the newly renovated **Hotel E Velasco**, built in 1902 and very grand. Just beside the hotel is the **Teatro Velasco**, now a cinema.

Sala de Conciertos ⓘ *Contreras (79) entre Ayuntamiento (288) y Santa Teresa (290), T45-267032.* The Sala has been beautifully restored by Atenart, a local group of artists and conservationists, who also worked on the restoration of the Museo Farmacéutico. Every detail of the neoclassical decor has been faithfully preserved or replicated; you would never know what a terrible state the building had fallen into prior to its restoration. The Sala de Conciertos reopened in 2015 as the home of the Matanzas symphony orchestra. It is on three levels and has space for a huge orchestra with 120 musicians accompanied by a choir. There is also a reception area, a gallery of photos of the city and a café. The interior patio contains a ceramic mural and a bronze, homage to the first *danzón*, performed here in 1879. See also Music in Matanzas, page 98.

Museo Farmacéutico ⓘ *Milanés (83) 4951 entre Santa Teresa y Ayuntamiento, T45-223197, Mon-Sat 1000-1700, Sun 1000-1600, CUC$3, camera charge, CUC$1.* On the south side of the plaza is this beautifully preserved museum containing the original equipment, porcelain jars, recipes and furnishings of the Botica La Francesa, opened in 1882 by the Triolet and Figueroa family. Both men founded a pharmacy in Sagua la Grande before visiting Matanzas together and establishing the new pharmacy; Triolet later married into the Figueroa family. It was a working pharmacy until 1964, when it was nationalized and then converted into this fascinating museum, believed to be unique in Latin America. The pharmacy shelves are all made of cedarwood and divided by Corinthian columns – all made from one tree trunk. The shelves are filled with 19th-century French porcelain jars, which contain medicinal plants, imported European products and North American goods. The museum exhibits lists of formulas, pill makers, the original telephone, baby bottles, gynaecological equipment and scorpion oil. You can also go upstairs to see the living quarters. Curator Patria Dopico is very helpful.

Calle Milanés

East of the plaza, on the street that bears his name (Calle 83), is the former home of local poet José Jacinto Milanés (1814-1863); it is now the **Archivo Histórico**. There is also a statue of the poet on Milanés, outside the elegant **Catedral de San Carlos Borromeo**. The cathedral was first built in 1693 but rebuilt in a neoclassical style in 1878 after a fire, with frescoed ceilings and walls. It is now undergoing restoration that will cover up the frescoes. The **Museo Provincial Palacio de Junco** ⓘ *Milanés entre Magdalena y Ayllón, T45-243195, Tue-Fri 1000-1800, Sat 1300-1900, Sun 0900-1200, CUC$2*, is a royal blue building that houses the provincial museum, built by a wealthy plantation owner and dating from 1840. The historical exhibition includes an archaeological display and exhibits on the development of sugar and slavery in the province. It includes the remains of a slave

Essential Matanzas city

Finding your feet

The town lies 104 km east of Havana along the Vía Blanca, which links the capital with Varadero beach, 34 km further east. If you are travelling by car the drive is unattractive along the coast and can be smelly because of the many small oil wells producing low-grade crude en route, but once you get into the hills there are good views of the countryside. Long-distance buses between Havana and Varadero all pass through Matanzas and you can request a stop here. You can also get here by train, although this is unreliable, either en route from Havana to Santiago, or on the Hershey Railway, the only electric train in Cuba. The 2½- to four-hour journey from Havana to Matanzas is memorable and scenic if you are not in a hurry.

Getting around

Most of the places of interest are within walking distance, but if you get tired you can board a horse-drawn *coche* or hail a bicitaxi. Taxis can be hired for day trips out of town. Some of the city's historic sights (San Severino fort, Cuevas de Bellamar and Tropicana) can be reached using the hop-on hop-off **MatanzasBusTour** between Varadero and Matanzas, which passes through the city centre. See also Transport, page 105.

> **Tip...**
> The **Mirador de Bacunayagua** is a spectacular lookout on the route between Havana and Matanzas, where the highest bridge in Cuba spans the gorge of the Yumurí valley. Most buses make this a rest stop.

ON THE ROAD
Music in Matanzas

Matanzas is a quiet town in all senses but one. If you listen carefully you can hear its unique heartbeat: one, two, one two three.

With its docks and warehouses, Matanzas provided the ideal birthplace for the rumba and it is still the world capital of this exhilarating music and dance form. Families here are virtually born into the rumba: the latest incarnation of the *Muñequitos de Matanzas* has a young boy keeping the beat on the bamboo *guagua*. The *Muñequitos* are the fathers and mothers of contemporary rumba, having set the standards for *rumberos* on their tours across the globe. Of course, the *rumba Matancera* bears not the slightest resemblance to its ballroom namesake.

The rumba at the Casa de la Trova was famous for its intricate drumming, vocal improvisations and dancing, which is by turns graceful, audacious, devotional and downright dirty. Rumba is a communal art form – the *Columbia* style was created by workers on the Columbia railway line; however, great names of the past are recalled in *Columbias* such as 'Malanga Murió'. On your way to a rumba, don't forget to stop at a bar and put a record by Matanzas' own Arsenio Rodríguez on the 1950s jukebox. Without Arsenio, there would have been no *conjunto son* and thus no Latin salsa. If you've got time, go and pay homage at the site of the dance hall where on a hot January night in 1879 Miguel Faílde created the *danzón cubano*, still the only authentic, unselfconscious marriage of orchestral sounds with African rhythms. It is now the Sala de Conciertos José White de Matanzas, Calle 79 entre 288 y 290. *Danzón* is currently enjoying a revival: across Cuba, music is being reissued and orchestras formed. The world has much to thank Matanzas for.

who was thrown into a pit with his chains still attached and stocks to hold the feet of slaves. There are guns and pistols from the capture of silver boats of Dutchman Piet Heyn on 8 September 1628.

Plaza de la Vigía

Teatro Sauto ⓘ *T45-243420, daily 0830-1600, CUC$2, 14 performances per month; ticket prices vary.* This magnificent neoclassical building dominates the Plaza de la Vigía south of Milanés. It was designed by Daniel Dallaglio, an Italian, who won the commission by competition; Dallaglio also built the church of San Pedro Apóstol, see page 100. The theatre dates from 1862-63 and seats 650 people in cream, wrought-iron seats in three-tiered balconies. Performances in the past have included Enrico Caruso and Anna Pavlova, who toured Cuba in 1917. French actress Sarah Bernhardt, musician José White, singer Rita Montaner and Alicia Alonso, director of the Cuban National Ballet, have all appeared here. It was restored after the Revolution and further renovation works take place from time to time. In the entrance there are Carrara marble statues of Greek goddesses and a painting of Piet Heyn, the Dutch admiral (see box, page 101) and, in the hall, the muses are painted on the ceiling. Most unusually, the floor can be raised to convert the auditorium into a ballroom.

Opposite the theatre is the restored, pale orange **Palacio de Justicia**, built in 1826 and rebuilt in 1911.

Matanzas

Valle de Yumurí

Río Yumurí

AREC HAVALETA

(Estero) 292

Mirador de Monserrate

† la Ermita de Monserrate

BALCON DEL YUMURI

Humbolt Cespedes

(Cuarta)

(Tercera) 23 San Juan 288

(Segundo) 27

(Primero) 37

(Arostegui) 41

San Hipólito 47

(San Juan) 49

(Versalles) 51

(Santa Rita) 53

(San Alejandro) 55

57

(Gómez) 59

(Isabel) 63

Arostegui 69

VERSALLES

San Pedro Apóstol

To Castillo de San Severino

Carretera Yumuri 67

LOS MANGOS

SIMPSON

57

(Reforma) 59

(Fortuna) 61

Jesús María 63

Methodist

(Jáuregui) 65

Seminario

Gran Chibango 314

Buena Vista 312

Domingo Mújica 306

San Gabriel 308

San Carlos 304

Compostela 302

(Salamanca) 71

(Daoíz) 75

MATANZAS ESTE

Hershey Terminal

Pentecostal

Contreras (Bonifacio Byrne)

América 300

Santa Teresa 290

(Maceo) 77

Los Carmelitas

Parque René Fraga

Presbiteriana

(Milanés) 83

Parque Libertad

† **Catedral de San Carlos Borromeo**

MATANZAS OESTE

Zaragoza

2 De Mayo

101

Bahía de Matanzas

La Caridad

(Río San Severino) 93

(Cuba) 95

(Alvarez) 97

(Embarcadero Blanco) 99

(Zargazozo) 101

Guachango 314

San Fabián 318

Río San Juan

(Recurso) 103

(Refugio) 105

To Cuevas de Bellamar & Castillo del Morrillo

2

(San Andrés) 109

(San Sebastián) 115

(San Juan Bautista) 117

(San Francisco) 119

(La Merced) 121

San Ambrosio 288

San Vicente 276

San Carlos 274

(San Juan de Dios) 123

PUEBLO NUEVO

(San Rafael) 127

(Santa Rita) 125

Estadio Victoria de Girón

332

Interprovincial

Línea 300

San Luis 298

(Espíritu Santo) 131

Long Distance (Víazul)

Mosquito 264

Manglar 262

Descanso 258

ARMANDO MESTRE

(San Fernando) 135

(Buen Viaje) 139

(Tenaza) 145

Destino

Palmar del Junco

(Maurri) 173

NARANJAL SUR

LA JAIBA

(Calzada de Esteban) 171

175

177

179

181

(Carretera de Cidra) 302

(Av 1) 175

(Av 31) 177

(Av 51) 181

(Av 71) 183

(Av 9) 183

Av 4ta

179

258

276

CAMILO CIENFUEGOS

To Madruga

Paseo 204

MIRET

N

500 metres

500 yards

➡ **Matanzas maps**
1 Matanzas, page 99
2 Matanzas centre, page 100

Entertainment ◑
Cabaret Restaurante
Monserrate **1**

There are several bridges in the town, but the one you are most likely to notice is the steel **Puente Calixto García**, built in 1899 at the edge of Plaza de la Vigía and next to the neoclassical fire station, **Parque de los Bomberos**. Just below the bridge is a **mosaic memorial** to Che Guevara. Opposite the fire station is **Ediciones Vigía** ① *daily 0900-1600*, founded in 1985, where you can see books being produced, ranging from fairy tales to those commemorating important events, embracing a variety of formats: books, magazines, loose sheets and scrolls, mostly poetry, short stories, literary criticism and children's literature. These are all handmade and in first editions of only 200 copies, so they are collectors' items, particularly if you get one signed. The **Galería de Arte Provincial** ① *also on the plaza, daily 0900-1700*, has rotating displays of contemporary Cuban art.

Northeast of the centre

North of the Río Yumurí in Reparto Versalles near the Hershey terminal is the **Iglesia de San Pedro Apóstol** ① *Calle 57 y 270, open Mon-Sat mornings and 1530-1930*. Cross the park in front of the terminal and walk up the street in the far corner; the church will soon be towering above you on the left. The interior is mustard yellow and has an imposing altar piece with four Ionic columns and a rather lovely stained glass of Saint Peter.

Museo de la Ruta de los Esclavos ① *Castillo de San Severino, Av del Muelle, Tue-Sat 1000-1900, Sun 0900-1200, CUC$2, CUC$1 for pictures, CUC$5 for a video camera*. Beyond Reparto Versalles, towards the northeast, is the **Castillo de San Severino**. This muscular, colonial castle was built in 1693 as a solid lookout post on the Bay of Matanzas to prevent pirate

Matanzas centre

→ Matanzas maps
1 Matanzas, page 99
2 Matanzas centre, page 100

Where to stay
Casa Rabelo cp 1
Hostal Alma cp 2
Hostal Azul cp 3
Hotel E Velasco 4

Restaurants
Bistro Kuba 1
Le Fettucine 2
Restaurante Romántico
  San Severino 3

Entertainment
Casa ACAA 1
Teatro Sauto 2

200 metres
200 yards

attack. The original coat of arms is still above the main entrance. Originally water lapped at the castle entrance but a road was built in front of it in 1910. The moat, however, was never filled with water. This was the place where slaves were unloaded from ships, having crossed the Atlantic in appalling conditions, before being sold. San Severino was also used as a prison until the 1980s. (One man was incarcerated here for six years for being a Jehovah's witness.) It is said the prison was divided by a wall, with political prisoners on one side and homosexuals on the other. With UNESCO support, the castle has been turned into a **museum of slavery**, including displays of ceramics and pipes and other materials found at the castle as well as exhibits on Afro-Cuban religion.

Northwest of the centre

La Ermita de Montserrate, a good hike north up Domingo Mujica (306) from the Parque de la Libertad (or take the hourly bus No 12 from beside the Museo Farmacéutico), was built in 1872 in honour of the Virgin of Monserrat. The roof caved in after storm damage but has now been rebuilt. From the hilltop it is perched on, you can see the city and the bay rolled out before you and, on the other side, the verdant **Valle de Yumurí**, although the perfection of the view is slightly marred by the pylons marching towards the horizon. This is an excellent place to walk, and there is a bar and restaurant in the park for refreshment.

South of the city

The road out to Varadero goes past the university and the Escuela Militar. One kilometre past the university you come to the **Río Canímar**, which flows into the Bahía de Matanzas. (Trips along the river can be arranged from Varadero.) Just before the bridge over the river, take the road running alongside the river towards the bay to the **Castillo del Morrillo.**

ON THE ROAD
Cuban all stars

Celebrities have always had a fascination for Cuba and there has always been a steady stream of rich and famous visitors to the 'Pearl of the Antilles'. In 1898 the young Winston Churchill narrowly missed being hit by a bullet on his 21st birthday when he visited to see what the Spanish-American War was all about. He returned, older and wiser, to paint and to smoke cigars, creating the ever-popular image of the wartime British leader puffing on a great fat *Habano*.

The US Prohibition Act of 1919 gave tourism in Cuba an unexpected boost, when drinking customers and whole bars moved to the island. The Irish-owned Donovan's Bar was relocated, lock, stock and barrel to a building opposite the Capitolio in Havana, and Cuban bartenders became world famous for their cocktails. Constante Ribalaigua, at the **Floridita**, was already an established expert before Hemingway discovered his daiquirís (he allegedly regularly drank 11 double, sugarless daiquirís before 1100), but the author gave him the crowning touch by writing about his cocktails in the novel *Islands in the Stream*. He also invited his friend Marlene Dietrich to sample them and she became a regular visitor to Havana. Another actress visitor, Mary Pickford, had a cocktail created for her in the **Hotel Sevilla Biltmore**.

George Gershwin was so taken with the music and rhythms of Cuba that he composed the *Cuban Overture*, first performed in 1932. Frank Sinatra was a regular visitor and even had a modernist house in the former Country Club district. Many others came down in their yachts to sail around the cays and drink in the bars. Photos of Errol Flynn, Gary Cooper, Spencer Tracy, Ava Gardner, Carmen Miranda and other glamorous figures still grace the walls of the **Bodeguita del Medio** bar.

There were also, of course, the less salubrious visitors – gangsters like Al Capone, Lucky Luciano, Meyer Lansky and George Raft – who were attracted by the money to be made in the casinos and by bootlegging alcohol. George Raft had a penthouse apartment (now a restaurant) on top of the **Capri** casino hotel. The **Hotel Nacional** and the **Riviera** were also linked to mafia money. The bar of the **Nacional** has a rogues' gallery of photos of its famous guests.

Today, celebrities continue to flock to this last bastion of Communism in the Western world. Famous names have included Sir Paul McCartney, Francis Ford Coppola, Naomi Campbell, Kate Moss, Leonardo di Caprio (whose entourage was so large he took over whole hotels), Paris Hilton, Rihanna, Beyonce and Jay-Z, while the annual Latin American Film Festival attracts a clutch of actors and directors, notably Robert de Niro, Arnold Schwarzenegger, Ken Loach, Jack Nicholson, Helen Mirren, Kevin Spacey and Kevin Costner.

Castillo del Morrillo ① *Tue-Sun 1000-1700, CUC$1 entrance, CUC$1 for guide*. Built in 1720 to protect the area, the castle is now a museum in memory of Antonio Guiteras Holmes, who was shot, along with the Venezuelan revolutionary Carlos Aponte Hernández, by Batista's troops near the bridge. Bronze busts of the two men can be seen underneath a mahogany tree. Guiteras Holmes was a student leader who started a revolutionary group called *Joven Cuba* (Young Cuba) in 1934. He served briefly in the government that replaced

Machado, but fell foul of the rising Batista. It was when he and Aponte came to Matanzas in 1935 to try and find a boat to take them into exile in Mexico that they were caught and executed. The castle also has a *sala* of aboriginal archaeology and a large rowing boat.

Cuevas de Bellamar ⓘ *Southeast of town at Finca La Alcancía, T45-261683. Mon-Sat 0900-2030, Sun 0900-1700. Tours daily at 0930, 1030, 1130, 1315, 1415, 1515, 1615, CUC$5, CUC$8 includes the extra 100-m stretch, parking CUC$1, CUC$5 for cameras, no bags allowed in. Take bus No 12, CUP$1, from Parque Libertad to the caves, leaves every 2 hrs. Tours from Varadero including brief city tour, CUC$30.* This cave system, discovered in 1862 by somebody working the land, stretches for 23 km, and is stuffed full of stalactites, stalagmites (one 12 m tall) and underground streams. Tour parties come from Varadero, so you may get herded along with a bus load. In any case, all visitors must be accompanied for the 750-m walk through the caves; you can go a further 100 m with torches. There are 154 steep steps down into the cave. Wear appropriate footwear because the caves can be wet, muddy and slippery, and the surface is uneven. The complex has a small museum with items found in the caves and explanations in English and Spanish, plus a restaurant, shop and children's playground.

Other caves around Matanzas There are also caves at **Las Cuevas de Santa Catalina**, near Carbonera, 20 km east of Matanzas, where there are believed to be 8 km of tunnels. The caves were used as an Amerindian burial site and feature paintings close to the entrance. **Refugio de Saturno** is a large cave often visited by scuba-divers, although anyone can enjoy a swim here. It is 1 km south of the Vía Blanca, 8 km east of the Río Canímar.

Listings Matanzas city and around *maps pages 99 and 100.*

Where to stay

Hotels

$$$-$$ Hotel E Velasco
Contreras entre Santa Teresa y Ayuntamiento, Parque de la Libertad, T45-253880, www. hotelescubanacan.com.
Newly renovated with a beautiful reception hall, intricately painted and with marble columns. 17 a/c rooms which open onto central atrium, except for suites, which are more spacious and have windows onto the square. Rooms are not large but are well-equipped and comfortable. Wi-Fi in the lobby. Reserved parking in the square. Food is fine and service is friendly.

$$ Canimao
Km 4.5 Ctra Matanzas a Varadero, T45-261014, www.islazul.cu.
A modern, but nice-looking hotel on the outskirts of Matanzas opposite the **Tropicana** cabaret. It has 120 rooms on a hill above the Río Canímar, with excursions offered on the river or to caves. Nearby is a natural canyon, the Cueva de Los Cristales, which had evidence of aboriginal infanticide. The hotel is past its best but the food and service are OK and the location makes up for its shortcomings.

Casas particulares

$ Casa Rabelo
Zaragoza (292) entre Milanés (83) y Medio (85), T45-243433, morirabelo@gmail.com.
Moraima (Mori) Rabelo, speaks English, is very helpful and full of advice. She has 3 rooms with a/c and fan, all on ground level, although there are steps. Walk through the house to the pretty courtyard garden where you have breakfast, dinner or just relax. This *casa* is popular with cyclists; Mori can recommend routes with lodging and will store bike boxes for the return flight if you are leaving from Varadero airport. Garage for parking.

$ Hostal Alma

Milanés (83) 29008 Altos entre Sta Teresa (290) y Zaragoza (292), T45-290857, 5283 1479 (mob), hostalalma@gmail.com.

Huge and grand 19th-century house with beautiful *vitrales*, large, multi-level terraces for drinks, meals or just sunbathing, and fabulous roof view, with 3 rooms on the 2nd floor with private bathroom, fridge, minibar. 1 room can hold a couple and child. Dinner is also offered to non-guests, but ring beforehand to book. Mayra, her friendly family and their attractive house make this a very popular option.

$ Hostal Azul

Milanés (83) 29012 entre Santa Teresa (290) y Zaragoza (292), T45-242449, T5-273 7903 (mob), hostalazul.cu@gmail.com.

Well-preserved 1870s mansion with original tiles. Very spacious, 4 rooms with high ceilings; the room up a spiral staircase has a balcony. There is a bar/café with vaulted ceiling in the front room of the house overlooking the street. Sometimes live music here. Run by husband and wife team Yoel Baez and Aylin Hernández, who are very helpful. Having worked for many years in Sol Meliá hotels in Varadero, Yoel is experienced in hospitality and speaks English and Italian.

$ Hostal Villa Mar

Calle 127 (San Rafael) 20809 entre 208 y 210, Rpto Playa, T45-288132, 5296 9894 (mob), lictik87@gmail.com.

A stylish 1950s villa on the waterfront away from the city centre, offering 2 rooms, one of which is an independent unit. English-speaking hosts, charming and hospitable and maintaining an excellent standard of accommodation. You have the option of dining overlooking the sea or relaxing with a cocktail enjoying the view but there are *paladares* in walking distance if you want to go out. If you fancy a swim, there are steps down through the rocks, coming out on a rocky overhang at the water's edge.

$ Villa Costa Azul

Calle 127 (San Rafael) 20817 entre 208 y 210, Rpto Playa, T45-261460, 5244 5223 (mob).

A modern house on the waterfront with 2 rooms, one on top of the other, with private entrance. The upstairs room has a terrace overlooking the sea, but the downstairs room also has a sea view and access to the garden. Meals can be taken in the gazebo by the sea. Teresa and Fernando are very hospitable and helpful and their son, Fernán, speaks good English. There is no access to the water, but a small beach is only a block away. Several *paladares* close by, although Teresita is a good cook.

Where to eat

$$$-$$ El Bukan

Calle 110 entre 127 y 129, Playa, T45-289999, www.elbukan.com. Thu-Tue 1200-2230.

On the top floor of a building overlooking the bay. The young men running this bar and restaurant with home-delivery service are professional and friendly. The cocktails are great, the beer frosty and the wine selection good. The food is varied, appealing to any member of a family, although some dishes are a heart attack waiting to happen and the portions are vast, so ask for leftovers to be bagged up for another meal or share one (meat skewer, for example) between 2 people.

$$$-$$ Mallorca

Calle 334 7705 entre 77 y 79, T45-283282. Wed-Sun 1230-2130.

A smart, modern *paladar* with screens for music videos or sports, but there is also live music and entertainment. The chef used to work for Meliá and the food is beautifully and professionally presented. Plenty of variety, fusion food, generous portions, menu in English. Quite a distance from the centre, a taxi is CUC$3.

$$$-$$ Restaurante Romántico San Severino

Calle 290 7903 Altos entre 79 y 83, T45-281573, Thu-Tue, 1200-late.

Upstairs in a grand old building overlooking Parque de la Libertad, sensitively renovated keeping the old tiles, light fittings and other fixtures. The best tables are the 3 on the balcony overlooking the plaza, good for people-watching by day but particularly in the evening when all the birds come to roost in the trees. Food is average to good. Cash only.

$$-$ Le Fettucine
C Milanés 29018 entre Zaragoza y Santa Teresa, T5412 2553 (mob), see Facebook. Fri-Wed 1200-2130.
New in 2015, starting small but bound to expand because of its instant popularity; queues outside. Home made pasta and pizza, limited selection but all delicious and menu changes according to availability of ingredients. Cash only. Takeaway service.

Bars

Bistro Kuba
C Milanés 29014 entre Zaragoza y Santa Teresa, T45-261465, see Facebook. Open 1100-0200.
Bar and café serving tapas and larger dishes. Modern and stylish, this is a great bar open after Le Fettucine has closed. Good cocktail list, cold beer, live music.

Entertainment

The **Centro de Promoción y Publicidad Cultural** (Independencia (85) entre Ayuntamiento (288) y Sta Teresa (290)), has a *cartelera* in the window displaying all entertainment fixtures. The Plaza de la Vigía is the place to go in the evenings; locals congregate here to chat, play dominoes or draughts, or make music. The **Teatro Sauto**, see page 98, usually has live performances at the weekends.

Cabaret
Cabaret Las Palmas (Artex), *Calle 254 (Levante) esq 127 (Gen Betancourt), T45-253252. Tue-Thu 2000-2400, Fri, Sat 2100-0200, Sun 1700-2100.* Mostly Cuban clientele, live shows,

comedy or recorded music. Sun afternoon dancing. Entry usually CUC$2-4 per couple, depending on the event.
Cabaret Restaurante Monserrate, *Mujica (306) final, T45-244222. Wed, Fri, Sat, Sun 2100-0200. CUC$1 or pay in CUP$. Bus No 12 takes you there.*
Tropicana Matanzas, *Autopista Varadero Km 4.5, T45-265380, reservas@tropimat. co.cu. Show Thu-Sun 2200-2330 then disco until 0200, adults CUC$49 (children CUC$34) which includes ¼ bottle of rum and cola and snacks. A lesser show Tue, Wed is CUC$39.*
The Matanzas version of the famous cabaret is in a spectacular outdoor setting opposite the **Hotel Canimao**. CUC$5 to use a camera.

Live music and dance
Casa ACAA (Asociación Cubana de los Artistas Artesanos), *Calle 85 entre 282 y 280.* Live music with trios and pianists. Also has a café.

Festivals

20-26 Aug Carnaval de Matanzas.

Transport

Bus
The bus station, T45-291473, open 24 hrs, is at Calle 131 y 272, Calzada Esteban esq Terry (Coppelia is opposite the terminal). **Viazul**, T45-916445, passes through on its **Havana–Varadero** route, 3 daily. There are taxis and *coches* at the bus station.

The hop-on hop-off **MatanzasBusTour** leaves Matanzas' Parque Libertad at 1115, 1445, 1545 and 1715. It passes the city centre historic sights and goes on to the San Severino fort, Cuevas de Bellamar and Tropicana arriving at Varadero at 1245, 1415, 1715 and 1845. It returns from Varadero at 0930, 1100, 1400 and 1530. CUC$10. **Transtur** operates the service and passengers wishing to return from Varadero later can take any **Transtur** bus heading to the city.

Train

There are 2 stations: the Hershey terminal and main terminal. The Hershey terminal is north of the Río Yumurí in Versalles at 282 y 67. There are no facilities here and the ticket office, T45-244805, has erratic opening hours. There are 3 trains daily on this electric line to and from Casablanca in **Havana**. Trains from Casablanca to **Hershey** leave at 0445, 1221, 1635. Tickets CUC$2.80, children half price, but you may never get charged. If there is no electricity it doesn't run.

The newer, main station south of the town at Calle 181, Miret (open 24 hrs, T45-292409), receives trains from Havana en route to **Santiago**.

Varadero

life's a beach

Cuba's chief beach resort, Varadero, is built on the Península de Hicacos, a thin, 23-km-long peninsula. Two roads run the length of the peninsula lined with dozens of large all-inclusive hotels, some smaller ones, and several chalets and villas, many of which date from before 1959. Sadly, some of the hotel architecture is hideous.

Varadero is still undergoing large-scale development, and joint ventures with foreign investors are still being encouraged. However, with the relaxation of restrictions on self-employment, it is no longer a state monopoly. You can now sleep in a *casa particular* and eat in a *paladar*.

The southwestern end of the resort is the more low key, with hustlers on the beaches by day and *jineteros* in the bars at night. The village area feels like a real place, not just a hotel city, and, in contrast to some other tourist enclaves (such as the northern cays),

Essential Varadero

Finding your feet

Varadero's **international airport** is 26 km west of the hotel strip, so, if you are booked into one of the new hotels at the far eastern end of the peninsula, you will have a journey of some 40 km to get there. The **Viazul** bus pulls in to the airport on its way to the central bus terminal and has recently opened a ticket office here. If you are travelling by car from Havana there is a good dual carriageway, the Vía Blanca, which runs to Varadero, 142 km from the capital. The toll at the entrance to the resort is CUC$2 for cars. The easiest way to get to and from Havana is on a tour or transfer bus, booked through a hotel tour desk, which will pick you up and drop you off at your hotel. There are daily buses from Havana, and also from Santiago de Cuba, from Trinidad via Sancti Spíritus and Santa Clara with **Viazul**.

Getting around

Distances should not be underestimated. Avenida 1, which runs southwest–northeast along the peninsula, has a tourist bus service (see Transport, page 112) that takes about an hour to cover the entire length, taking into account dropping-off times. Calle numbers begin with lowest numbers at the southwest end and work upwards to the northeast. Car rental is available at the airport and at numerous hotel and office locations along the peninsula. Most hotels also rent bicycles or mopeds, which will allow you to get further, faster. Taxis wait outside hotels, or you can phone for one. There are also horse-drawn carriages for a leisurely tour and a handful of *cocotaxis*. See also Transport, page 112.

ON THE ROAD
Diving around Varadero

Varadero is one of the most developed areas in Cuba for diving. There are several sites around the offshore cays suitable for novice or advanced divers. Interesting sites include the wreck of the *Neptune*, a 60-m steel cargo ship thought to be German, lying in only 10 m. This is home to a number of fish including massive green moray eels and very large, friendly French angelfish. The wreck is very broken up, but the boilers are still intact, and there are places where the superstructure (shaft and propeller) is in good condition and interesting to explore with good photo sites. Among the many reef dive sites in the area are Clara Boyas (Sun Roof), a massive 60-sq-m coral head in 20 m of water, with tunnels large enough for three or four divers to swim through. These connect with upward passages where the sunlight can be seen streaming through. Another site, Las Brujas (the Witches), is only 6 m deep. Large coral heads protrude from the sandy bottom, with coral holes and crevices, adorned with sea fans, home for large schools of snapper. Playa Coral is a site on a 2-km barrier reef west of Varadero, beginning at Matanzas Bay, with a large variety of fish and coral. This is usually a shore dive, although if you go over the wall, where you can find black coral and gorgonians in deep water, it can be a boat dive. If you are based in Varadero on a dive package, you may be offered a trip to Playa Girón for good shore diving, and to the Refugio de Saturno for an inland cave dive, as part of your package.

Cubans do actually live here. The far northeastern end is where the international hotels are located. Most are all-inclusives, although you can pay to use their facilities even if you are not staying there.

Sights

The relatively recent development of Varadero means there is little of historical or architectural interest; visitors spend their time on the beach, engaging in watersports or taking organized excursions. The **Museo de Varadero** ⓘ *C 57 y Av de la Playa, daily 1000-1900, CUC$1*, is worth a visit if you want something to do away from the beach. The house itself is interesting as an example of one of the first beach houses. Originally known as Casa Villa Abreu, it was built in 1921 by architect Leopoldo Abreu as a summer house in blue and white with a lovely timber veranda and wooden balconies all round, designed to catch the breeze. Restored in 1980-1981 as a museum, it has the usual collection of unlabelled furniture and glass from the early 20th century, stuffed animals in a natural history room (a revolutionary guard dog, Ima, appears to be suffering from mange), and an Amerindian skeleton (male, aged 20-30, with signs of syphilis and anaemia). However, the most interesting exhibit is a two-headed baby shark washed up on these shores. There are several old photos of the first hotels in Varadero, including Dos Mares (1940), Internacional (1950) and Pullman (1950), as well as items of local sporting history, a shirt of Javier Sotomayor and a rowing boat from the Club Náutico

Tip...
Between Cárdenas and Varadero there are oil wells, which release gas into the air, often in the middle of the night. The smell of sulphur drifts as far as Varadero if the wind is in the wrong direction; it is particularly obvious if you stay at the southwestern end of the peninsula.

BACKGROUND

Varadero

Salt was the first economic catalyst in the area, followed by cattle, timber and sugar. A plan was drawn up in 1887 for the foundation of a city, but development of the peninsula did not really begin until 1923, when it was discovered as a potential holiday resort for the seriously rich. The Dupont family bought land in the 1920s, sold it for profit, then bought more, constructed roads and built a large house, now the **Mansión Xanadú**. There are some old wooden houses left from this period, with rocking chairs on the verandas and balconies, but the village area at the western end of the peninsula was not built until the 1950s.

de Varadero. The house is in serious need of renovation again and the upstairs floor can no longer be used for exhibits.

The **Parque Josone**, Avenida 1 y 57, is a large park with pool and several restaurants. You can take a pedalo out on the boating lake. The bar/café closest to the entrance is renowned for its piña coladas, made with fresh ingredients.

At the far end of the peninsula 450 ha of the land has been designated the **Varadero Ecological Park** (Parque Ecológico Varahicacos) ① *Centro de Visitantes at the road entrance to Hotel Paradisus Varadero, daily 0900-1630, CUC$5; the tourist bus stops nearby*. The reserve includes 700 m of shoreline with different plant species, including scrub and cactus, a lagoon where salt was once made, several kilometres of sandy beach and two caves. The **Cueva de Ambrosio**, 30 minutes' walk from the main road, is where dozens of Amerindian drawings were discovered in 1961. **Cueva de Musulmanes** contains aboriginal fossils. You can see hummingbirds and other birds, lizards, crabs and bats in the caves. Allow 1½ hours for the walk. Wear stout footwear because the paths are rough, and take water, insect repellent, hat and sunscreen because it is fiendishly hot.

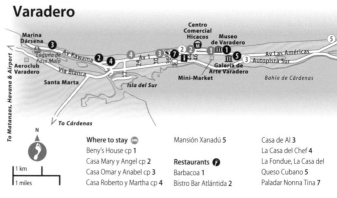

Varadero

Where to stay 🛏
Beny's House cp **1**
Casa Mary y Angel cp **2**
Casa Omar y Anabel cp **3**
Casa Roberto y Martha cp **4**

Mansión Xanadú **5**

Restaurants 🍴
Barbacoa **1**
Bistro Bar Atlántida **2**

Casa de Al **3**
La Casa del Chef **4**
La Fondue, La Casa del
Queso Cubano **5**
Paladar Nonna Tina **7**

Beaches

Varadero's sandy beach stretches the length of the peninsula, broken only occasionally by rocky outcrops which can be traversed by walking through a hotel's grounds. Some parts are wider than others; as a general rule, the older hotels have the best bits of beach. The **Internacional**, for instance, which was the **Hilton** before the Revolution, has a large swathe of curving beach, whereas the newer **Meliá Las Américas** and its sister hotels, **Meliá Varadero** and **Sol Palmeras**, have a disappointingly shallow strip of sand and some rocks. That said, all the beaches are beautifully looked after and cleaned daily, and the water is clean and nice for swimming. For good **snorkelling**, however, you're advised to take one of the many boat trips out to the cays (see below).

> **Fact...**
> Despite the SPAW agreement, to which Cuba is a signatory, dolphins are caught in the wild and kept in dolphinariums for tourists' amusement or allegedly exported to other Caribbean islands for the same purpose. No zoo in the world now takes animals caught in the wild, relying instead on breeding in captivity, but Cuba does not apply this rule to dolphinariums.

Cays

The cays around the **Hicacos Peninsula** were once the haunt of French pirates, and it is supposed that the name 'Varadero' comes from *varados* (stranded), due to the fact that ships ran aground here. There are many **sailing tours** to the offshore cays, which usually include lunch, an open bar and time for swimming and snorkelling. **Cayo Mono** lies five nautical miles north-northeast of Punta de Morlas. During the nesting season in mid-year it becomes a bird sanctuary for the brown noddy (*Anous stolidus*; known as the *gaviota negra* in Spanish), the sooty tern (*Sterna fuscata; gaviota monja*) and the bridled tern (*Onychoprion annaethetus*), during which time you can only pass by and watch them through binoculars. **Cayo Piedra del Norte** is two miles southeast of Cayo Mono and has a lighthouse. Other cays visited by tour boats include Cayo Blanco, Cayo Romero and Cayo Diana.

Entertainment ◉
Cabaret Cueva del Pirata **1**
Casa de la Música **2**
La Comparsita **3**
Mambo Club **4**

Palacio de la Rumba **5**

Tourist information

State tour agencies can be found in all the hotels. Although their main purpose is to sell tours, they operate as tourist information offices and can help with hotel reservations, tickets and transfers. **Infotur** has an office at Calle 13 esq Av 1, T45-662966. There are also offices in the airport and at Centro Comercial Hicacos, Av 1 entre 44 y 46, T45-667044. Most are open daily 0800-1700.

Where to stay

The building of new hotels and renovation of older ones is continuing all along the peninsula and there are now some 18,000 rooms, with some encroaching on the edge of the nature reserve. Overdevelopment is a real issue. The newer international hotels are located at the northeastern end of the peninsula, very remote from the shopping area and independent restaurants. Unless you specifically want an all-inclusive beach holiday in an international hotel, it is best to stay in the village area, where restaurants, bars and shops are within walking distance, and the beach is just as good. We do not list the all-inclusives in this guide.

It is now legal for Cubans to rent rooms to foreigners in Varadero; *casas particulares* are generally a better option than the few small hotels (cleaner, friendlier, better food). You could also choose to stay in Matanzas and get the bus in to Varadero.

$$$$ Mansión Xanadú
Ctra Las Americas, Km 8.5, T45-668482, www.varaderogolfclub.com.
The beach house built for the Du Pont family in the 1920s is now the clubhouse for the golf course, offering the smartest, boutique type accommodation in Varadero. The mansion sitting on a bluff overlooking the sea and backed by the golf course offers 5 doubles

and 1 single room, each with balcony. Furnished with period pieces and very prettily decorated, golf is usually included in the package. Restaurant and bar. Away from the hustle and bustle of the beach resorts. Guests use all the facilities and the beach at the next door **Meliá Las Américas**.

$$ Beny's House
Calle 55 124 entre Av 1 y 2, Varadero, T45-611700, www.benyhouse.com.
Very good, very popular house within 80 m of the beach, Parque Josone and the Beatles Bar. Spacious rooms and an apartment with quality fixtures and fittings, pleasant garden and patio. Food is tasty and plentiful. English spoken. Friendly and helpful family and staff. Sunbeds provided for you to take to the beach.

$$ Casa Mary y Angel
Calle 43 entre Av 1 y 2, Varadero, T45-612383, marisabelcarrillo@yahoo.com.
Good location, short walk to beach, 3 rooms with good bathrooms around a patio. Friendly and helpful family, English spoken. Plenty of outside space for relaxing, plus outdoor shower when you come back from the beach. Parking.

$$ Casa Omar y Anabel
Calle 31 104 entre Av 1 y 3, T45-612587, sherlyday@yahoo.es.
A suite with its own entrance, very comfortable, immaculate, a/c, kitchenette and fridge, TV, patio with table and chairs outside the door, convenient location, beach towels provided. Omar and Anabel are experienced hosts, very friendly and helpful and will do their best for you. English spoken. Good food. Parking.

$$ Casa Roberto y Martha
Calle 17 102A entre Av 1 y 2, T45-612958, varr@nauta.cu.
Roberto is the epitome of a genial host: he's a mine of information about where to eat and

what to do and can sort out accommodation all over the island. 3 rooms, of which 1 is a suite with kitchen, 1 is rather small, but all are well-equipped and spotless. Rooms have own access. Close to the beach but also close to a night club which can be noisy Sat night. Delicious food and particularly good breakfasts. Special diets catered for.

Where to eat

$$$ Barbacoa
Calle 64 esq Av 1, T45-667795. Daily 1200-2300.
Good surf and turf with indoor and alfresco dining. Huge lobster tails will feed 2 for CUC$22, or a smaller one for CUC$18. The steak is Canadian. Extensive wine list. Reservations advised in high season, but they will usually find room for you.

$$$ Casa de Al
Villa Punta Blanca.
A stone building with blue painted wooden attributes, which used to belong to Al Capone. It's a quiet spot for a sunset drink (with outdoor tables on the terrace) or a meal of Mafia Soup, Godfather Salad, Fillet Mignon "Lucky Luciano" and cold blood ice cream. The service is a little on the slow side but not annoyingly so. Worth a visit.

$$$ La Fondue
La Casa del Queso Cubano, Av 1 entre 62 y 64, T45-667747. Daily 1200-2300.
Powerful a/c and smart tables. Serves a variety of fondues including lobster fondue and chocolate fondue as well as breaded pork, chicken and grilled fish. Service often lacking.

$$$-$$ Bistro Bar Atlántida
Av 1 entre 6 y 7, Santa Marta, T5283 6972, atlantidabistro@gmail.com.
A great bar and bistro with a wide range of drinks and a good Spanish menu. Welcome cocktails, tapas as well as main dishes, all beautifully presented and tasty. Owner Félix is friendly, and the service is exemplary compared with the state restaurants.

$$$-$$ La Casa del Chef
Av 1 y 12, T45-613606. Daily 1230-2200.
Seafood restaurant with good value lobster, indoor or outdoor seating, pleasant live music.

$$$-$$ Paladar Nonna Tina
38 5 entre Av 1 y Playa, T45-612450, www. paladar-nonnatina.it. Daily 1200-2300.
Tina is Italian married to a Cuban and cooks authentic Italian food, delicious pizzas and pastas. Very popular, especially with Italian visitors, queues outside. Resort hotels are worlds away.

Bars

Every hotel has several bars to choose from and it can be fun to work your way through the barman's list of cocktails during your holiday. Even here, however, you may be told *'no hay'*, with tomato juice and other mixers often unavailable. Stick to the traditionally Cuban and you won't be disappointed.

Outside the hotels, the **Bar Mirador Casa Blanca**, on the top floor of the **Mansión Xanadú** at the Golf Club is worth a visit for the view and relaxed atmosphere, if not the prices. Several *paladares* have good bars for before or after your meal, while *casas particulares* often have a cocktail list for a relaxing evening on the patio.

Beatles Bar
Calle 59 y Av 1.
You can't miss it thanks to the statues of The Beatles outside. An after-dinner bar where you can catch tribute bands to the fab four and other rock music in an outdoor setting. It is also open during the day for a salad lunch and to look at all the old photos on the walls. Reasonably priced cocktails.

Entertainment

Live music
Buena Vista Social Club, *at Plaza América, call Paradiso travel agency to reserve, T45-614759.* A group performs live every 1st and 3rd Wed of the month at 2200.

Casa de la Música, *Av Playa entre 42 y 43, T45-668918. Tue-Sun 2230-0300, CUC$10 entrance.* Lots of live bands every night, good for dancing, also DJ. *Jineteros* can be pushy. Run by EGREM, the state music company. A *cartelera* in the window advertizes events.

Nightclubs and cabaret
Cabaret Cueva del Pirata, *Autopista Sur Km 11, T45-667751. Show in a cave, CUC$10. Check opening times.* Music is a mix of traditional Cuban with more modern Cuban and international music. Lots of dancing. Cool on a hot night. Toilets are unhygienic. Take toilet paper.

La Comparsita, *Calle 60 y Av 3, T45-667415.* Dancing under the stars at this nightclub. A mix of entertainment, from live salsa band to DJ playing European music. Most nights cover is CUC$7 and drinks are free, although limited in choice and availability is restricted by the tiny size of the bar, more like a window. Upstairs there is karaoke for an extra charge.

Mambo Club, *Ctra Las Morlas Km 14, T45-668565. CUC$15. Temporarily closed in 2015, so call ahead.* A club stuck in a 1950s time warp.

Palacio de la Rumba, *Av Las Américas, Km 4, T45-668210. Daily 2200-0300. CUC$10-15, depending on whether drinks are included.* Indifferent staff at bar, live salsa bands at weekends. Frequented by Cubans and foreigners but often empty mid-week.

Transport

Air
The **Juan Gualberto Gómez airport** (VRA), T45-247015, www.varadero-airport.com, receives international scheduled and charter flights.

Bus
The interprovincial bus station is at Autopista Sur y C 36. **Viazul**, T45-614886, has daily buses to/from **Havana**, **Trinidad** and **Santiago de Cuba**, via **Santa Clara** and **Holguín**. There is also a ticket office at the airport, just outside **Arrivals**, T45-663396.

The hop-on, hop-off, open-topped tourist bus, **Varadero BeachTour** (**Transtur**, T45-668212) runs every 30 mins daily 0930-2100, along Av 1 southwest–northeast the length of the peninsula, with 45 stops at hotels and shops, CUC$5 per day. Don't lose your ticket or hand it in on alighting, or you will have to pay again. There is also the **MatanzasBusTour**, which leaves Varadero at 0930, 1100, 1400 and 1530, arriving in **Matanzas** at 1100, 1230, 1530 and 1700. It returns to Varadero at 1115, 1245, 1545 and 1715; CUC$10 per day.

Car/moped hire
Agencies have offices all over town and in nearly all the hotels. **Cubacar** at many of the hotels, main office: T45-667326. **Transtur**, T45-667715. **Vía Rent a Car**, T45-619001. **Havanautos**, T45-614409. Hiring a moped is a good way to see the peninsula but you will have no insurance and no helmet. The **Servi Cupet** petrol station is at 54 y Autopista, 17 y Autopista, Vía Blanca Km 31.

Taxi
Cubataxi, T45-614444. Most trips cost CUC$5-15 depending on where you need to go along the peninsula. The best place to hail a taxi is at any hotel, as they usually wait there for fares. Horse-drawn vehicles act as taxis, usually just for a tour around town.

West of
Havana

The west of Cuba is dominated by one of the island's three main mountain ranges, the Cordillera de Guaniguanico, divided into the Sierra del Rosario in the east and the Sierra de los Organos in the west. A fault line creates a sharp boundary between these mountains, with a wide expanse of rolling farmland to the south.

The forested Sierra del Rosario encompasses the Biosphere Reserve at Las Terrazas, a must for anyone with an interest in tropical flora and fauna, as well as the orchidarium at Soroa. The Sierra de los Organos, meanwhile, is famous for the landscape of steep-sided limestone mogotes and flat, fertile tobacco fields around the Valle de Viñales. This is where you will find the world's best dark tobacco, which is hand-processed into the finest cigars. The valley attracts thousands of visitors, due to its spectacular scenery and good walking opportunities. The only major city west of Havana, Pinar del Río can be a good base for excursions to this area as transport starts from here. The coast offers undeveloped beaches and some sensational scuba diving.

Essential West of Havana

Finding your feet

Pinar del Río, 157 km from Havana, is the main transport hub for the area. It is connected to Havana by a slow and unreliable train service and by daily **Viazul** buses, which continue on to Viñales; they will stop on request at Las Terrazas and San Diego de los Baños. A dual-carriageway has been completed almost as far as Pinar del Río, although some of the slip roads are still unsurfaced mud and stones. It takes nearly three hours to get from Havana to Pinar del Río on the *autopista* (see page 139) or four hours 10 minutes on the old main road.

Getting around

From Pinar del Río, it is easy enough to get a bus to Viñales, but public transport to other destinations is limited to local peso buses. A local train runs from Pinar del Río to Guane but is not recommended. Apart from the long-distance **Viazul** buses (see above), there is very little public transport at all in the Sierra del Rosario. Car hire is available in Pinar del Río and Viñales and is recommended for independent excursions: driving distances from Pinar del Río are 103 km to Las Terrazas, 88 km to Soroa, 25 km to Viñales. There are also plenty of organized tours to caves, cigar factories, tobacco farms and other local attractions. Long-distance travel by taxi is possible but you will need very good Spanish to negotiate effectively.

When to go

The driest time in the Sierra del Rosario is from January to April, when it is easiest to hike in the mountains. The orchids at Soroa are good then too. The wet season begins around May, but storms can be expected between September and November. This is also the wettest time in the Sierra de los Organos. Pinar del Río holds its carnival in July and Viñales has one in March.

Time required

Las Terrazas and Viñales are often visited as day trips from Havana, but to do the area justice you need at least three days. If you want to visit beaches or cays on the north coast, allow another day or two.

★ Sierra del Rosario

follow trails through thick forest and old coffee plantations, full of birds and butterflies

Heading west from Havana the land is initially low-lying and unimpressive. Soon, however, the green mountains of the Sierra del Rosario come into view, stirring anticipation of exploration and discovery. The Sierra incorporates a 260-sq-km biosphere reserve, giving recognition to its ecological diversity and richness. Birdwatching is rewarding around Las Terrazas, the main centre for nature tourism. Lovers of flora will also appreciate the orchidarium at Soroa, although there are many and varied plants to be found by anyone who hikes up and down the hills.

Reserva de la Biósfera Sierra del Rosario

Admission CU$10 although it can be cheaper in low season. Admission includes a drink and all park facilities, including Río San Juan and Río Bayate. There is a map at the entrance.

A barrier marks the entrance to the biosphere reserve, which covers 25,000 ha of the Sierra del Rosario mountain range, and has the best example of evergreen forest in western Cuba. There are three nuclei in the reserve: El Salón, Las Peladas and Las Terrazas. The latter has an ecological station and the local community is directly involved with protecting the environment. Birdwatching is rewarding and you may see the bee hummingbird. There are nearly 800 plant species, of which 34% are endemic.

Las Terrazas

Las Terrazas was built in 1971 as a forestry and soil conservation station, with nearby slopes terraced to prevent erosion. It is a pleasant settlement of white-painted houses and a long apartment block overlooking the lake of San Juan, which now houses an ecological research centre. On the hillside, **Hotel Moka** (see Where to stay) is run as an ecotourism centre. This is an unusual opportunity to stay in a nature reserve, with tropical evergreen forests, 850 plant species, 82 bird species, an endemic water lizard, the world's second smallest frog and world-class experts on tap. Elsewhere in Las Terrazas there is a vegetarian restaurant, a *paladar*, as well as craft workshops, a gym, a cinema and a museum which sometimes holds *canturías* or folk music sessions. Nearby there are waterfalls where you can picnic. Other activities include riding, mountain biking, rowing on the lake and fishing. There is also a zip line, **Canopy Las Terrazas**, which crosses the lake into the trees (CUC$25 for foreigners, CUC$15 for hotel guests, CUC$7 for Cubans).

Following the death in a car accident of the popular singer, Polo Montañez in 2002, his lakeside house was opened as a museum, run by his brother. In nearby San Cristóbal, a clay statue of the singer has been put on display. Formerly a woodcutter, he rose to fame as a singer/songwriter and had many hits in the three years before his death, touring Latin America and Europe.

Hiking around Las Terrazas The hills behind Hotel Moka rise to the **Loma del Salón** (564 m). There are several easy hiking trails: to the partly restored 19th-century **Buenavista** coffee plantation (restaurant has *pollo brujo*, cheaper for hotel guests than for others); 3 km along the San Juan River to the old **La Victoria** coffee plantation and sulphur springs; 4 km along La Serafina path to the ruins of the 19th-century **Santa Serafina** coffee plantation, excellent for seeing birds like the Cuban trogon, the solitaire, woodpeckers and the Cuban tody; 8 km along the Cañada del Infierno valley to the **San Pedro** and **Santa Catalina** coffee plantations. There are also more demanding whole-day hikes with a professional ecologist as a guide (CUC$33-41 for one person, falling to CUC$14-18 per person with six people).

Essential Sierra del Rosario

Getting around

On the *autopista*, 51 km west of Havana, a roadside billboard announces the turning to Las Terrazas/Moka, 4 km north of the *autopista*. However, after that there is little signposting through a confusing series of side roads; if you are driving, you may have to ask the way.

Public transport is negligible. Long-distance buses go along the *autopista*, occasionally to Las Terrazas, but not to other sites of interest. Taxis are expensive and can only be arranged in Havana, Pinar del Río or Viñales. Therefore, the easiest way of getting to Soroa or Las Terrazas is to book yourself on an organized tour from Havana. A day trip (10 hours) to Las Terrazas, with walking, river bathing and a ghastly lunch is around CUC$50 at any tour agency. Other trips include overnight stays at the hotels and some take in Soroa as well. Alternatively, hire a car and take your time, but note that rooms at **Hotel Moka** need to be booked in advance.

Soroa

If travelling by car, you can make a detour to Soroa, a spa and resort in the Sierra del Rosario, 81 km southwest of the capital, either by continuing 18 km west then southeast from Las Terrazas through the Sierra del Rosario, or directly from the *autopista*, driving northwest from Candelaria. As you drive into the area from the south, a sign on the right indicates the **Mirador de Venus** and **Baños Romanos**. Past the baths is the **Bar Edén** (open till 1800), where you can park before walking up to the **mirador** ⓘ *25 mins, free on foot, CUC$3 on a horse.* From the top you get fine views of the southern plains, the forest-covered Sierra and Soroa itself. There are lots of birds, butterflies, dragonflies and lizards around the path; many flowers in season and birdwatching is very popular here.

Further north is a **Jardín Botánico Orchidarium** ⓘ *T48-522558, guided tours daily 0830-1140, 1340-1555, CUC$3, camera CUC$1, birdwatching, hiking and riding CUC$3 per hr, parking CUC$1,* with over 700 species of which 250 are native to Cuba, as well as ferns and begonias (check if the orchids are in bloom before visiting). Alberto at the desk speaks good English and some French, and there is also a restaurant, **Castillo de las Nubes** (1200-1900). There is an excursion to **El Brujito**, a village once owned by French landlords, where the third and fourth generations of slaves live. Across the road from the Orchidarium is a **waterfall** (250 m along a paved path, CUC$2), which is worth a visit if you are in the area. You can do a day trip from Havana or stay overnight.

Parque Nacional La Güira

A few kilometres west of **San Diego de los Banos**, an impressive neo-Gothic gateway leads to the Parque Nacional La Güira. Inside, there are extensive neglected 19th-century gardens, pools and statues, with the ruins of a Gothic mansion. There is a small bar near the entrance. Behind, the road winds up through the hills to an army recreation centre; behind this there is an enormous, cheap and rather run-down restaurant. The **Cueva de las Portales** just north of here was Che Guevara's HQ during the Cuban missile crisis and there is a small exhibition of military and personal relics. The national park covers an area of 22,000 ha and protects a number of endemic species.

Listings Sierra del Rosario

Where to stay

Las Terrazas
Hotels

$$$-$$ Hotel Moka
T48-578600, www.hotelmoka-lasterrazas.com.
Above the village is this 26-room hotel complex run in cooperation with the Cuban Academy of Sciences as an ecotourism centre. It is beautifully designed and laid out in Spanish colonial style with tiled roofs. Breakfast and dinner packages available, transfers from Havana, a/c, satellite TV. Staff are friendly and knowledgeable: even the hotel receptionist has an ecology PhD. Gardens behind have a tennis court and a pleasant pool where you can have food and drinks.

Casas particulares
All *casas particulares* are outside the park, a short distance away on the Cayajabos road.

$ Casa Hospedaje Villa Duque
Finca San Andrés, road to Cayajabos, T5322 1431 (mob).
2 km from Las Terrazas entrance, this 2-storey house is in a lovely rural setting on a hillside with views for miles over the countryside. 2 a/c rooms in very good condition with independent access, roof terrace for cocktails and star gazing. Delicious food from the

garden and the home-grown, home-roasted coffee should not be missed. The owners have a 1955 Chevy if you want to go anywhere. Some English spoken.

$ Villa Juanita
Calle 1 601, Finca La Pastora, Cayajabos, 3 km from las Terrazas, T5221 0634 (mob).
3 a/c rooms with fridge, apartment upstairs has independent access. Meals available, good food, very welcoming *casa particular*, a little English and expressive, slow Spanish spoken. Parking.

Soroa
Hotels

$$$-$$ Villa Soroa
T48-523534.
Cabins and self-catering houses used mostly by tour groups, restaurant, disco, bar, Olympic-sized swimming pool, bike rental, riding nearby. A peaceful place on a hillside but the rooms and bathrooms are in need of renovation. The hotel runs 1-day, 17-km, gently paced hikes around the main sights of the area with picnic.

Casas particulares

$ Casa Los Sauces
Jorge y Ana Lidia, on the road up to Villa Soroa, about 1 km from the autopista, T5228 9372, lossauces@nauta.cu.
Ana Lidia works at the orchidarium and her own garden is a mini botanical garden. 3 a/c rooms each with double and single bed, fridge, rocking chairs on shady terrace, the 3rd room is upstairs, meals available. A good *casa*, experienced hosts.

$ Hospedaje Estudio de Arte
Km 8.5, 300 m outside Soroa next to a primary school in converted church, T48-598116, infosoroa@hvs.co.cu.
Jesús is an artist and has a contract with UNEAC; the hotel organizes tours to his Estudio de Arte in the house, where he sells his paintings. His wife, Aliuska, runs the house, 1 room, large and decorated with Jesús' art, excellent *comida criolla*, food recommended by Cubans.

Where to eat

Las Terrazas

$$ El Romero
T48-578555. Daily 0900-2200.
Vegetarian restaurant, exceptional for Cuba. Service and food suffer if a large party is in and sometimes menu items are not available, but overall it is a pleasant change from regular Cuban food with liberal use of fresh vegetables, fruit, herbs and their own honey. Pleasant view from the terrace.

$$ La Fonda de Mercedes
Edif 9, Apto 2, T48-578647. Daily 0900-2100.
Best to make reservations as this small *paladar* is very popular. Mercedes prepares excellent meat dishes to traditional recipes and serves them on her patio in the apartment block just below Hotel Moka.

$ Café de María
Las Terrazas.
This is the place to come for coffee, locally grown, home-roasted, ground and brewed. María ran this café for 40 years and now her family continue in her memory. Generally considered to serve the best coffee in Cuba.

Pinar del Río gives a good taste of provincial Cuba. About 70% of Cuba's tobacco crop is grown in the region and almost every agricultural area is dotted with *vegas*, curious tent-shaped windowless structures made of palm thatch, which are used for drying tobacco leaves. The cigar factory in Pinar del Río city has regular tours and in the harvest season it is possible in most villages to visit an *escogida de tabaco*, where the best leaves are selected for further processing (see box, page 120).

Sights

Pinar del Río is a lively city and there is always something going on, but it is not particularly attractive. The centre consists of single-storey neoclassical houses with columns, some with other interesting architectural details. Under the porches are thriving one-person businesses, ranging from selling snacks to repairing cigarette lighters. Horse-drawn vehicles vie for space alongside bicycles and battered old cars on the roads, while the pavements are full of people jostling and weaving in and out of the pillars and other obstacles.

The main shopping street and centre of activities is José Martí, which runs west-east through the town. At the west end is the **Centro de Artes Visuales** ① *Martí, opposite Parque Independencia, T48-752758, Mon-Fri 1000-1700, Sat 0800-1200, CUC$1.* Walk along

Essential Pinar del Río

Finding your feet

There is a **train** from Havana, which is cheap but has the disadvantage of being very slow with lots of stops and is very dark, so there is a risk of theft. You have to hang on to your bags all the time and take particular care of your pockets in the tunnels. The **bus station** is reasonably central and all buses use the same terminal. **Viazul** air-conditioned buses come from Havana on a route that continues to Viñales. On arrival in Pinar del Río you must expect to be hassled by crowds at the bus or train stations, who are touting for your business (see Where to stay, page 122). Even if you come in by car they will be waiting for you at the road junctions. Young men on bicycles are a particular hazard and very persistent. Always say you have a reservation. See also Transport, page 124.

Getting around

The town has changed its street names, but locals continue to use the old ones as well as the new official names. It can be confusing when names on the map conflict with what people really call the streets: for example, 20 de Mayo is now Primero de Mayo; Vélez Caviedes is also Ormani Arenado, while Virtudes is also Ceferino Fernández. Pinar del Río is not large and it is easy to walk around the centre and to most of the places of interest, such as the rum and tobacco factories.

When to go

Carnival is in July but it is not on the scale of Santiago's or Havana's. At any time of year you can find something going on in and around the city. Expect storms between September and November, although heavy showers can happen at any time, usually in the afternoon. This area was badly hit by the hurricanes in 2008 but is now largely rebuilt.

José Martí to the east to a renovated building opposite the Wedding Palace: the **Palacio de Computación** ⓘ *Martí esq González Coro, Mon-Sat 0800-2100, theatre, cafeteria and classrooms for teaching computer skills,* which was inaugurated by Fidel Castro in January 2001. It is very photogenic if seen from Parque de la Independencia. The **Casa de la Cultura Pedro Junco** ⓘ *Martí esq Rafael Morales, Mon-Sat 0800-1800,* is in a huge colonial house and includes an art gallery, a hall for parties and seven classrooms for teaching dancing, painting, singing, etc. There are evening activities according to scheduled programmes. The old **Globo** hotel, right in the centre near the corner of José Martí and Isabel Rubio, is only for Cubans, but it has a beautiful tiled staircase worth a peep, and its clock is a local curiosity for its accurate time-keeping. The **Museo Provincial de Historia** ⓘ *Martí 58 entre Isabel Rubio y Colón, T48-754300, Mon-Fri 0830-1830 Sat 0900-1300, CUC$1,* renovated and reopened in 2015 details the history of the town and displays objects from the Wars of Independence. On the same side of the street is the **Teatro José Jacinto Milanés** ⓘ *Martí esq Colón.* Built in 1883, this is one of the most beautiful theatres in the country. Renovated and reopened in 2006, it is true to its original style and decor, with its

Pinar del Río

Where to stay 🛏
Casa Colonial Jose
  Antonio Mesa cp **1**
Vueltabajo **2**

Restaurants 🍴
Doña Neli **1**
El Gallardo **2**
El Mesón **3**

Entertainment 🎭
Bar La Esquinita **1**
Casa de la Cultura **2**
Casa de la Música **3**
Casa del Joven Creador **4**

400 metres
400 yards

ON THE ROAD
Cuban cigars

During Columbus' second journey to the New World, he landed at Gibara in Cuba. Forays inland brought reports that the local inhabitants were smoking roughly rolled dried leaves for ceremonial or religious purposes, which they called *cohibas*. The Spaniards soon acquired the taste for tobacco and in the 17th century introduced it to the European market with great success. The first tobacco plantations in Cuba were established by the Río Almendares (Havana), in the centre of the island and around Bayamo. Tobacco planting spread in the 18th century, becoming particularly successful in the west, and by the 19th century tobacco planters and merchants were extremely prosperous. By the time Cuba achieved its independence, there were 120 cigar factories around the island.

Nowadays tobacco is cultivated in the west of Cuba in the province of Pinar del Río, in the centre in the provinces of Villa Clara and Sancti Spíritus, and in the east in the provinces of Granma and Santiago de Cuba, although the tobacco regions are known as Vuelta Abajo, Semi Vuelta, Partidos, Remedios and Oriente. Only Partidos and Vuelta Abajo can grow tobacco of a high enough quality for the Grandes Marcas of cigars (*Habanos*), and only Vuelta Abajo (Pinar del Río) produces all the leaves necessary for a cigar. Lower quality tobacco is made into cigarettes.

Tobacco is extremely labour intensive, and in Cuba it is grown, harvested and processed entirely by hand. Seedlings are transplanted from the nursery between October and December when they are 18-20 cm, and great care is taken not to damage the delicate roots. After a week they are weeded and after two weeks they are earthed up to maintain humidity and increase the plants' assimilation of nutrients. This is done with the help of oxen rather than a tractor, to avoid compacting the soil. When the plant reaches 1.4-1.6 m, side shoots are removed and the plant is encouraged to grow tall with only six to nine pairs of leaves. Harvesting takes place between January and March, during which time the leaves are collected by hand, two or three at a time, every five days, starting at the bottom. They are then taken to a *vega*, a huge, thatched barn, where they are sewn together in pairs and hung on a pole to dry. The leaves turn yellow, then reddish gold and are considered dry after about 50 days. They are then piled in bundles or stacks for about 30 days, during which time the first fermentation takes place at a temperature not exceeding 35°C, before being classified according to colour, size and quality for wrappers or fillers. At this stage the leaves are stripped off the main vein, dampened, flattened and packed in bigger stacks for up to 60 days of fermentation at a temperature not exceeding 42°C. Finally they are stored and aged for months, or maybe years, before being taken to be rolled by the expert hands of factory workers.

Five types of leaves are used in the manufacture of a cigar. In the middle (*tripa*) are a mixture of three types, *ligero*, *seco* and *volado*. These are wrapped in the *capote*, which is then enveloped in the *capa*, which is the part you see and determines the appearance of the cigar. There are two types of tobacco plant: the *corojo*, and the *criollo*. The former produces only the *capa*, but it comes in several colours. It is grown beneath vast cotton shrouds to protect it from the sun's radiation and keep it soft and silky. The latter provides the other four leaves needed to make up the cigar, which determine the flavour. It is grown in full sunlight to get intense flavours. Each of the five leaves is processed and aged differently before reaching the factory floor for mixing according to secret recipes and rolling.

Hundreds of workers sit at tables in the factory, equipped only with a special knife called a *chaveta*, a guillotine and a pot of gum. A skilled artisan (*torcedor*) makes an average of 120 cigars a day. They used to sit and listen to readings from the press or novels, a tradition which started in 1865 but has recently been replaced by the radio or recorded music. Although many of the people rolling cigars are women, it is unfortunately a myth that Cuban cigars are rolled on the thighs of dusky maidens. The women sorting the leaves do, however, place them across their laps on each leg and this may have been where the erotic image originated.

Quality control is rigid. Any cigars which do not meet the standards of size, shape, thickness and appearance are rejected. Those which do make it are stored at a temperature of 16°-18°C and at a humidity of 65-70% for several weeks until they lose the moisture acquired during rolling. A specialist then classifies them according to colour (of which there are 65 tones) and they are chosen for boxes, with the colours ranging from dark to light, left to right. They have to remain exactly as they are placed in the cedar wood box and the person who then labels each cigar has to keep them in the same order, even facing the same way.

Finally the boxes are stamped and sealed with the government's guarantee, which looks rather like a currency note and carries the words: 'Cuban Government's warranty for cigars exported from Havana' in English, French and German as well as Spanish.

Always buy your cigars from a state shop, not on the street, where they are bound to be fakes, no matter how good a deal they appear. Check the quality of each cigar. They should be tightly rolled, not soft; they should have no lumps or other protuberances; if you turn them upside down nothing should come out; the colour should be uniform and the aroma should be strong. The box should be sealed with the four-language warranty, which should not be a photocopy, and on the bottom you should find the stamp: Habanos s.a. HECHO EN CUBA *Totalmente a mano*.

Cigars are like fine wines or whiskies and there are many different types from which to choose. Fidel Castro used to smoke *Cohiba* cigars, which were created in 1966 exclusively for the diplomatic market. In 1982 the *Cohiba Lanceros*, *Coronas Especiales* and *Panatelas* were created for public sale, followed in 1989 by the *Espléndidos*, *Robustos* and *Exquisitos*, which together make up the Classic Line (*La Línea Clásica*). In 1992, to mark the 500th anniversary of the landing of Columbus, they brought out the 1492 Line (*La Línea 1492*), with its five centuries: *Siglo I, II, III, IV, V*. The *Espléndidos* now sell for up to CUC$385 a box.

As well as the *Cohiba* brand, there are *Montecristo*, *Romeo y Julieta*, *Bolívar*, *Punch*, *Hoyo de Monterrey*, *H Upmann*, *Partagás*, *Quintero*, *La Flor de Cano*, *El Rey del Mundo* and *Rafael González*, all of which have their company histories and logos, mostly dating from the 19th century.

three-tiered auditorium and antique chairs. Further along Martí is the **Museo de Ciencias Naturales Tranquilino Sandalio de Noda** ⓘ *José Martí 202 esq Av Comandante Pinares, T48-753087, Mon-Sat 0800-1700, CUC$1*, with geological and natural history exhibits: not large, not much explanation, not much on typical Cuban animals. The great thing, however, is the eclectic building, formerly the Palacio Guasch, which is the most ornate in the region, with Gothic towers, spires and all sorts of twiddly bits.

The cigar factory, **Fábrica de Tabaco Francisco Donatién** ⓘ *Maceo 157 y A Tarafa, T48-723424/773069, Mon-Sat 0800-1700, CUC$5 for a short visit, no photos or videos allowed*, is one of the town's main tourist attractions. It reputedly makes the best cigars in Cuba, and it will give you a better appreciation of how cigars are made than you would gain on a tour in Havana. Even when the factory is shut,

> **Tip...**
>
> Avoid the youngsters selling cigars outside. Workers in the factory will also try and sell you cigars. Remember there is a limit on the number of cigars you can take out of the country without a receipt so any illegally bought cigars should be smoked in Cuba. See page 142.

you can still buy the very finest cigars in the town from the shop opposite, Casa del Habano: you'll get the genuine article, even if it is pricey.

Also worth a visit, if you're interested, is the rum factory, **Fábrica de Guayabita** ⓘ *Isabel Rubio 189 entre Ceferino Fernández y Frank País, Mon-Fri 0900-1530, Sat 0900-1230, CUC$2 for a tour and stop at the tasting room*, which makes a special rum flavoured with miniature wild guavas, *Guayabita del Pinar*, which comes in either dry or sweet varieties. The bottles on sale are cheaper than those in the shops. Between the two is the pretty cream-coloured cathedral of **San Rosendo** ⓘ *Maceo 2 Este esq Gerardo Medina*.

Listings Pinar del Río *map page 119.*

Where to stay

Hotels

$$ Hotel Vueltabajo
C José Martí 103 y Rafael Morales, T48-759381, carpeta@vueltapr.co.cu.
Pleasant hotel, nice rooms with very high ceilings, but those facing the street can be noisy, particularly at weekends, internal rooms are quiet, safety deposit box, satellite TV. Pricey meals of poor quality but fast service, restaurant open 0715-0930, 1200-1445, 1900-2145. Bar open 1700-2330, very crowded with locals, who offer cigars to foreigners (beware fakes), drink inside or outside, but the porch is close to the road. Car rental, excursions, tourism bureau, currency exchange.

$$ Finca La Guabina
Carretera a Luis Lazo Km 9.5, T48-757616.

Outside Pinar del Río is this 1000-ha ranch where they breed horses and other animals. There are 5 a/c rooms in the main house and 3 in cabins overlooking the lake, which are very peaceful and relaxing. Lots of outdoor activities such as walking, riding, trips in horse-drawn carriage, taking a boat out on the lake and watching traditional rural pastimes. The restaurant serves fresh and tasty food and the breakfasts are substantial. English-speaking guides available for tours. Horse riding CUC$7 per hr through the mountains and countryside on good horses. Tour parties come here for the day from Viñales and Pinar del Río and there are rodeo shows Mon, Wed, Fri 1000-1200, 1600-1800.

Casas particulares

There is a mafia of young men on bicycles who will meet you on arrival, whether by car, bus or train, and pester to take you to a *casa particular*, *paladar*, or whatever. Sometimes they say they are from **Formatur**, the tourism school. Sometimes they tell you there is a salsa festival in town to get you to stay here rather than go on to Viñales. They are after a commission, set by them at CUC$5 per person per night and have been known to be violent with Cuban landlords who refuse to pay. Avoid them if you can and make your own way using the map. If you accept any help with directions they will ask the Cuban family for money. Taxi drivers are in the same game; if your driver says he can't find the address, refuse to pay unless he goes to the right house. He will try and take you somewhere else to get his commission.

$ Casa Colonial José Antonio Mesa
Gerardo Medina 67 entre Adela Azcuy y Isidro de Armas, T48-753173.
A gem of a colonial building, single storey with pillars and decorative topping, spacious, high ceilings, stained glass, tiled floors, rooms have fridge and fan, lovely courtyard garden with jacuzzi in a gazebo, meals available.

$ Casa Villa Maury
Ceferino Fernández 186 entre Antonio Tarafa y Antonio Guiteras, T48-771735, 5371 4505 (mob), domipimientav@gmail.com.
Maura Padrón Cruz rents 2 rooms with a/c and fan, terrace, patio, parking, English and Portuguese spoken. The house is recognizable by its orange and pink paint.

$ Villa Manuela
Garmendia 10 entre Antonio Guiteras y Volcán, T48-773274, www.casaparticular-manuela.sitew.com.
Rental rooms upstairs above the multi-generational family quarters. Friendly and welcoming, French and English spoken, Manuela is Cuban and Gérard (Pepe) is French. However, the house is run by Sandy and other staff, as the owners live in France part of the year. Good home cooking eaten under the thatched palapa on the multi-level terrace, chairs outside for street-

watching, all clean, spacious and well cared for. Parking CUC$2.

Where to eat

$$$-$$ Rumayor
2 km on Viñales road.
Open 1200-2200, closed Thu.
State-run restaurant which specializes in *pollo ahumado* (smoked chicken), at CUC$6.50. Also *Tropicana*-style show, Fri, Sat and Sun (see Entertainment, below).

$$ El Gallardo
José Martí 207 entre Comandante Pinares y Celestino Pacheco, opposite the Museo de Ciencias Naturales, T48-778492, 5283 3603 (mob), restaurantgallardo@nauta.cu.
Good comida *criolla*, attentive and prompt service. Good for lunch or dinner, also rooms to rent, **Casa Roger**.

$$ El Mesón
José Martí 205, opposite the Museo de Ciencias Naturales, T48-822867.
Mon-Sat, 1200-2200.
Good, fresh food served in this *paladar*, run by Rafael, a former teacher, Cuban menu popular with local families, grilled pork with vegetables CUC$5.50.

$ Doña Neli
Gerardo Medina 24.
Bakery. Open daily 0700-1900 for bread, 0830-2300 for pastries and cakes.

Entertainment

The town is very lively on Sat nights and, to a lesser extent, on Fri, with music everywhere: salsa, *son*, Mexican music, international stuff.

Music
During the day you can hear traditional music (mambo, rumba, cha-cha-cha, *danzón*) in Parque Roberto Amarán. Baseball fans gather here for heated discussions about sport. Parque de la Independencia is quieter and a place to enjoy the breeze at night, a popular hangout for the young crowd.

Opposite the **Hotel Vueltabajo** is a bar where locals gather to drink draft beer made from grapefruit and perform *canturías*. Open daily but best on Fri evening. Other places to try include **Artex** (Martí 36, daily 0900-0200), and **Bar La Esquinita** (Isabel Rubio, daily 2000-0200), for live guitar music.

Casa de la Cultura, *Rafael Morales esq Martí*. Band play every Sun evening with a dance contest for the elderly, fantastic, free, photos allowed.

Casa de la Música, *on Gerardo Medina next to Coppelia*. Live music daily except Mon.

Casa del Joven Creador, *José Martí 113A, opposite the Chess Academy, T48-774672*. An organization for music and the arts where young musicians gather at night and arrange concerts. A band that rose up through this system is the ethno-metal **Tendencia**, led by singer and director Kiko, a former high school English teacher. They have travelled abroad and now have a national reputation.

Nightclubs

Disco Pista Rita, *on González Coro*. An open-air venue popular with teenagers, where they play loud, US-style disco music and rock, entry CUP$2, the only drink on sale is neat rum at CUP$25 a bottle. **Pinar Rock**, a national rock festival, is held here the 2nd weekend of Mar.

Rumayor, *2 km on road to Viñales. Restaurant (1200-2200, closed Thu)*. A *Tropicana*-style show, Fri, Sat and Sun CUC$5, very good, lots of security. Starts 2300 (get there before 2200 to get a table) and lasts about 1½ hrs, followed by disco until 0300 or so. Held in small amphitheatre with proper sound and lighting system. No photography or videos allowed. The complex is in a pleasant garden with lots of trees.

Transport

Bus

The bus station is on Colón, north of José Martí, near Gómez. Head downstairs for tickets for provincial buses and trucks, upstairs for buses to **Havana**.

Viazul, T48-752572/755255, runs a daily bus service from Havana continuing to **Viñales**, see page 125. It stops on request at **Las Terrazas** and **San Diego de los Baños**.

Car hire

Transtur, Martí 109 near Restaurant La Casona, T48-750104, commercial.pri@ transtur.cu. **Servi Cupet** station on C Rafael Morales esq Frank País, on the road to San Juan y Martínez.

Taxi

Cubataxi has an office in the bus station with an a/c waiting room and an officer who can show you a brochure of trips and fares (no English spoken), Mon-Sat 0700-1800, Sun 0700-1200.

Train

The railway station in Pinar del Río is on Av Comandante Pinares, T48-752106/752272. From **Havana**, departs 19 de Noviembre (Tulipán) station at 0610 every other day, arriving at 1325. It returns the next day at 0900, getting in at 1455, CUC$7. This service is not recommended as it is very slow and robberies are common: take a torch for the tunnels and hang on to your luggage; don't sleep. The line continues to **Guane**, CUC$3.

North of Pinar del Río, the road leads across pine-covered hills and valleys for 25 km to Viñales, a delightful small town in a dramatic valley in the Sierra de los Organos. The area has a distinctive landscape, with steep-sided limestone mogotes rising dramatically from fertile flat-floored valleys, where farmers cultivate the red soil for tobacco, fruits and vegetables. This unique countryside is recognized as a UNESCO World Cultural Landscape. As in so much of rural Cuba, horses, pigs, oxen, zebu cattle and chickens are everywhere, including on the main road.

Viñales town

Viñales itself is a pleasant town, with single-storey houses with red-tiled roofs and wooden colonnades along the main street. Visitors come here to relax, hike in the hills and maybe visit a beach on the north coast. The main street is Salvador Cisneros and a walk along it will reveal nearly all the attractions Viñales has to offer. Streets running parallel or across it are residential and contain many *casas particulares*. Viazul drops you off half way along the street, opposite the main square with a little-used church. This is the Wi-Fi hotspot for the town so there are always people about (buy Etecsa cards at the office around the corner). There is also a little municipal museum on Salvador Cisneros and a **Casa de la Cultura** on the square with an art gallery. An informative curator here speaks English. There are several bars and restaurants along Salvador Cisneros, but hardly of the quality to warrant the thousands of visitors who come here every year.

On the edge of Viñales is **Caridad's Garden** ⓘ *turn left at the gas station at the end of Salvador Cisneros on the road to Cueva del Indio, no entry fee, but a tip of CUC$1 is appreciated.* The garden contains a beautiful collection of flowers and fruit trees from Cuba and around the world. Chickens scratch about in the shady undergrowth with their chicks. The garden was first planted in the 1930s. A guide will show you around, pointing out all the different species and you will be invited to try all the different fruits. They are generous with their produce but appreciate contributions to the upkeep of the garden.

Mural de la Prehistoria

Two kilometres west of Viñales is the Mural de la Prehistoria, painted by **Lovigildo González**, a disciple of the Mexican Diego Rivera, between 1959 and 1976, generally disliked as a monstrous piece of graffiti. If you are fit and active you can climb up the rocks to the top for a great view. No guide needed. One hundred metres before the mural is **Restaurant Jurásico**, from where you can see the paintings; there is a swimming pool nearby. A new attraction in this area is a zip line, **Fortín Canopy Tours** ⓘ *CUC$7 for Cubans, CUC$25 for foreigners*, which opened

Essential Valle de Viñales

Finding your feet

Viazul has a daily bus service from Havana via Pinar del Río. The nearest train station is at Pinar del Río.

Getting around

Viñales town is small and easy to walk around, although there's also a hop on/hop off bus that runs between the hotels, daily 0830-1800, CUC$5 for a 40-minute round trip. Many visitors hire a car or scooter to get around the nearby attractions, although there are also horses for hire and local buses between villages.

in September 2015 and is only the second in the country after Las Terrazas (see above). The zip line runs for 1100 m between the mogotes, over the tobacco fields and across the valley.

Los Acuáticos

Four kilometres from Viñales is the community of **Los Acuáticos**, where the villagers worship water. It was founded in 1943 by Antoñica Izquierdo, a *santera*, who recognized the importance of hygiene and clean water for health. The few families in the hamlet on the mountainside are self-contained and they bathe three times a day. Despite excellent rural healthcare in Cuba, the community refuses medical assistance for anyone who has an accident or is sick. It is recommended that women do not come here on their own.

Caves

Six kilometres north of Viñales is the **Cueva del Indio** ⓘ *avoid 1130-1430 when tour parties arrive and there are long delays, CUC$5,* a cave which you enter on foot, then take a boat, with a guide who gives you a description, very beautiful. There is a restaurant nearby where tour parties are given a lunch of suckling pig (*lechón*). The tour includes lunch but not the cave, and no drinks; even water is an 'extra'. Beyond the restaurant is a small farm, well kept, with little red pigs running around, oxen and horses. There are trips to a disco in the **Cueva de San Miguel**, west of Cueva del Indio (much better to go on your own

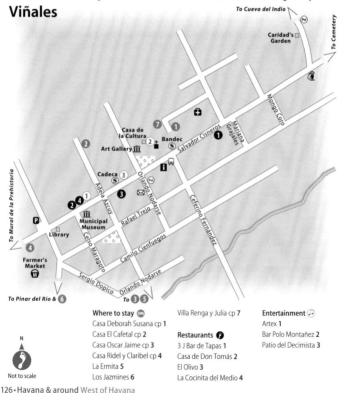

Viñales

To Cueva del Indio

To Cemetery

Caridad's Garden

Casa de la Cultura

Bandec

Art Gallery

Salvador Cisneros

Mariana Grajales

Monga Coro

Cadeca

Orlando Nodarse

Cefetino Fernández

To Mural de la Prehistoria

Adela Azcuy

Rafael Trejo

Municipal Museum

Celso Maragoto

Library

Camilo Cienfuegos

Farmer's Market

Sergio Dopico

Orlando Nodarse

To Pinar del Río & 6

To 3 5

N

Not to scale

Where to stay
Casa Deborah Susana cp 1
Casa El Cafetal cp 2
Casa Oscar Jaime cp 3
Casa Ridel y Claribel cp 4
La Ermita 5
Los Jazmines 6

Villa Renga y Julia cp 7

Restaurants
3 J Bar de Tapas 1
Casa de Don Tomás 2
El Olivo 3
La Cocinita del Medio 4

Entertainment
Artex 1
Bar Polo Montañez 2
Patio del Decimista 3

ON THE ROAD
Rocks, caves, valleys and mogotes

The rocks around Viñales are pure limestone formed in the Jurassic period around 160 million years ago. Unlike most other rocks, limestone can be dissolved by rainwater. Rivers and streams often flow underground through extensive cave systems; most of the 10,000 recorded caves in Cuba are in Pinar del Río province and one cave system in the Valle Santo Tomás consists of a total of 25 km of underground passages. Where a valley is formed in tropical limestone, often by downwards faulting of the rock, it may be filled with fertile red soil. Rotting vegetation increases the acidity of the groundwater on the valley floor. This 'aggressive' water eats into the valley sides, undercutting the rocks and producing steep cliff-like features. The valley floor is broken by isolated steep-sided hills, known to both English- and Spanish-speaking geologists by their Cuban name: mogotes. Other valleys (narrow gorges) are produced when the roof of a large cave collapses. Similar tropical limestone landscapes can be seen in parts of Puerto Rico and Jamaica.

Rapid drainage of rainwater into the rock produces dry growing conditions for plants. The limestone hills have a distinctive vegetation type, with palms (including the curious cork palm), deciduous trees, succulents, lianas and epiphytes. More than 20 species are endemic, found only in the Viñales area. The isolation of the mogotes has also produced distinctive animal species, with some types of snail found only on a single mogote.

and have the cave to yourself), short hiking trips to a mogote, visits to various caves and **El Palenque de los Cimarrones**, a restaurant and craft shop with a display of Cuban folklore. These are advertized as daily events, but don't rely on it. See Entertainment, page 130.

The **Valle de Santo Tomás** (with 25-km cave system) contains the **Gran Caverna Santo Tomás** 17 km southwest from Viñales in a community called El Moncada. A guide will show you the cave; prices depend on which walk you choose. Near El Moncada is the 3-km ecological path, **Maravillas de Viñales**.

Listings Valle de Viñales *map page 126.*

Tourist information

There is a visitor centre, **La Casa del Visitante**, on the main road heading out to Pinar del Río, near **Hotel Los Jazmines**, daily 0730-1800.

Where to stay

Hotels

$$$-$$ La Ermita
Ctra de la Ermita, Km 2, 3 km from town with magnificent view of the valley and town, especially at sunset, T48-796122/796071, www.hotelescubanacan.com.

62 rooms, a/c, shop, tennis court, wheelchair access, pool (not always usable), food not recommended, better to walk into the village for evening meal, breakfast included, nicer public areas than at Los Jazmines.

$$$-$$ Horizontes Los Jazmines
Ctra de Viñales, Km 23.5, 3 km before the town, in a superb location with travel brochure view of the valley, T48-796123/796205, www.hotelescubanacan.com.

62 rooms and 16 cabañas, nightclub, breakfast buffet CUC$5 if not already included, unexciting restaurant, bar with snacks available, shops, swimming pool (CUC$5

including towels for day-visitors and CUC$5 in vouchers for bar drinks), riding, easy transport.

Casas particulares

There are more than 500 registered *casas particulares* in Viñales. Many were rebuilt after the 2008 hurricane and are of a good standard. Tourist rooms tend to be built on to the side of houses with their own, independent entrance. Most charge CUC$20-25 a night, with breakfast at CUC$3-4 and dinner at CUC$7-10, depending on your menu choice. Many offer juice, coffee or *mojito* but do not say whether it is free or not; ask to avoid nasty surprises on the final bill. *Casa* owners will meet you at the bus station.

$ Casa Deborah Susana
Calle C Final 1, T48-796207, T5283 2018 (mob), deborahsusana7@nauta.cu.
Deborah Alfonso and Juan Carlos (barman at **Don Tomás**) are very caring and friendly and both speak English. They offer 2 airy rooms at the back of the house with a/c, fan, fridge, lots of power points, good bathrooms and independent access, which open out onto a pretty patio garden with comfy chairs and hammock under cover. The *casa* is very quiet, behind the main street at the back of Banco Nacional, and there is no traffic noise, despite being very central.

$ Casa El Cafetal
C Adela Azcuy Norte Final s/n, T5223 9175, 5331 1752 (mob).
Lovely rural and peaceful location, last house on the road, detached cottage in a lush garden which produces lots of fruit and coffee for the household. The food is wonderful and you eat overlooking the garden and the mogotes. Marta and Amador Martínez run this *casa* with Marta's son, Edgar Rivery, a climbing guide who speaks English. 2 a/c bedrooms with 2 double beds and private bathroom.

$ Casa Oscar Jaime
Adela Azcuy 43, T48-793381.
Oscar Jaime Rodríguez and Leida Robaína Altega offer a friendly and welcoming home shared by 3 generations of family, including cousins, which is a mecca for climbers. Oscar was one of the first local people to get involved in climbing the mogotes and is very experienced and knowledgeable about routes. He can lend you equipment. 3 new rooms and a *paladar* built in 2015, making 6 in total on different levels and all to a high standard. Great food and delicious juices and (strong) mojitos.

$ Casa Ridel y Claribel
C Salvador Cisneros (Pasaje B), on western outskirts of town, T48-695127, 5823 3677 (mob), www.ridelyclaribel.altervista.org.
Very friendly and helpful hosts who can arrange trips and transport, and go out of their way to make your stay memorable. 2 comfortable a/c rooms, 1 has its own patio but there is also a roof terrace for sunset watching looking over the town roofs to the mogotes. Good food: you won't go hungry.

$ Villa Renga y Julia
C Salvador Cisneros Interior 1a, T48-798333, 5331 1817 (mob), http://casavinales.jimdo.com.
Immaculate house run by Julia's daughter Meily. Modern furnishings, disco lighting around the beds in the a/c bedrooms, jacuzzi outside. Excellent mattresses, safe box, large new bathrooms, all good quality. Very good food too, with huge and varied breakfast. Very close to Casa Deborah Susana, so also quiet but central.

$ Villa Tery
Calle 4 31 entre 5 y 7, Rpto La Colchonería, T48-696662.
Simple house in quiet, rural area, a short walk to centre, large comfortable rooms with a/c, fan and fridge, the room at the back has its own entrance. Very friendly, kind and informative family. Guillermo, the father, will answer all your questions, Jolie, his daughter is an excellent cook and speaks English, while her grandfather has a tobacco farm and will show you how to make cigars. Parking. Bicycle hire.

Where to eat

$$$-$$ 3 J Bar de Tapas
Salvador Cisneros 45, T48-793334,
5531 1658 (mob).
A tapas bar with a good menu. Rum cocktails
as strong as you like and they'll top up your
glass with rum until you're happy. Modern,
stylish decor in a renovated old house. Sit
on the veranda or inside. Pleasant staff and
friendly owner. A good place to sit with a
book for a couple of hours, day or night.

$$$-$$ Buena Vista
On the road to Hotel Los Jazmines,
T5223 8616 (mob), buenavista@nauta.cu.
Look for the blue and white thatched and
tiled house. Tables outside on the veranda
or inside, with glorious view over the valley
to the mogotes, quiet and peaceful. Very
good *comida criolla*, tasty lobster, plentiful
side dishes. There are also rooms to rent
so you can wake up with the same view
in the mornings.

$$$-$$ Casa de Don Tomás
Salvador Cisneros 140, T48-796300.
Open 1000-2200.
The oldest house in Viñales (1879), totally
renovated after the 2008 hurricanes, very
pretty with a spectacular orange climbing
begonia (*lluvia de oro*) on a pergola at the
back. Food very average, eggs the only option
for vegetarians, but the cocktails are good and
it's pleasant to sit and listen to live music with
a Ron Collins or Mary Pickford. Most cocktails
are CUC$2, but the house special, *Trapiche*, is
CUC$2.20 (rum, pineapple, sugar cane syrup,
served with ice and a stick of sugar cane). A
bottle of rum is not much more than in a shop
and a shot of rum starts at CUC$0.30.

$$$-$$ El Olivo
Salvador Cisneros 89, T48-696654,
olivo.vinales@nauta.cu. Open 1200-2200.
A small, smart town centre *paladar* with
a wide range of menu options including
Mediterranean food and professional service.
Good fish, paella, spaghetti, plenty of

vegetarian options and interesting starters.
Rabbit in chocolate sauce is worth trying
and the goats cheese salad with raisins and
hazelnuts (all imported) has very crisp, fresh
lettuce. Most pasta dishes CUC$5-6, cocktails
CUC$2.50-3.50. Eat inside or on the veranda.
Always popular, queues outside.

$$$-$$ Fernando's
Ctra de la Ermita, Km 1, T48-696628.
Paladar within walking distance of the town
centre, tables al fresco on patio among plants
overlooking countryside and mountains.
Lunch and dinner, with live music at night,
good *criollo* food, lobster at CUC$15 the most
expensive dish, several courses included,
excellent service.

$$$-$$ La Casa Verde
50 m from Hotel Los Jazmines, T5223 8626.
Friendly, rustic, open air *paladar* with a great
view over the valley to the mogotes, simple
food but much better than anything on
offer in the hotel and well worth the short
walk for lunch or dinner. Usually a choice of
chicken, fish or pork and sometimes lobster,
with rice, beans, salad, sweet potato or
plantain, followed by fresh fruit salad laced
with liqueur. Vegetarians catered for. Meals
usually CUC$10-12.

$$$-$$ La Cocinita del Medio
Salvador Cisneros 122, T48-796414.
Open 1200-2300.
Good, simple *comida criolla*, grilled or
stewed meat comes with all the usual
trimmings: rice and beans, salad, yuca
or plantain, generous portions.

Cafés

Mogote Café
Pasaje Ceferino Fernández 1, T5440 7238.
Drinks with a view. Lovely open-air
seating on a veranda overlooking the
mogotes, very peaceful. Good coffees
and cocktails with happy hour in the
afternoon. Soak up the mojitos with
bruschetta or canapés. Sometimes live
trios, otherwise international music.

Entertainment

Live music

Artex, *Salvador Cisneros*. Bar, live music, shop 1000-2000.

Bar Polo Montañez, *next to Casa de la Cultura on the plaza, CUC$2*. Live music every night from 2100-2400 with different bands, followed by DJ until 0200. Valle Son plays Tue and every other Sat, Afro-Cuban night Wed. Large dance floor.

Los Jazmines, *see Where to stay, above*. Disco 2000-0300, CUC$5.

Palenque de los Cimarrones, *4 km north of Viñales at Km 32 Ctra a Puerto Esperanza, T48-796205*. Fri-Sat there is a cabaret show and after midnight a disco, very popular. Take a sweater with you in case you stay until very late.

Patio del Decimista, *Salvador Cisneros 112A, T48-796014*. Tables on the pavement or in the courtyard. Live music 1730-2030 in the open-air courtyard and from 2100 until late in the inner patio. Bands switch every other night, good mix of locals, tourists and professional salsa dancers. Good fun, small and intimate, everyone gets up to dance, no cover charge.

Transport

Bus

Bus terminal at Salvador Cisneros 63A. **Viazul**, T48-793195, daily from **Havana** via Pinar del Río. Local buses from **Pinar del Río** to **Puerto Esperanza**, **La Palma** and **Bahía Honda** all pass through Viñales. Tour buses from Havana will drop you off if you want to stay more than a day and collect you about 1600 on the day you want to return.

Bicycle/scooter

On the plaza **Cubanacán**, daily 0900-1900, rents bicycles by the hour, the day or longer. Alternatively rent a bike on the street for CUC$10 for the afternoon. It is illegal to rent bicycles from *casas particulares*, but it happens and is cheaper. Scooters and bicycles can be rented from **Don Tomás** restaurant.

Car hire

Havanautos and **Transtur** at the end of Salvador Cisneros by the gas station, T48-796305/796330, Mon-Fri 0830-1800, hire cars and small jeeps. **Cubacar**, also by the gas station, T48-796060, Mon-Fri 0800-1700, Sat 0900-1300, is not always open but has good rates.

Taxi

Taxi fares vary and can be negotiated for long distances. To **Cayo Jutías** is CUC$60-70, depending on waiting time, with a surcharge later in the afternoon.

North coast

pale sand beaches, turquoise water and superb diving or snorkelling

It is a lovely drive southwest through the valley, via El Moncada, and then north through Pons and the former copper mining centre of Minas de Matahambre up to Cayo Jutías on the north coast near Santa Lucía, 50 km. The road is well signed on the way there, but not at all on the way back.

Cayo Jutías

Day trip to Cayo Jutías with a tour operator from Viñales, CUC$50 per person including lunch; or taxi transfer, CUC$60-70 (up to 4 people), 1 hr.

Cayo Jutías, a 6.7-km cay, is attached to Cuba by a long causeway through mangroves. There is a restaurant/bar on the beach (very busy with groups at lunchtime), plus thatched shade umbrellas, a beach volleyball pitch and a toilet. Sunbeds cost CUC$1.50 per day. You can also rent towels and pedalos.

There is no hotel, and the beach therefore remains an undeveloped narrow strip of curving white sand with mangroves at either end. The far west end is quieter and better. The sea is calm, warm and multi-coloured with starfish, but there are patches of weed and not much snorkelling unless you can swim quite far out to the reef, which is marked by buoys. There is a lot of sand and sea grass on the way out to the reef, which can get stirred up with poor visibility, depending on the weather, but the reef itself is shallow with excellent visibility, especially when the sun is shining. There is some good brain coral and anemones here but, although there is a good variety, the fish are quite small. **Mégano**, an islet just offshore, is reached by boat, 12 minutes.

Cayo Levisa

Ferries depart from Palma Rubia daily 1000 and 1800 (15 mins), returning from Cayo Levisa at 0900 and 1700, CUC$15 including drink. Hired cars can be left at the terminal building at Palma Rubia.

Cayo Levisa is part of the **Archipiélago de los Colorados**, with a long, sandy beach and reef running parallel to the shore that offers good snorkelling and scuba diving (lots of fish). The ferry jetty is on the south side of the island from where you follow a boardwalk through the mangroves to get to the hotel on the north side. The island is very quiet and peaceful with nothing much to do on land except walk a circuit of the island, which takes about three hours. It is very relaxing and charming, but take insect repellent.

Diving There are about 23 dive sites between 15 m and 35 m deep and none is more than 30 minutes away by boat. The underwater scenery is characterized by big sponges and enormous black coral trees. Angel fish are very numerous, as are barracuda and schools of jacks. The current is generally quite gentle, so it is an ideal place for beginners and experts alike. There are several bits and pieces of old galleons, most of which have been covered by corals. In season you can windsurf or go on sailing and snorkelling trips to other cays and beaches, but from September when the sea gets rougher there is less available, so check beforehand.

Listings North coast

Where to stay

Cayo Levisa

$$$ Cayo Levisa
T48-756501, www.hotelescubanacan.com.
Book in Havana through any tour agency that deals with **Cubanacán**; packages include transport from Havana, some or all meals and often watersports. Cabins on beach, thatched, with verandas, built in 2 rows but staggered so that each gets a sea view, a/c, TV, fridge, comfortable but not luxurious, spacious, also newer apartments further along the beach and more being built. The restaurant serves bland and boring food and service is awful, the beach bar at the far end serves fresh fried fish or chicken which is preferable, bar, live music. Even on an all-inclusive package you will probably have to pay for your drinks and beach towel rental. There are lots of day-trippers from Havana, but the beach doesn't feel crowded and once they've gone back, you could be on a desert island. Take plenty of insect repellent against mosquitoes and sand fleas/*jejenes*.

BACKGROUND
Afro-Cuban religion

From the mid-16th century to the late 19th century, countless hundreds of thousands of African slaves were brought to Cuba. Torn from dozens of peoples between the Gulf of Guinea and southern Angola, speaking hundreds of languages and dialects, they brought from home only a memory of their customs and beliefs as a shred of comfort in their traumatic new existence on the sugar plantations. The most numerous and culturally most influential group were the Yoruba-speaking agriculturalists from the forests of southeast Nigeria, Dahomey and Togo, who became known collectively in Cuba as *lucumí*. It is their pantheon of deities or *orishas*, and the legends (*pwatakis*) and customs surrounding these, which form the basis of the syncretic Regla de Ocha cult, better known as **Santería**.

Although slaves were ostensibly obliged to become Christians, their owners, anxious to prevent different ethnic groups from uniting, turned a blind eye to their traditional rituals. The Catholic saints thus spontaneously merged or syncretized in the *lucumí* mind with the *orishas*, whose imagined attributes they shared.

Santería, which claims to have at least as many believers as the Roman Catholic Church in Cuba, enshrines a rich cultural heritage. For every *orisha* there is a complex code of conduct, dress (including colour-coded necklaces) and diet to which his or her *hijos* must conform, and a series of chants and rhythms played on the sacred *batá* drums.

Santería is non-sectarian and non-proselytizing, co-existing peacefully with both Christianity and the **Regla Conga** or **Palo Monte** cult brought to Cuba by *congos*, slaves from various Bantu-speaking regions of the Congo basin. Indeed many people are practising believers in both or all three. Found mainly in Havana and Matanzas provinces, **Palo Monte** is a much more fragmented and impoverished belief system than **Regla de Ocha**. Divided into several sects, it is basically animist, using the forces of nature to perform good or evil magic and predict the future in ceremonies involving rum, tobacco and at times gunpowder. The focus of its liturgy is the *nganga*, both a supernatural spirit and the earthenware or iron container in which it dwells along with the *mpungus* or saints. **Regla Conga** boasts a wealth of complex magic symbols or *firmas*, and has retained some exciting drum rhythms.

The **Abakuá Secret Society** is, as its name suggests, not a religion but a closed sect. Open to men only, and upholding traditional *macho* virtues, it has been described as an Afro-Cuban freemasonry, although it claims many non-black devotees. Found almost exclusively in Havana (particularly in the Guanabacoa, Regla and Marianao districts), and in the cities of Matanzas, Cárdenas and Cienfuegos, it has a strong following among dock-workers; indeed, outsiders often claim its members have *de facto* control over those ports. Also known as *ñañiguismo*, the sect originated among slaves brought from the Calabar region of southern Nigeria and Cameroon, whose Cuban descendants are called *carabalí*. Some **ñáñigos** claim the society was formally founded in 1836 in Regla, across the bay from Havana, but there is evidence that it already existed at the time of the 1812 anti-slavery conspiracy. **Abakuá** shares with freemasonry the fraternal aims of mutual assistance, as well as a series of seven secret commandments, secret signs and arcane ceremonies involving special vestments.

Practicalities

Getting there

Flights from the UK
Direct flights take about nine hours. **Virgin Atlantic** flies from London direct, while **Air France**, **Iberia** and **KLM** operate connecting services via Paris, Madrid and Amsterdam respectively. Indirect flights can be cheaper, but are more time consuming and less convenient.

Flights from the rest of Europe
Direct flights are available from Amsterdam, Frankfurt, Madrid, Milan, Munich, Paris, Rome and Zurich depending on the season and the Cuban airport. All flights from Europe arrive in Havana around 2000-2130, returning overnight.

Flights from North America
Since 1962, US citizens have only been permitted to visit Cuba providing they can prove they are travelling for journalistic, cultural, sporting or scientific purposes, although many defied the ban and travelled via a gateway city, such as Nassau, Mexico City, Cancún or Grand Cayman. However, in 2015-2016 the rules were relaxed allowing 12 categories of travel, and more US citizens are now flying to Cuba, initially on chartered flights from Los Angeles, Miami and Tampa, mostly either on people-to-people programmes or Cuban Americans visiting relatives. In December 2015, the governments of the USA and Cuba announced the resumption of direct commercial flights for the first time since the early 1960s and airlines such as **American Airlines** are expected to start flying in 2016. Up to 30 US flights a day will be allowed.

There are lots of charter and scheduled flights from Canada (Montréal and Toronto) to various airports in Cuba, particularly in winter.

Flights from the Caribbean and Latin America
There are flights from the Dominican Republic, Grand Cayman and Martinique and frequent flights to Havana from several Mexican cities. **Avianca** ⓘ *www.avianca.com*, flies to Cuba from most Central and South American countries. The Cuban charter airline **Aerogaviota** ⓘ *www.aerogaviota.com*, also connects Cuba with a growing list of other Caribbean and Central American countries.

Flights from Australia and New Zealand
There are no direct flights to Cuba from Australia or New Zealand; all flights connect in a European, Canadian or Latin American city. Even if you fly **Virgin** all the way, you will have to change airports in London (Heathrow–Gatwick). Round-the-world tickets offer the best deals, with Cuba added onto a South or Central American itinerary.

Airport information
Cuba has several airports classified as international, but Havana's José Martí airport is by far the largest. Terminal 1 is for domestic flights. Terminal 2 is for US charters. Terminal 3 is for international flights.

Arriving at José Martí International Airport Terminal 3 has exchange facilities open during normal banking hours, snack bars, shops and a 24-hour tourist information bureau (**Infotur**, limited information). Car hire desks are outside the door to your right. The airport is safe at night, which is when the European flights arrive. There is no airport hotel and you will need to take a taxi to any accommodation. See page 30 for transport from Havana airport into the city.

Immigration can be very slow with long queues. You should expect to take 1½ hours to clear Immigration, pass through security and collect your bags if arriving on a busy flight, eg **Virgin Atlantic** from London.

Departures Allow plenty of time for check-in. The seating everywhere at Havana airport is uncomfortable. The restaurant upstairs, before you go through passport control, is okay for sandwiches or full meals and will be your last chance to hear a live Cuban band while eating. The food on offer in the departure lounge is awful, with a choice between a microwaved hot dog or a soggy pizza. As most European flights leave late at night this can be a problem if you have a long wait for a (delayed) **Air France** or **Iberia** flight, but you can savour your last mojito in this vast, uncomfortable shed. The selection of shops is limited but there is lots of rum, coffee and biscuits on sale. The selection of cigars is poor; if you know which brand you particularly want, get it in a specialist shop before you get to the airport. Rum costs much the same as elsewhere. The Cubita coffee, on the other hand, is marginally cheaper than in town.

Sea

There are no ferry services between Cuba and neighbouring islands, but a ferry to link Havana with Florida, USA, is in the planning stages. Havana, Cienfuegos and Santiago receive tourist cruise vessels.

Getting around

Shortages of fuel and spare parts in Cuba still cause difficulties in the supply of transport. The government has segregated tourists from Cubans and encourages them to hire cars or travel on dedicated buses to maximize foreign exchange income. The cheapest forms of transport are reserved for Cubans.

Internal flights are frequent and efficient but generally only link Havana with other towns, so you cannot criss-cross the island by air. **Roads** are in need of resurfacing, but there is little traffic, except in Havana, which is a bit of a nightmare if you have just arrived. Out of the city, roads are fairly empty and you can often travel for miles without seeing another vehicle. **Buses** operated by Viazul and paid for in CUC$ run on long-distance routes between cities commonly visited by foreigners, while the more extensive **Astro** bus network is reserved for Cubans. All long-distance travel by foreigners is paid for in CUC$. **Tour buses** are flexible, allowing you to stay a night or two in, say, Pinar del Río, before rejoining the tour for the return to Havana. **Transtur** now runs some of its tour buses as a scheduled service, for example between Havana and Trinidad. **Car hire** is available, although you may not get the car you want unless you arrange it in advance from abroad. The disadvantage of car hire is that it is expensive and petrol stations are not always conveniently located, but you will have the freedom of going where you want, when you want and you will have the roads almost to yourself. A good way of getting around and meeting the people is to hire a local taxi to take you out for a day. If there are two or three of you it can work out cheaper and more enjoyable than taking an organized excursion on a tour bus. Most **rail** journeys are fraught with difficulties and generally are subject to breakdowns and long delays. There have also been some fatal accidents. Repairs and new rolling stock are awaited.

Air

There are **Cubana de Aviación** or **AeroCaribbean** services between Havana and most of the main towns and beach resorts to the centre and east. **Aerogaviota** ⓘ *www.aerogaviota. com*, is a charter airline owned by the armed forces, with flights from Playa Baracoa airport outside Havana. Tourists must pay air fares in CUC$. It is advisable to pre-book flights at home as demand is very heavy, although you can get interprovincial flights from hotel tour desks if you are on a package deal. It is difficult to book flights from one city to another when you are not at the point of departure, except from Havana; the computers are not able to cope.

Rail

Train journeys are only recommended for the adventurous and patient traveller, as long delays and breakdowns must be expected. Arrive at the station at least one hour before the scheduled departure time.

> **Tip...**
> Take your own food with you on train journeys. Cold fried meat with rice and black beans is sometimes sold in a cardboard box for CUP$15 – you have to tear off a piece of the box to use as an eating tool – but this is sold soon after leaving Havana and there will be nothing else available for the rest of the trip, however long that may be. You may be able to get something at intervening stations, but make sure you have pesos cubanos with you.

Fares are reasonable but have to be paid for in CUC$, which will usually entitle you to a waiting area, seat reservation and to board the train before the big rush starts. There is a CUC$ ticket office in every station. Long-distance trains allow only seated passengers. All carriages are smoking areas; they are extremely cold unless the air conditioning is broken, so take warm clothes, a torch (needed for the toilets) and toilet paper. Bicycles can be carried but often cost more than the fare for a person. The best source of information on trains, timetables and fares is **The Man in Seat 61** ① *http://www.seat61.com/Cuba.*

Road

Bus

Local The local word for a bus is *guagua*. Urban transport is varied: there are regular buses in Havana and other major centres, but you're likely to see horse-drawn *coches* in provincial towns. The urban bus fare throughout Cuba is 40 centavos. Urban tickets can only be bought in pesos cubanos and it helps to have the exact fare. The government prefers foreigners to use taxis rather than local buses.

> **Tip...**
> Do not forget the etiquette for queues when buying tickets at **Viazul** head office and always ask who is last in line ('*El ultimo?*').

Long distance For bus transport to other provinces from Havana there are two companies: **Viazul** and **Astro**, but foreigners can only travel on **Viazul** (**Viajes Azul**) ① *Av 26 entre Av Zoológico y Ulloa, Nuevo Vedado, Havana, T7-881 1413, www.viazul.com, ticket sales 0700-1700, 1900-2230.* The buses are reasonably comfortable and air conditioned; films are shown on longer journeys. Tickets can be bought online, but you pay 8% more than in the ticket offices. Children under 12 pay half price; those small enough not to need a seat travel free. It is essential to book in advance during peak season, especially in August, which can be very busy with an increased number of Cuban tourists. Even booking up to two or three days in advance may not be sufficient to guarantee a seat, especially if you are a family with children or travelling in a group. There is a weight limit for luggage of 20 kg.

Astro ① *Terminal de Omnibus Nacional, Boyeros y 19 de Mayo, Havana, T7-870 3397/9401, daily 0700-2100,* is mainly used by Cubans who often have to book tickets (in pesos cubanos) months in advance at busy times of the year. Away from the capital and off the beaten track, it is less

> **Tip...**
> Baggage handlers in Havana have an irritating habit of demanding a tip even though they hardly touch your bag. Any small coin will satisfy them.

controversial for tourists to travel on **Astro** to minor towns and pay in pesos; in fact you may have no other option. The **Viazul** terminal in Havana is a long way from the centre and you will have to get a taxi, but in other cities **Viazul** and **Astro** use the same bus terminal.

Car

In view of the difficulties of getting public transport to out-of-the-way places, you can save a considerable amount of time and hassle by hiring a car. However, it is the most expensive form of travel. Breakdowns are not unknown and you may be stuck many kilometres from the nearest town. Be careful about picking up hitchhikers, although this can be an interesting way of meeting Cubans and of acquiring useful navigational information. Cubans drive on the right-hand side of the road.

Fuel Petrol stations are not self-service. Petrol and diesel are available in **Servi Cupet** stations and must be paid for in CUC$ at around CUC$1.10 per litre for Regular and diesel and CUC$1.30 for Especial. Car hire companies will fill the tank at the beginning of your rental period and you must return the car empty at the end. A number of hire cars use diesel, which can be more difficult to get hold of than petrol. Only the main fuel stations sell diesel.

Main roads *Autopistas* were incredibly empty of traffic during the 1980s and 1990s, but as the economy picked up, traffic increased. Cubans often use the hard surface for other purposes, such as drying rice on the roadside. Oxen, horses, donkeys, bicycles and tractors will be sharing the fast lane with you. The dogs on the side of the road are often not dead, just asleep. Watch out for low-flying vultures preying on any animals that really are dead. Cubans slow right down and give them a wide berth; they can do enormous damage to your car if you do hit one. Main roads can be good places to shop for fresh fruit and vegetables; vendors stand by the roadside (or in the road) or sell from broken down trucks.

Finding your way Most ordinary roads are in reasonable condition, but minor roads can be very badly maintained and signposting is uniformly atrocious or non-existent. Even where there are road signs, they are usually so bleached by the sun that they are illegible until you draw level with them. Finding your way across a large city like Havana can present problems, in spite of the courteous assistance of police and pedestrians. Your best bet is to get the *Guía de Carreteras* (Road Guide, published by Directorio Turístico de Cuba) and follow the distances marked between junctions. Getting into towns is usually easy; finding a road out again is more difficult.

Safety There are numerous police checks on the roads. Always have all your documentation to hand. Driving at night can be extremely hazardous and is not recommended. Even in major cities, you are likely to encounter horses, cattle, pigs, goats and sheep monopolizing the road without any semblance of lighting. In addition, cyclists, bullock carts and other vehicles without lights are common. It is best to travel early in the day and reach your destination before nightfall. During the winter months, November to March, sunrise is at 0700 and sunset at 1830 (2000 in summer months).

Car hire
There are state rental companies at international airports and most large hotels, or contact the companies direct. During July and August it is extremely difficult to hire a car without booking well in advance. It is advisable to arrange car hire from home before you travel. Drivers need to be a minimum 21 years of age, although for some vehicles the age limit goes up to 25 years. You must present your passport and home driving licence.

Costs All car rental agencies are state owned and operated, so there is no real competition on prices. **Cubacar** ⓘ *www.transtur.cu*, **Havanautos** ⓘ *www.havanautos.cu*, and **Rex** ⓘ *www.rex.cu*, all belong to **Transtur** ⓘ *www.transtur.cu*. **Vía Rent-a-Car** belongs to **Gaviota** ⓘ *www.gaviota-grupo.com*. **Rex** is the most expensive but also the best, with excellent customer service and good cars. Rental costs a minimum of CUC$40 a day (or CUC$50 for air conditioning) with limited mileage of 100 km a day plus CUC$10-20 a day for insurance, or CUC$50-88 per day with unlimited mileage. Weekly rental offers better rates. Most vehicles are Japanese or Korean makes; Suzuki jeeps can be hired for six to 12 hours in beach areas. Moped rental (*moto*) is around US$25 per day, cheaper for longer.

Non-US credit cards are accepted for the rental. If you pay cash it will have to be in advance and the company will still need a credit card for a deposit, which may be debited for the whole rental even if you have paid up front. In practice, you may find car hire rates prohibitively expensive when small cars are 'unavailable' and a four-door sedan costing CUC$93 per day (unlimited kilometres, insurance included) is your only option. Staff have been reported to be 'unhelpful' in finding the car you want. However, it pays to shop around, even between offices of the same company.

Make sure the tank is really full when you start; you should leave it empty when you return the vehicle. If you hire a car in Havana but want to drop it off at the airport, companies will charge you an extra CUC$10 or so, although this is sometimes waived if you bargain hard.

Security Always take out full insurance and on return beware of extra charges for dirty exterior, dirty interior and scratches on the paintwork caused by flying stones. Watch out for theft of the windscreen wipers, licence plates, radio and spare tyre; you will have to pay about CUC$350 if your spare tyre is stolen unless you take out the costly extra insurance. Always arrange secure parking overnight, usually by paying someone to watch your car for CUC$2. If you are stopped by the police, do not pay an on-the-spot fine. Instead, your misdemeanour should be noted on your car rental documents, and you pay the hire company at the end of your lease.

Cycling

For people who really want to explore the country in depth and independently, cycling is an excellent option. A good-quality bicycle is essential if you are going to spend many hours in the saddle, although that does not mean it has to be very sophisticated. We have heard from cyclists who have toured Cuba without gears, although they did have plenty of muscle.

Safety Look out for potholes. Cuba has an extensive network of tarmac and concrete roads, which are in good condition in areas of heaviest tourist use, but suffer from lack of maintenance and storm damage in rural areas. The old cars, buses and trucks on the roads may be fascinating to see, but they belch unpleasant fumes from their exhausts, which are difficult to avoid in towns. Watch out for railway crossings that have no barriers or warning lights. They often look unused, but it is absolutely essential that you stop and look for approaching trains, particularly in sugar-growing areas. Plan to finish each journey in daylight, as cycling in the dark is dangerous. Street lighting can be subject to power cuts. Other vehicles on the road often do not dip their headlights for bikes. Book your accommodation in advance to check they can safely store bikes.

Hitchhiking

With the shortage of fuel and decline in public transport after 1991, Cubans took to organized hitchhiking to get about. At every major junction outside towns throughout Cuba you will find the *Amarillos*: traffic wardens who organize a queue, stop traffic to find out where the trucks or vans are going, and then load them with passengers. Foreigners are not allowed to use this service, nor to travel on trucks. Cubans also hitchhike (*a botella*) unofficially and get rides in ancient cars, trucks and other makeshift vehicles. Cubans are not allowed to carry paying foreigners in their vehicles unless they have a licence to operate a taxi, so be aware that if a Cuban agrees to give you a lift, he/she could get into trouble if the vehicle is stopped by the authorities.

Taxis

There are three types of taxi: **tourist taxis**, **Cuban taxis** (*colectivos*) and **private taxis** (*particulares*). **Tourist taxis**, paid for in CUC$, can be hired for driving around; you pay for the distance, not the waiting time. On short routes, fares are sometimes metered. **Cuban taxis**, or *colectivos*, also operate on fixed routes and pick you up only if you know where to stand for certain destinations. The flat rate fare is CUP$10. Travelling on them is an adventure and a complicated cultural experience. **Private taxis**, *particulares*, are cheaper than other taxis. A *particular* who pays his tax will usually display a 'taxi' sign, which can be a hand-written piece of board, but have a private registration plate. Some have meters; in others you have to negotiate a price in CUC$.

For long distances you can negotiate with official taxis as well as *particulares*, and the price should be around CUC$10 per hour. Taxis can work out cheaper than going on organized tours if you are in a group and are prepared to bargain. As a general rule, the cost will depend on the quality of your Spanish and how well you know the area. One family paid CUC$80 to travel from Havana to Viñales by taxi, although someone else was quoted CUC$50 for the return journey.

Essentials A-Z

Accident and emergency

Ambulance: T104. **Fire**: T105. **Police**: Policía Nacional Revolucionaria (PNR) T106. The main police station in Havana is at Dragones entre Lealtad y Escobar, Centro, T7-863 2441.

Clothing

This is generally informal and summer calls for the very lightest clothing. Sunglasses, a high-factor sun lotion and some kind of head cover are recommended. A jersey and light raincoat or umbrella are needed in the cooler months; a jersey or fleece is also needed if you plan to travel on a/c internal flights, buses (particularly overnight on **Viazul** bus) or trains, which are very cold. You should be appropriately dressed to go into a church or temple. Cubans dress up to go out at night.

Customs and duty free

Duty-free allowances include personal baggage and articles for personal use, as well as 1 carton of cigarettes and 2 bottles of alcoholic drinks. You may take in up to 10 kg of medicine, so long as it is in its original packaging. It is prohibited to bring in fresh fruit and vegetables, which will be confiscated if found. On departure you may take out only 20 cigars without a receipt; 50 cigars in their original package, unopened, sealed with the official hologram, and up to an amount not exceeding CUC$5000 in the original packaging, unopened, sealed with the official hologram, with a formal sales invoice from the authorized store where they were bought. You can also export up to 6 bottles of rum and personal jewellery.

To take out works of art you must have permission from the **Registro Nacional de Bienes Culturales de la Dirección de Patrimonio del Ministerio de Cultura**. Books that are more than 50 years old may not be taken out of the country, nor those belonging to Ediciones R. For further details on customs regulations, see www.aduana.co.cu.

Disabled travellers

There are few facilities for disabled people. In the resort areas new hotels have been built with a few rooms adapted for people using wheelchairs, but the older, state-run, 3-star hotels usually have no facilities and neither do *casas particulares*. Cuba is not easy to get around in a wheelchair and a certain amount of determination is required. Pavements are usually built up much higher than the roads, because of rain and flash flooding, which makes crossing the road hazardous. Potholes and loose paving stones compound the difficulties. If you are travelling independently it is not impossible to get around and stay in private accommodation, but you will have to do plenty of research first to make sure you can have a ground-floor room and that passages and doorways are negotiable with wheels. You can use the bus company **Viazul** if you have someone to help you, or you can hire your own vehicle. Don't be discouraged, you will not be the first disabled person to travel around Cuba and Cubans are tremendously helpful and supportive.

Electricity

110 volts, 3 phase 60 cycles, AC. Plugs and sockets are usually of the American flat 2-pin type, so bring an adaptor from home if necessary. In some new tourist hotels however, European plugs are used, with 220 volts, check in advance if it is important to you. Some *casas particulares* now have both 110v and 220v, which is better for charging laptops, phones, etc. Do not be surprised if there are power cuts.

Embassies and consulates

A list of embassies in Havana can be found at http://embassy goabroad.com.

Festivals

January

New Year is celebrated around the country with great fanfare, largely because it coincides with **Liberation Day**, marking the end of the Batista dictatorship, on 1 Jan. There is lots of music and dancing, outdoor discos and general merriment, fattened pigs are roasted, washed down with copious quantities of rum.

Cubadanza is a twice-yearly dance festival with workshops and performances. Contact Danza Contemporánea de Cuba, www.dccuba.com.

February

Havana International Book Fair is held at La Cabaña; a commercial fair in the castle, immensely popular with book-hungry families, who come for a day out. Look out for new book launches. Also held in many cities around the island, www.cubaliteraria.com.

Vuelta a Cuba is a cycle race from east to west of the island.

Cigar Festival, www.festivaldelhabano.com, is for true aficionados of Habanos. Held at the Palacio de las Convenciones, you can learn about the history of cigars and there are opportunities for visits to tobacco plantations and cigar factories.

March

Bienal de la Habana is held over a month and takes place every 2 years (next in 2017), gathering over 200 artists from 40 countries in the Centro de Arte Contemporáneo Wifredo Lam, Centro de Arte La Casona, Parque Morro-Cabaña, Pabellón Cuba and other venues, www.bienalhabana.cult.cu.

Spring in Havana: International Festival of Electroacoustic Music in Havana, with workshops and performances.

May

Ernest Hemingway International Billfishing Tournament is one of the major events at the Marina Hemingway. www.internationalhemingwaytournament.com.

Festival Internacional de Poesía de La Habana, at Cuba Poesía, Hospital esq 25, http://www.cubapoesia.cult.cu.

June

Festival Danzón Habana, held at the Teatro América, Centro Hispanoamericano de Cultura y Unión Fraternal, at the end of the month, musicians and dancers celebrate *danzón* and each year it is dedicated to a different Latin American country; contact ireartes@hotmail.com.

July

Cuballet de Verano is a summer dance festival with workshops and courses for dancers and dance teachers organized by Laura Alonso and ProDanza, www.prodanza.cult.cu.

August

Cubadanza, the 2nd of the year, with workshops and courses, see Jan for details.

October

Havana International Ballet Festival, held every other year in the 2nd half of the month at the Gran Teatro, Teatro Nacional and Teatro Mella. Run by Alicia Alonso, head of the Cuban National Ballet, www.festivalballethabana.cult.cu.

November

Havana Contemporary Music Festival, held at UNEAC and theatres mid-month. www.musicacontemporanea.cult.cu.

Marabana, Havana's marathon, on the 3rd Sun of the month. www.inder.cu/marabana.

December

International Festival of New Latin American Cinema, shows prize-winning films (no subtitles) at cinemas around

Havana. This is the foremost film festival in Latin America with the best of Cuban and Latin American films along with documentaries and independent cinema from Europe and the USA. See the stars as well as the films, as the festival attracts big-name actors and directors, www.habanafilmfestival.com.

International Jazz Plaza Festival is held at theatres and the Casa de la Cultura de Plaza. It is one of the world's major jazz festivals with the best of Cuban and international jazz. There are masterclasses and workshops available and the event is organized by Grammy winner Jesús 'Chucho' Valdés. http://jazzcuba.com.

Gay and lesbian travellers

Cuba has in the past been notoriously homophobic and after the Revolution many homosexuals were sent to hard labour camps to be 'rehabilitated'. The Mariel exodus was characterized as being the flight of criminals and homosexuals, who could no longer stand their human rights being flouted. However, attitudes gradually changed, and although Cuba is still a macho society, there is an increasing tolerance of gays just as there is more religious freedom. The film, *Fresa y Chocolate*, did much to stimulate debate and acceptance. For an excellent account of Cuban attitudes to homosexuals, before and after the Revolution and up to the present, read Ian Lumsden's *Machos, Maricones and Gays, Cuba and Homosexuality*, published by the Temple University Press, Philadelphia and Latin American Bureau, London. Gay travellers will not generally encounter any problems in Cuba: there are no laws against homosexuality and physical assaults are rare. However, in practice, there can be difficulties with accommodation if you want to stay in *casas particulares*, as some owners prefer not to rent rooms to same-sex partners, particularly if one of them is Cuban.

Gifts

Some items are in short supply in Cuba and will be much appreciated: T-shirts (preferably with something written on them), household medicines such as paracetamol or aspirin, cosmetics, cotton wool, tampons, soap, pens, pencils, notebooks and writing paper. Those with access to CUC$, such as *casa particular* owners, generally have access to imported goods, but schools, churches and other community organizations can distribute your gifts to those genuinely in need.

Health

Cuba has a high-quality national health service and is one of the healthiest countries in Latin America. Travel in Cuba poses no health risk to the average visitor provided sensible precautions are taken. It is important to see your GP or specialist travel clinic at least 6 weeks before departure for general advice on any travel risks and necessary vaccinations. Check the details of your health insurance for Cuba and take a copy of your insurance policy with you. Also get a dental check, know your own blood group and if you suffer a long-term condition such as diabetes or epilepsy, obtain a Medic Alert bracelet/necklace (www.medicalert.co.uk). If you wear glasses, take a copy of your prescription.

Vaccinations

It is important to confirm your primary courses and boosters are up to date. There are no vaccinations demanded by immigration officials in Cuba, however it is advisable to vaccinate against **tetanus**, **typhoid** and **hepatitis A**. Vaccines sometimes advised are **hepatitis B**, **rabies** and **diphtheria**. **Yellow fever** vaccination is not required unless you are coming directly from an infected country in Africa or South America. Although **cholera** vaccination is largely ineffective, immigration officers may ask for proof of such vaccination if coming from a country where an epidemic has occurred. Check www.who.int for updates. **Malaria** is not normally a danger in Cuba.

Health risks

The most common affliction of travellers to any country is probably diarrhoea and the same is true of Cuba. Tap water is good in most areas of the country, but bottled water is widely available and recommended. Swimming in sea or river water that has been contaminated by sewage can be a cause of diarrhoea; ask locally if it is safe. Diarrhoea may also be caused by viruses, bacteria (such as E-coli), protozoal (such as giardia), salmonella and cholera. It may be accompanied by vomiting or by severe abdominal pain. Any kind of diarrhoea responds well to the replacement of water and salts. Sachets of rehydration salts can be bought in most pharmacies and can be dissolved in boiled water. If the symptoms persist, consult a doctor.

There is no malaria in Cuba but dengue fever has been reported and there are lots of mosquitoes in the wetlands, so take insect repellent and cover up to avoid being bitten. Sleep off the ground and use a mosquito net and some kind of insecticide. DEET (Di-ethyltoluamide) is the gold standard. Apply the repellent every 4-6 hrs but more often if you are sweating heavily. If a non-DEET product is used, check who tested it. Validated products (tested at the London School of Hygiene and Tropical Medicine) include Mosiguard, Non-DEET Jungle formula and non-DEET Autan. If you want to use citronella remember that it must be applied very frequently (ie hourly) to be effective.

The climate is hot; Cuba is a tropical country and protection against the sun will be needed. To reduce the risk of sunburn and skin cancer, make sure you pack high-factor sun cream, light-coloured loose clothing and a hat.

Medical services

Medical services are no longer free for foreign visitors in areas where international clinics (Clínicas del Sol) and pharmacies (Farmacias Internacionales) exist; see www.healthservicecuba.com for a list. These services are designed specifically for tourists and charge in CUC$ (credit cards accepted), although charges are generally lower than those in Western countries. Visitors requiring medical attention will be sent to these clinics wherever possible; emergencies are handled on an ad hoc basis. Away from Havana and tourist enclaves with on-site medical services, visitors are still treated free of charge. Make sure you have adequate insurance (see below). Remember you cannot dial any toll-free numbers abroad so make sure you have a contact number. The following are a list of medical services in Havana:

Clínica Central Cira García, 20 4101 esq 41, Playa, Havana, T7-204 2811, www.cirag.cu. Payment in CUC$, emergency health care, also the place to go for emergency dental treatment. There are other branches at the Hotel Comodoro, Sevilla, Habana Libre, Marina Hemingway, Terminal 3 at the airport and at Clínica Playas del Este, Villa Tarará, and Villa Panamericana to the east.

The **pharmacy** at the **Clínica Central Cira García** (open 24 hrs) T7-204 2880, sells prescription and patent drugs and medical supplies that are often unavailable in other pharmacies, as does the **Farmacia Internacional**, Av 41, esq 20, Playa, T7-204 4350, daily 0900-2100, and the **Habana Libre**, L y 23, Vedado, T7-838 4593. **Camilo Cienfuegos Pharmacy**, L y 13, Vedado, T7-8323507, ext 113, daily 24 hrs.

There are international clinics around the country in tourist resort areas such as Varadero. Medical procedures for foreigners, or health tourism, are run by **Servimed**, www.healthservicecuba.com.

Useful websites

www.bgtha.org British Global and Travel Health Association.

www.cdc.gov Centres for Disease Control and Prevention (USA).

www.fco.gov.uk British Foreign and Commonwealth Office travel site has useful information on each country, people, climate and a list of UK embassies/consulates.

www.fitfortravel.scot.nhs.uk A-Z of vaccine/health advice for each country.

www.itg.be Institute for Tropical Medicine, Antwerp.

www.nathnac.org National Travel Health Network and Centre (NaTHNaC).

www.nhs.uk/nhsengland/ Healthcareabroad/pages/ Healthcareabroad.aspx UK National Health Service.

Insurance

Travel health insurance is mandatory for entry into Cuba and must include sufficient cover for medical evacuation by air. We strongly recommend that you invest in a good insurance policy that covers you for theft or loss of possessions and money, the cost of medical and dental treatment, cancellation of flights, delays in travel arrangement, accidents, missed departures, lost baggage, lost passport and personal liability and legal expenses. Also check on inclusion of 'dangerous activities'. These generally include climbing, diving, horse riding, parachuting and even trekking. Always read the small print carefully. Not all policies cover ambulance, helicopter rescue or emergency flights home, and not all policies cover Cuba.

All loss must be reported to the police and/or hotel authorities within 24 hrs of discovery and a written report obtained. This is notoriously difficult to obtain in Cuba. **Asistur**, www.asistur.cu, is linked to overseas insurance companies and can help with emergency hospital treatment, repatriations, robbery, direct transfer of funds to Cuba, financial and legal problems, travel insurance claims, etc. For (24-hr) emergencies go to the main office: Prado 208, entre Colón y Trocadero, La Habana Vieja, T7-866 8339/866 8920, www.asistur.cu. There is also an office in Varadero.

Internet

Cubans' access to the internet is tightly controlled and limited to those who can afford to pay in CUC\$. The only Cubans who are permitted to use the internet at home are civil servants, doctors and party representatives, on a regular phone line paid for in pesos; others have to pay in CUC\$. However, restrictions on access to the internet are being relaxed as part of the negotiations with the USA. Wi-Fi hotspots have been introduced in most towns of any size and more are coming. These are usually in plazas, outside tourist hotels or outside the phone company's offices, and can be easily identified by groups of Cubans using their smart phones or tablets and chatting to friends and relatives abroad. Be careful of theft if you decide to do likewise. The telephone company, **Etecsa**, sells prepaid cards that give you an access code and a password code for when you log in; these cost CUC\$2 per hr throughout the island. Touts will sell you cards at a premium if you don't want to queue at Etecsa, or if they have 'run out'.

Foreign tourists using the internet will invariably be asked to show their passport. If you need a computer terminal, the large, international hotels of 4 or 5 stars, such as the **Nacional**, **Habana Libre**, **Parque Central** and **Meliá Cohiba** in Havana, have business centres with computers for internet access, but this is the most expensive way of checking emails. Nearly every hotel for foreigners now has internet access for its guests in some form or other and this is always worth trying even if you are not staying there. Most hotels now have 1 or 2 terminals in the lobby, which are not reserved for guests. The main telephone office in each town usually has internet access, but if not, look for **Telepunto** offices, or **Etecsa** cabins (large blue telephone boxes) with international and national phone services and a computer for internet access. The best place in La Habana Vieja is Etecsa's **Telepunto**, Habana 406 entre Obispo y Obrapía, T7-866 0547, daily 0830-1900, which has 12 terminals for internet access.

Language

Spanish is the official language, spoken fast with some consonants dropped. In the main tourist areas you will find staff often speak several languages, but off the beaten track you will need Spanish or very efficient sign language. English is becoming more commonly used; it is a university entrance requirement and encouraged by the influx of Canadian and now American tourists. German, Italian and French are spoken by many people working in the tourist industry and tour guides are usually multilingual. Many older people also speak Russian.

Money

CUC$1=US$1, CAN$1.30, €0.90, £0.77 (Jul 2016).
Cuba operates a dual currency system with a domestic peso and a convertible peso. There are plans to unify them, but no timetable has been announced.

The **peso cubano** (CP$ or CUP$), also referred to as *moneda nacional* (MN) has notes for 1, 3, 5, 10, 20, 50, 100, 200, 500 and 1000 pesos, and coins for 5, 20 and 40 centavos and 1 and 3 pesos. You must have a supply of coins if you want to use the local town buses (CUP$0.20 or 0.40). The 20 centavo coin is called a *peseta*. Cubans are paid in pesos cubanos and pay for most of their goods in the same currency.

The **peso convertible** (CUC$, pronounced 'cook') has a different set of notes and coins. It is fully exchangeable with authorized hard currencies such as euro, sterling and Canadian dollars. Foreigners are expected

to pay for their accommodation, meals, transport and other items with the peso convertible. In some tourist enclaves, such as Varadero, the euro is accepted as well. Remember to spend or exchange any pesos convertibles before you leave as they are worthless outside Cuba. The exchange rate fluctuates around 24 pesos cubanos (CUP$) to the peso convertible (CUC$).

There is no black market. Food in the *agromercados* (markets), at street stalls and on trains, as well as books and popular cigarettes (but not in every shop), can be bought in pesos cubanos. You will need pesos cubanos for the toilet, rural trains, food at roadside *cafeterías* during a journey and drinks and snacks for a bus or train journey. Away from tourist hotels, in smaller towns, you will need pesos cubanos for everything. Visitors on pre-paid package tours do not need pesos cubanos.

Exchange

In 2016 Cuba announced it would rescind a 10% tax on exchange transactions involving the US dollar but the measure appears to be dependent on the USA removing restrictions on Cuban bank accounts, so the tax remains for the time being. It is therefore still better to bring currencies such as the euro, sterling, or Canadian dollars. It is best to bring lots of cash but take care not to bring any notes with writing or extraneous stamps on them as they will not be accepted. There are **banks** and **Cadecas** (*casas de cambio*) for changing money. The latter have longer opening hours and are usually open at weekends. If arriving at Havana airport, change what you need for a couple of days at the exchange desk there, then go to a Cadeca in town for larger amounts. Wear a money belt to store your cash safely.

Plastic/Banks (ATMs)

Credit cards issued in the USA will not be accepted. A British credit card issued by a US bank (eg **MBNA**) is not valid. Visa or MasterCard **credit cards** are acceptable in most places. American Express, no matter where issued, is unacceptable.

You can obtain cash advances with a credit card at banks and Cadecas, but it is best to bring plenty of cash to avoid hefty fees and commissions. ATMs (dispensing CUC$ only) have been installed in most banks, but it is often quicker and easier to queue at the counter. All credit card transactions are converted from CUC$ into US dollars at point of use, and your bank or credit card company will then convert that into your own currency, making all credit card transactions very costly when you include the US dollar conversion tax. There are no toll-free numbers for you to call if your credit card is lost or stolen. You will have to phone home to the financial institution that issued you the card in order to put a stop on its use. Make a note of this number before you leave home, together with your credit card account number and keep them separate from your card. If you get really stuck and need money sent urgently to Cuba, you can get money transferred from any major commercial bank abroad direct to a Cuban bank, to **Asistur** (see Insurance, page 146) immediately for a 10% commission, or to **Western Union** which is used largely by Cubans abroad to send money home to relatives.

Cost of living/travelling

Raúl Castro has increased wages and removed the cap on salaries to allow bonuses to be paid but still most state employees earn no more than CUP$300-500 a month, whatever their profession. Housing, education and medical care is provided at no cost and some basic foodstuffs are still rationed and heavily subsidized (see Food and drink, page 20), but making ends meet is extremely hard. Most consumer goods are priced in pesos convertibles, and families have to have access to CUC$ to buy nice things for their home and family. It is therefore not surprising that Cubans will do almost anything to earn *divisa* (hard currency) and many families make sure that at least one member works in the dollar economy, eg tourism. The entire peso economy is subsidized, and although there are opportunities for travellers to use pesos cubanos, it is understandable that you will be expected to pay your way in CUC$. You earn hard currency, so you pay in hard currency.

It is important to remember that Cuba is competing in the Caribbean market, and its neighbours are selling themselves as luxury destinations. Compared with islands like the Bahamas or the Virgin Islands, it is cheap, but if you have just come from a backpacking trip through Central or South America and want a stop-off on an island before you go home, you will find your last few dollars don't go very far. However, by Caribbean standards, Cuba has it all. You can stay at luxury hotels (over CUC$100 a night for a double room), dine in elegant restaurants (up to CUC$50 per person) and frequent world-famous nightclubs, or for those on a mid-range budget you can stay in pleasant colonial hotels (CUC$60-80 for a double room), eat reasonably well (CUC$15-20 for a decent dinner) and find plenty to do in the evenings in the clubs, theatres and cinemas (CUC$2-10).

Anyone with a more restricted budget should consider staying with Cuban families in the *casa particular* system (CUC$25-35 per room in Havana), which is the equivalent of a bed and breakfast place in Europe. You can eat at private restaurants (CUC$7-15) or on the street, changing a few dollars into pesos to make resources stretch further, and head for a **Casa de la Trova** (CUC$1-5) for entertainment. At the bottom end of the scale you could get by on CUC$40 a day, including transport, but few treats. It depends what you want to do, after all, sitting on the beach is free if you don't want a sunbed. A beer can cost CUC$1-3 depending on where you go and a mojito can vary from CUC$2 in a local bar to CUC$5 in the touristy **Bodeguita del Medio** in Havana, a Hemingway haunt. Based on 2 people sharing, this budget would include

CUC$3-5 for breakfast, CUC$10 for transport or an excursion and CUC$10 for snacks, entry fees and entertainment. Increasing that budget by 50% would give you flexibility to take advantage of opportunities when they arise, stay in a more comfortable *casa* and have the freedom to explore a bit more.

Public holidays

See also Festivals, page 143.

1 Jan New Year coincides with **Liberation Day**, marking the end of the Batista dictatorship. Liberation Day is celebrated around the country with great fanfare.

1 May **Labour Day**.

25, 26, 27 Jul **Revolution Day**.

10 Oct **Beginning of War of Independence**.

25 Dec **Christmas Day**.

Other festive days which are not public holidays are **28 Jan** (birth of José Martí, 1853), **24 Feb** (anniversary of renewal of War of Independence, 1895), **8 Mar** (International Women's Day), **13 Mar** (anniversary of 1957 attack on presidential palace in Havana by a group of young revolutionaries), **19 Apr** (anniversary of defeat of mercenaries at Bay of Pigs, 1961), **30 Jul** (martyrs of the Revolution day), **8 Oct** (death of Che Guevara, 1967), **28 Oct** (death of Camilo Cienfuegos, 1959), **27 Nov** (death by firing squad of 8 medical students by Spanish colonial government, 1871), **7 Dec** (death of Antonio Maceo in battle in 1896). These dates are often marked by speeches and displays by school children.

Safety

The island is generally safer than many of its Caribbean and Latin neighbours and most Cubans are very hospitable. It is a serious crime to do anything to harm tourism and the penalties are extremely severe with long prison sentences. However, visitors should remember that some of the local population will do anything to get hard currency, from simply asking for money or foreign-bought goods, to mugging.

Foreigners will be offered almost anything on the street – from cigars to cocaine to *chicas* (girls). Buying cigars on the street is not illegal, but they are often not genuine and may be confiscated at customs if you have more than 20 and cannot produce an official receipt of purchase.

Visitors should never lose sight of their luggage or leave valuables in hotel rooms (most hotels and some *casas particulares* have safes). Do not leave your things on the beach when going swimming. Guard your camera closely. Pickpocketing and purse-snatching on buses is quite common in Havana. Also beware of bag-snatching by passing cyclists. Street lighting is poor so care is needed when walking or cycling in any city at night. Some people recommend walking in the middle of the street. Dark and crowded bars can also be a haven for thieves.

The police are usually (but not always) helpful and thorough when investigating theft. Ask for a stamped statement for insurance purposes, although this is reported to be like getting blood out of a stone from some police stations. In the event of a crime, make a note of where it happened.

Take extra passport photos with you and keep them separate from your passport.

Single travellers

Whether you are a man or a woman travelling on your own, and whatever your age and physique, you will be approached by hustlers, known as *jineteros/as* looking to make a quick buck out of you. Be careful who you allow to become attached to you, for obvious reasons, and if you choose to have a companion make sure that the terms and conditions are fully understood by both parties. The age of consent in Cuba is 18 so if you are introduced to a young girl make sure it is not a blackmail trap. Single men and women are targeted by Cubans of the opposite sex, not only for their dollars, but also as a way out of the country if they can find a marriage partner. Single women will encounter the usual macho attitudes found in all Latin American countries and can expect to receive stares, hissing and comments on their attributes. Rape is not common, but the usual precautions should be taken to avoid getting into a compromising situation, trust your intuition, as always.

Tax

Airport departure tax is now included in air fares. Only the private sector (*casas particulares*, *paladares*) pays taxes. There is no sales tax.

Telephone *Country code +53.*

Empresa Telecomunicaciones de Cuba (**Etecsa**) is on Av 3 esq 76, Centro de Negocios Miramar, Edif Beijing, Miramar, in Havana, with offices elsewhere called **Telepunto**. There are also **Minipunto** cabins dotted around the city for phone services, internet and prepaid phone cards. There are phone boxes all over Havana, taking coins or phone cards; it is written on the side whether they are for local, national or international calls. **Cubacel**, which operates mobile phone service, is part of **Etecsa**.

To make a call to another province, dial 0 then the code and then the number. If you need the operator's help, dial 0, pause, then dial 0 again. Many public phones now take prepaid cards (*tarjetas*) which are easier to use than coins. If you do use a phone which takes coins, they only accept 20-centavo or 1-peso coins. For domestic, long-distance calls try and get hold of a peso phone card, eg 10 pesos, which works out much cheaper than the CUC$ cards, but which are not technically available to foreigners. There are 2 sorts of cards: '*chip*' and '*propria*', but only the latter has cheaper rates at night, otherwise they cost the same. The *propria* cards can be used to make calls from a private phone or from a cabin, dialling the personal code on the upper part of the card.

To phone abroad on a phone with **international dialling** facility, dial 119 followed by the country and regional codes and number. Many hotels and airports have offices where international calls can be made at high prices or you may be able to direct dial from your room. Look for the **Telecorreos**, **Telepunto** or **Etecsa** (www.etecsa.cu) signs. Collect (reverse charge) calls are possible to Argentina, Brazil, Canada, Colombia, Costa Rica, France, Italy, Mexico, Nicaragua, Panama, Puerto Rico, Spain, UK and USA. Dial 012, choose option 0 and follow instructions.

Phonecards (*tarjetas propias*) are green if used for international calls as well as domestic calls. They come in CUC$5, CUC$10, CUC$15, CUC$25 denominations and are valid for 6 months. CUC$1.95 per min (CUC$1.40 1800-0600) to USA and Canada, US$2.60 per min (US$2.20) to Mexico, Central America and the Caribbean, CUC$2.35 (CUC$1.65) to South America, CUC$3.05 (CUC$2.10) to the rest of the world CUC$3.65 (CUC$2.55).

Mobile/cell phones are commonly used in Cuba. If you want to rent a cell phone you can do so from **Cubacel**, at Telepunto, Habana 406 entre Obispo y Obrapía, Havana, or other **Telepunto** or **Etecsa** offices nationwide, T5264 2266, www.etecsa.cu. To call a Cuban cell phone from abroad, dial 53 + the phone number.

Time

Eastern Standard Time, 5 hrs behind GMT; Daylight Saving Time, 4 hrs behind GMT. However, Cuba does not always change its clocks the same day as the USA or the Bahamas. Best to check in the spring and autumn so that you are not caught out with missed flights and buses, etc.

Tipping

Rules regarding tipping have changed: it is now definitely recommended to tip a small amount (not a percentage) in hotels and restaurants. Some restaurants add a service charge; others leave it to your discretion. At times taxi drivers will expect (or demand) a tip. **Viazul** porters ask for tips in some bus stations (eg Trinidad) just for putting your luggage in the hold, but in others (eg Camagüey) they will do almost anything for you in return for a friendly chat. There is no service charge or tip for food or lodging at *casas particulares*. The attendants in toilets expect a tip in return for a sheet or 2 of toilet paper, pesos cubanos are useful for this. Musicians in bars and restaurants depend on your tips. Leaving basic items in your room, like toothpaste, deodorant, paper, pens, is recommended.

Tourist information

Various colourful, glossy brochures are produced by the tourist authorities, available in tourist offices worldwide, but for hard information you are better looking on the internet. Some of the best unofficial websites for travel information and news are **www.cubajunky.com**, **www.cubacasas.net**, **www.havana** **times.org** and **http://havanajournal.com**. Other useful sources include:

http://autenticacuba.com Has lots of information as well as details and addresses of hotels, tour operators, car hire companies, etc, but is not always up to date.

www.cubalinda.com run by former CIA agent, Philip Agee, is particularly helpful for travellers from the USA. You can book tickets and excursions online.

www.gocuba.ca The Canadian tourist office site is better than most.

www.infotur.cu Background information and maps for sale as well as details of events and excursions.

Tour operators

UK and Ireland

Càlédöñiâ, 33 Sandport St, Edinburgh, EH6 6EP, T0131-621 7721, www.caledonia worldwide.com. Cuba specialists for tailor-made trips, dance and music holidays, hiking and Spanish language.

Captivating Cuba, T 01438-310099, www.captivatingcuba.com.
Cuba Direct, T020-3811 1889, www.cubadirect.co.uk.
Cubaism, Unit 30, DRCA Business Centre, Charlotte Despard Av, Battersea Park, London, W11 5HD, toll free T0800-298 9555, T044 20-7498 7671, www.cubasalsa holidays.com. Dance holidays in Cuba and one-to-one Spanish tuition.
Cuba Welcome, T020-7584 6092, www.cubawelcome.com.
Havanatour UK Ltd, T01707-537513, www.havanatour.co.uk.
Interchange, T020-8681 3612, www.interchangeworldwide.com.
Journey Latin America, T020-8622 8464, www.journeylatinamerica.co.uk.
Regent Holidays, T020-3553 0889, www.regent-holidays.co.uk.

Visas and immigration

Visitors from the majority of countries need only a passport, return ticket and **30-day tourist card** to enter Cuba, as long as they are going solely for tourist purposes. Tourist cards must be obtained in advance from Cuban embassies, consulates, airlines or approved travel agents, which is a hassle-free way of obtaining a card. UK residents and EU citizens can also get their tourist cards online at **www.visacuba.co.uk**. In the UK tourist cards cost £15 from the consulate or from travel agents (an administration fee may be charged). In other countries they cost US$15, Can$15, or up to AU$60-140 in Australia depending on how quickly you want it.

Nationals of countries without visa-free agreement with Cuba, journalists, students and those visiting on other business must check what visa requirements pertain and, if relevant, apply for an **official/business visa**.

Travelling from the USA
The US government does not normally permit its citizens to visit Cuba. US citizens should have a US licence to engage in any

transactions related to travel to Cuba, but tourist or business travel is not licensable, even through a 3rd country such as Mexico or Canada. However, the Obama administration is relaxing restrictions where possible and visits to Cuba are now permitted by Cuban Americans to visit relatives and by any American for professional, religious or cultural programmes and humanitarian projects. In effect, it means that US travellers may visit on people-to-people programmes and organized tours with a specialist theme. There are now 12 categories of permitted travel, although independent travel for recreation and general tourism is still not permitted. Any further relaxation of restrictions will depend on a vote in Congress. For further information on entry to Cuba from the US and customs requirements, US travellers should contact the **Cuban Embassy**, at 2630 16th St NW, Washington DC 20009, T202-797 8518. They could also contact the Friendship Associations listed below for the latest information on how to sidestep the regulations. US citizens on business in Cuba should contact **Foreign Assets Control**, Federal Reserve Bank of New York, 33 Liberty St, NY 10045.

Many US travellers conceal their tracks by going via Mexico, the Bahamas, or Canada, where the tourist card is stamped, but not the passport. On your return, make sure that you have destroyed all tickets and other evidence of having been in Cuba. US travellers returning via Canada may be stopped at the border and threatened with massive fines. If you are stopped by an immigration official and asked whether you have been to Cuba, do not lie, as that is an offence. If they want to take it further, expect a letter from the **Office of Foreign Assets Control** (OFAC; Department of the Treasury). This will either ask for information on your suspected unlicensed travel, in which case you should refuse to incriminate yourself, or it will be a pre-penalty notice assessing a civil fine, often US$7500, based on the money OFAC believes you would have spent in Cuba without a licence. The latter gives you 30 days to pay the fine or request an official hearing. The **National Lawyers' Guild** has drafted specimen letters you can use to reply to OFAC in either case; for further information see **www.cubalinda.com**.

Visa extensions

Immigration in Havana airport will only give you 30 days on your tourist card, but for CUC$25 you can get it extended for a further 30 days at Immigration offices in Nuevo Vedado: **Inmigración**, Factor esq Final, Nuevo Vedado, Mon-Fri 0830-1200. Go early, it gets busy and there are queues.

Index

*Entries in **bold** refer to maps*

Credits

Footprint credits
Editor: Nicola Gibbs
Production and layout: Emma Bryers
Maps: Kevin Feeney
Colour section: Patrick Dawson

Publisher: Felicity Laughton
Patrick Dawson
Marketing: Kirsty Holmes
Sales: Diane McEntee
Advertising and content partnerships:
Debbie Wylde

Photography credits
Front cover: Chepe Nicoli/Shutterstock.com.
Back cover top: Kamira/Shutterstock.com.
Back cover bottom: stevedavey.com.
Inside front cover: Kamira/Shutterstock.com,
stevedavey.com.

Colour section
Page 1: stevedavey.com.
Page 2: danm12/Shutterstock.com.
Page 4: Christian Kober/SuperStock.com,
Stefano Ember/Shutterstock.com,
lazyllama/Shutterstock.com.
Page 5: Toniflap/Shutterstock.com,
corlaffra/Shutterstock.com.
Page 6: Martchan/Shutterstock.com,
EsHanPhot/Shutterstock.com.
Page 7: stevedavey.com, Sergi Reboredo/
SuperStock.com, merc67/Shutterstock.com.
Page 8: Kamira/Shutterstock.com.

Duotone
Page 28: Kamira/Shutterstock.com.

Printed in Spain by GraphyCems

Publishing information
Footprint Havana
2nd edition
© Footprint Handbooks Ltd
September 2016

ISBN: 978 1 911082 07 1
CIP DATA: A catalogue record for this book is
available from the British Library

® Footprint Handbooks and the
Footprint mark are a registered
trademark of Footprint Handbooks Ltd

Published by Footprint
6 Riverside Court
Lower Bristol Road
Bath BA2 3DZ, UK
T +44 (0)1225 469141
F +44 (0)1225 469461
footprinttravelguides.com

Distributed in the USA by
National Book Network, Inc.

Every effort has been made to ensure that
the facts in this guidebook are accurate.
However, travellers should still obtain advice
from consulates, airlines, etc about travel
and visa requirements before travelling.
The authors and publishers cannot
accept responsibility for any loss, injury or
inconvenience however caused.